ADVANCES
IN CHILD DEVELOPMENT
AND BEHAVIOR

Volume 27

ADVANCES
IN
CHILD DEVELOPMENT
AND
BEHAVIOR

edited by

Hayne W. Reese
Department of Psychology
West Virginia University
Morgantown, West Virginia

Volume 27

ACADEMIC PRESS
San Diego   London   Boston
New York   Sydney   Tokyo   Toronto

Academic Press
A Harcourt Science and Technology Company
525 B Street, Suite 1900, San Diego, California 92101-4495, USA
http://www.apnet.com

Academic Press
24-28 Oval Road, London NW1 7DX, UK
http://www.hbuk.co.uk/ap/

International Standard Book Number: 0-12-009727-3

PRINTED IN THE UNITED STATES OF AMERICA
99 00 01 02 03 04 BB 9 8 7 6 5 4 3 2 1

Contents

From Form to Meaning: A Role for Structural Alignment in the Acquisition of Language

CYNTHIA FISHER

The Role of Essentialism in Children's Concepts

SUSAN A. GELMAN

Infants' Use of Prior Experiences with Objects in Object Segregation: Implications for Object Recognition in Infancy

AMY NEEDHAM AND AVANI MODI

Perseveration and Problem Solving in Infancy

ANDRÉA AGUIAR AND RENÉE BAILLARGEON

Temperament and Attachment: One Construct or Two?

SARAH C. MANGELSDORF AND CYNTHIA A. FROSCH

The Foundation of Piaget's Theories: Mental and Physical Action

HARRY BEILIN AND GARY FIREMAN

Contributors

Numbers in parentheses indicate the pages on which the authors' contributions begin.

ANDRÉA AGUIAR
Department of Psychology, University of Illinois at Urbana-Champaign, Champaign, Illinois 61820 (135)
RENÉE BAILLARGEON
Department of Psychology, University of Illinois at Urbana-Champaign, Champaign, Illinois 61820 (135)
HARRY BEILIN
Developmental Psychology Program, City University of New York Graduate School, New York, New York 10016 (221)
GARY FIREMAN
Department of Psychology, Texas Tech University, Lubbock, Texas 79409 (221)
CYNTHIA FISHER
Department of Psychology, University of Illinois at Urbana-Champaign, Champaign, Illinois 61820 (1)
CYNTHIA A. FROSCH[1]
Center for Developmental Science, University of North Carolina at Chapel Hill, Chapel Hill, North Carolina 27599 (181)
SUSAN A. GELMAN
Department of Psychology, University of Michigan, Ann Arbor, Michigan 48109 (55)
SARAH C. MANGELSDORF
Department of Psychology, University of Illinois at Urbana-Champaign, Champaign, Illinois 61820 (181)
AVANI MODI
Department of Psychology: Experimental, Duke University, Durham, North Carolina 27708 (99)
AMY NEEDHAM
Department of Psychology: Experimental, Duke University, Durham, North Carolina 27708 (99)

[1]Current address: Department of Family Resources and Human Development, Arizona State University, Tempe, Arizona 85287

Preface

The amount of research and theoretical discussion in the field of child development and behavior is so vast that researchers, instructors, and students are confronted with a formidable task in keeping abreast of new developments within their areas of specialization through the use of primary sources, as well as being knowledgeable in areas peripheral to their primary focus of interest. Moreover, journal space is often simply too limited to permit publication of more speculative kinds of analyses that might spark expanded interest in a problem area or stimulate new modes of attack on a problem.

The serial publication *Advances in Child Development and Behavior* is intended to ease the burden by providing scholarly technical articles serving as reference material and by providing a place for publication of scholarly speculation. In these documented critical reviews, recent advances in the field are summarized and integrated, complexities are exposed, and fresh viewpoints are offered. These reviews should be useful not only to the expert in the area but also to the general reader.

No attempt is made to organize each volume around a particular theme or topic, nor is the series intended to reflect the development of new fads. Manuscripts are solicited from investigators conducting programmatic work on problems of current and significant interest. The editor often encourages the preparation of critical syntheses dealing intensively with topics of relatively narrow scope but of considerable potential interest to the scientific community. Contributors are encouraged to criticize, integrate, and stimulate, but always within a framework of high scholarship.

Although appearance in the volumes is ordinarily by invitation, unsolicited manuscripts will be accepted for review. All papers—whether invited or submitted—receive careful editorial scrutiny. Invited papers are automatically accepted for publication in principle, but usually require revision before final acceptance. Submitted papers receive the same treatment except that they are not automatically accepted for publication even in principle, and may be rejected. The *Advances* series is generally not a suitable place of publication for reports of a single study or a short series of studies, even if the report is necessarily long because of the nature of the research. The use of sexist language, such as "he" or "she" as the general singular pronoun, is not acceptable in contributions to the *Advances* series; the use of "they" as a singular pronoun is incorrect. The use of "he or she" (or the like) is acceptable.

I acknowledge with gratitude the aid of my home institution, West Virginia University, which generously provided time and facilities for the preparation of this volume. I also thank Drs. Renée Baillargeon and Judy DeLoache for their editorial assistance and Mrs. Ann Davis for her excellent secretarial services.

Hayne W. Reese

FROM FORM TO MEANING: A ROLE FOR STRUCTURAL ALIGNMENT IN THE ACQUISITION OF LANGUAGE

Cynthia Fisher

DEPARTMENT OF PSYCHOLOGY

UNIVERSITY OF ILLINOIS AT URBANA-CHAMPAIGN

CHAMPAIGN, ILLINOIS 61820

I. Introduction

Knowledge of verbs plays a central role in our ability to interpret sentences. A verb is the syntactic and semantic heart of a sentence, determining both what oth-

ADVANCES IN CHILD DEVELOPMENT
AND BEHAVIOR, VOL. 27

er phrases can appear in the sentence and what semantic relation among these phrases the sentence will convey. The sentences in (1) illustrate both the syntactic selectivity of verbs and their fundamental contribution to sentence meaning: *Laugh* can appear intransitively but not transitively (Phil cannot laugh Fred), and *drop* and *fear* can appear transitively. *Put* and *explain* readily occur in sentences with three noun phrases, and *think* accepts an embedded sentence as its complement. Moreover, sentence pairs (b–c) and (d–e) share a syntactic structure, but describe very different semantic relations.

(1)   a. Phil *laughed* at Fred.
      b. Jeanine *dropped* the phone.
      c. Melanie *feared* thunderstorms.
      d. Emily *put* the cereal on the shelf.
      e. The director *explained* his ideas to the actor.
      f. Ron *thought* that he could get away with cheating on his taxes.

Both of these kinds of information—the syntactic requirements of verbs and the semantic relations they encode—must be part of what we know about each verb. Knowledge about verbs plays a major part in theories of sentence comprehension by adults (e.g., Carlson & Tanenhaus, 1988; Ferreira & Henderson, 1990; Trueswell, Tanenhaus, & Garnsey, 1994) and of syntax acquisition by children (e.g., L. Bloom, 1970; Braine, 1992; Grimshaw, 1981; Pinker, 1984, 1989). This chapter concerns how a child might acquire these necessary packages of linguistic information. Young children do learn both syntactic and semantic facts about verbs: For example, Tomasello (1992; Olguin & Tomasello, 1993) has observed that young talkers use new verbs appropriately, but largely conservatively, in the same sentence structures in which they have heard them modeled. Thus, in their first production of verbs, children reveal the beginnings of the combination of semantic and syntactic information about verbs that plays such a major role in adult language use.

A. THE PROBLEM OF VERB PERSPECTIVE

To learn the meaning of a new verb a listener must determine what relation among participants in some scenario is encoded by the sentence, without the aid of the primary linguistic device for conveying that information—the verb itself. In large part this determination must be made by attending to the nonlinguistic situation. For example, only by observing instances of kicking, paired with the verb, could a child learn what *kick* means. Important aspects of the meaning of a verb, however, are surprisingly indirectly related to the situation it comments on. Verb meanings depend not only on events but also on a choice of *perspectives* on events (e.g., Bowerman, 1985; Choi & Bowerman, 1991; E. Clark, 1990; Fillmore, 1977; Fisher, 1996a; Fisher, Hall, Rakowitz, & Gleitman, 1994; Gleitman, 1990; Goldberg, 1995; Grimshaw, 1994; Landau & Gleitman, 1985; Pinker, 1989; Rispoli,

1989; Slobin, 1985; Talmy, 1983, 1985). For example, "I'm *putting* the cup on the table" and "The cup *goes* on the table" could both accompany the same scene, but they describe relations among different subsets of the participants in the scene. Other perspective differences are reflected in the choice of sentence subjects (Fillmore, 1977). For example, the pairs of sentences in (2) and (3) differ in their focus on one or another participant's role in the same states or events.

(2) a. John gave a book to Mary.
     b. Mary got a book from John.
(3) a. Leo likes music.
     b. Music pleases Leo.

The unpredictability of verb perspective choices was emphasized by Rispoli (1989), who found that Japanese parents addressing 2-year-olds were as likely to use intransitive motion verbs (e.g., *hair*-'go in') as transitive ones (e.g., *ire*-'put in') when commenting on events in which a causal agent acted on an object. Clearly, the presence of an agent in an event does not demand that a speaker choose a verb that encodes the agent's role. Linguistic perspective on an event is influenced by many factors, including the speaker's current focus of attention (e.g., Forrest, 1996), beliefs and interests (e.g., Kuno, 1987; Osgood, 1980), and the momentary accessibility of various lexical items and syntactic structures (e.g., Bock, 1987; Bock, Loebell, & Morey, 1992; McDonald, Bock, & Kelly, 1993). Languages give speakers the flexibility to say different things about the same events. Furthermore, just as speakers can choose among verbs to describe their perspective on an event, different languages lexicalize different choices among perspective options (e.g., Bowerman, 1985, 1990; Choi & Bowerman, 1991; Grimshaw, 1994; Talmy, 1983), offering striking evidence for flexibility in the linguistic encoding of events.

B. CONSEQUENCES FOR VERB LEARNING

The indirect relationship between verb meaning and world events makes verb learning somewhat mysterious. How can the child get enough information about the intended perspective on an event to interpret a verb correctly? Several studies have demonstrated children's understanding of speaker cues such as eye gaze and pointing (e.g., Baldwin, 1993; Tomasello, 1992), and their ability to use other nonlinguistic cues to determine whether an object or action is being labeled (Tomasello & Akhtar, 1995). These investigations help to explain how children and adults achieve joint attention on the same event, a clear prerequisite for verb learning. The pervasive verb perspective problem addressed here, however, applies even after the intended event has been identified.

Here I will focus on a different source of information: Powerful additional clues to the verb's perspective on a scene could come from the rest of the sentence. As the examples above reveal, verbs differ not only in their meanings, but also in the structures of sentences in which they appear. When a parent labels a causal event using the verb *put* or *go,* the sentences in which those verbs appear will differ. Therefore, to a suitably knowledgeable child, the sentence itself can convey hints about what aspect of an event the verb encodes, constituting a linguistic "zoom lens" to help the child to adopt the verb's perspective. The use of sentence structure cues to guide verb learning is known as *syntactic bootstrapping* (Landau & Gleitman, 1985).

In this chapter, I explore how syntactic bootstrapping might work: (a) What aspects of sentence structure are meaningful to young children, (b) what kind of semantic information can sentence structures provide, and (c) what degree of syntactic knowledge will suffice to give children some guidance in verb learning? In section II I begin by sketching some of the evidence that children can use sentences to guide verb learning, and then consider this and other evidence in relation to several possible mechanisms for syntactic bootstrapping. To preview, I will argue that little or no language-specific syntactic knowledge is needed to give the child an initial sentence-structural guide for interpreting verbs. Instead, based on a partial or presyntactic description of sentences, children can obtain information about verb meaning essentially by structural analogy, aligning a sentence representation with a conceptual representation that shares its skeletal structural properties (Fisher, 1996a). For example, a child could arrive at different interpretations of transitive and intransitive verbs for the same event by aligning a transitive verb with a conceptual relation between two participants, and an intransitive verb with a conceptual predicate involving only a single participant. In section III I explore how learners might construct the simple structured representations of sentences needed to use this simple mechanism for syntactic bootstrapping.

II. Syntactic Bootstrapping: How Does It Work?

A. THE PHENOMENON: INITIAL EVIDENCE

Several experimental studies support the general claim that children's interpretations of novel verbs are affected by their sentence contexts. For example, Naigles (1990) showed young 2-year-olds a videotape depicting two concurrent events (e.g., a duck bends a rabbit over, while both duck and rabbit make arm circles). This composite scene was paired with a nonsense verb in either a transitive sentence ("The duck is kradding the bunny") or an intransitive sentence with both actors mentioned in subject position ("The duck and the bunny are kradding"). The two events were then separated onto two video screens, and the child was prompted to "Find kradding!" Children who heard the verb in a transitive sentence looked longer at the causal event (bending), while those who heard an intransitive sentence looked longer at the noncausal actions (arm circling). Two-year-olds used sentence cues to infer which event in a composite scene was relevant to the meaning of a new verb (see also Hirsh-Pasek & Golinkoff, 1996).

As suggested by the examples of section I.A, sentences could provide the same kind of information for different verbs describing a single event. Verb pairs that take different perspectives on the same event (e.g., *put/go* and *give/get*) should be particularly difficult to disentangle based on observation of events without sentence cues. Fisher et al. (1994) examined 3- and 4-year-olds' interpretations of novel verbs applied to single events that could be interpreted in two complementary ways. For example, one scene showed a rabbit feeding an elephant, who ate, and another showed a rabbit giving a ball to an elephant, who took it. Each event was described with a nonsense verb presented in one of two different sentence contexts, as in (4) and (5).

(4) a. The bunny is nading the elephant.
     b. The elephant is nading.
(5) a. The bunny is blicking the ball to the elephant.
     b. The elephant is blicking the ball from the bunny.

The sentence contexts included transitive/intransitive pairs as well as transitive pairs that differed in the order of noun phrases or the choice of a preposition. Preschoolers were asked what they thought the novel words meant, and their judgments were influenced by the sentence context. For example, children were more likely to take the verb in (4a) to mean "feeding" and the verb in (4b) to mean "eating." The effect of sentence context was maintained when only responses that were not single English words were examined (e.g., "giving him medicine" or "licking it off the spoon"), suggesting that these findings did not depend on the direct retrieval of a familiar verb that fit the sentence.

These preliminary investigations tell us that (a) sentence structure clues influence verb interpretation in young children, (b) these clues can be found in several different kinds of sentences including those that differ in transitivity, as in (4), and those that do not, as in (5), and (c) sentence context can direct children's attention toward different aspects of a single event. Given these basic phenomena, we can go on to ask how sentence structures might guide verb learning.

B. STRUCTURE AND MEANING IN THE VERB LEXICON: BACKGROUND ASSUMPTIONS

Any form of syntactic bootstrapping depends on a strong assumption about languages: Verbs that occur in similar sentence structures must also be similar in meaning. Principled relations between verb syntax and semantics are a basic part of current theories of the lexicon and of grammar (e.g., Chomsky, 1981; Dowty, 1991; Goldberg, 1995; Grimshaw, 1990; Jackendoff, 1987, 1990; Rappaport Hovav & Levin, 1988). Views of these relations differ in significant ways, but three

broad generalizations are consistent with most of the recent thinking about syntax
and semantics in the verb lexicon. These generalizations provide a starting point
for any view of how children might use sentence structures to interpret verbs (Fisher, Gleitman, & Gleitman, 1991).

1. Semantic Structure versus Semantic Content

One generalization relevant to verb interpretation is that sentence structures can
express only limited semantic information. The principal elements of sentence
structures are the number, type (e.g., noun phrase vs. sentence complement), and
positioning or marking (e.g., subject vs. object) of the verb's syntactic arguments.
Sentences also vary in markings of the temporal properties of events: Verbs can be
inflected for tense (e.g., past vs. present) and aspect (e.g., complete vs. continuing), and these features of sentences are also related to the semantics of verbs. For
example, some verbs seem more natural with the English progressive ending than
others (compare "I am knowing that" to "I am thinking about that"). The tendencies of various verbs to co-occur with different tense and aspect markers are reflected in children's earliest use of those markers (L. Bloom, Lifter, & Hafitz,
1980), and verb inflection can be shown to influence 3- and 5-year-olds' interpretations of novel verbs (Behrend, 1995).

With these materials to work with, sentence structure can be related only to
properties of verb meaning that affect the number and type of arguments associated with the verb, and the temporal structure of the event it names (Fillmore, 1968;
Fisher et al., 1991, 1994; Grimshaw, 1990; Rappaport Hovav & Levin, 1988,
1998)—what might be called its semantic structure rather than its semantic content (Grimshaw, 1993). For example, the different manners of motion encoded by
slide, roll, and *bounce* have no direct reflection in sentence structure. All of these
verbs describe the motion of an object; therefore, they have the same basic event
structure and can occur in the same sentence structures, as in (6).

(6)   The rock slid (rolled, bounced) down the hill.
       Bill slid (rolled, bounced) the rock down the hill.

Thus, in the novel verb-learning experiments described above, the sentences
could have directly told children nothing about the "arm-waving," "pushing," or
"feeding" aspects of the new verbs, and could outline only the general structure of
a semantic relation. This reveals a division of labor in the representation of verb
meaning and therefore in verb learning: Sentence structures can tell the child only
about the verb's semantic structure; observation of the event itself must provide
the event-specific semantic content (e.g., Fisher et al., 1991, 1994; Landau & Gleitman, 1985).

2. Semantic Structure and Syntactic Structure

A second generalization relevant to verb interpretation is that the semantic structure of a verb partly determines the sentence structures in which the verb can appear (e.g., Chomsky, 1981; Goldberg, 1995; Grimshaw, 1981, 1990; Jackendoff, 1987, 1990; Pinker, 1984, 1989; Rappaport Hovav & Levin, 1988). If a verb describes the motion of an object, for example, it will be able to specify that object as a noun phrase in sentences. Consequently, verbs occurring in different sentence structures differ in the semantic structures they encode. For this reason, terms like "argument structure" or "predicate-argument structure" are often used to refer both to the semantic structure of a verb (the relation it encodes and the participants required to embody that relation) and to its syntactic requirements when it occurs in a sentence.

Regularities between verb syntax and semantics reflect meaning differences that can be uncovered in simple linguistic judgments made by adults. Fisher et al. (1991) asked adults to judge the semantic similarity among verbs by selecting, for each of many sets of three verbs, the one least like the others in meaning. Verbs that occurred in similar sentence structures tended to be judged similar in meaning. Although the labeling of semantic properties of words is a difficult matter, these judgments provide evidence that aspects of the meanings of verbs can be predicted from their syntactic properties. Furthermore, the semantics of clusters of verbs derived from these similarity judgments could be characterized in ways consistent with the limitations of sentence structure as a device for representing meaning. For example, verbs that accept sentences as their complements (e.g., "Ben knew *he was in trouble*") describe relations between their subjects and an event or state; these verbs include verbs of cognition (*know, think*), perception (*see, hear*), and communication (*explain, say*). Verbs that take three noun-phrase arguments (e.g., "John mailed a letter to Bill") describe relations among the referents of those three noun phrases, typically transfer of position (*put, drop*), possession (*give, take*), or information ("John explained matters to Bill"). The same broad correspondences between verb syntax and meaning were found in Italian (Fisher et al., 1991) and Hebrew (Geyer, Gleitman, & Gleitman, 1991) using the same procedure. Finer-grained correspondences between verb syntax and meaning can also be detected in such judgments (Fisher, 1994).

Across and within semantic classes of verbs, the number, type, and position of arguments assigned to a verb are systematically related to meaningful differences in the type of relation encoded by the verb. Although the semantic correlates of syntax have to do with abstract semantic structure rather than event-related semantic content, these aspects of meaning are part of what ordinary speakers know about verbs, and part of what makes verb learning seem so difficult.

3. *Verbs versus Verbs in Sentences*

A third generalization relevant to the interpretation of verbs is that the semantic hints given by sentence structure directly pertain to the semantic structure of the verb *in that sentence,* and only indirectly to the verb in general. Most verbs can appear in a number of different structures, each of which results in a different interpretation (e.g., Fisher, 1994; Goldberg, 1995; Grimshaw, 1993; Gropen, Pinker,

Hollander, & Goldberg, 1991a; Levin & Rappaport Hovav, 1991; Pinker, 1989, 1994; Rappaport Hovav & Levin, 1998). For example, "The door opened" and "Bill opened the door" have the same verb, but the first describes the door's change in position and the second describes the act causing the change. Each time *open* is heard, the listener must use the sentence to determine its meaning on that occasion, causal or noncausal.

Verbs vary considerably in their syntactic restrictiveness (Ritter & Rosen, 1993). *Put,* for example, must always appear with each of its three possible arguments; thus, no variation in the semantic structure of *put* can be reflected in its syntactic structures. At the opposite extreme, the most frequent verbs in English occur in a bewildering variety of sentence structures and seem to have little meaning that persists across uses. For example, in (7) *have* conveys possession, in (8) it implies that Marie caused an event, and in (9) it suggests that Marie experienced a misfortune. In each case, the main verb *have* is little more than a place-holder for some semantic relation between its subject and its complement. Ritter and Rosen argued that the nature of that relation is determined both by the syntactic form and the lexical content of the complement phrases.

(7)   Marie had six dogs.
(8)   Marie had her assistant get her a cup of coffee.
(9)   Marie had her dog get run over by a car.

These examples demonstrate less a limitation of structural cues to verb meaning than their indispensability even in adult comprehension. Most verbs, like *open* and *have,* are compatible with more than one semantic structure. The learner who does not yet know the basic meaning of the verb and the adult who already does must both consult the syntax and lexical semantics of each sentence in order to determine the semantic structure of its current use. Therefore, a plausible conclusion is that sentence structures have meanings of their own, distinct from the words they contain. This is a basic claim of syntactic bootstrapping (Landau & Gleitman, 1985), and also of some approaches to grammatical theory (see Goldberg, 1995; Rappaport Hovav & Levin, 1998). If sentence structures are somehow linked with their abstract relational meanings, this could account for adults' ability to generate and comprehend novel uses of verbs like those in (10), adapted from Goldberg (1995). The examples in (11) are taken from Bowerman's (1982) analysis of children's speech. The latter cases, like the adult uses in (10), suggest that the speaker knows the meanings of various syntactic structures and combines them with words to achieve the desired sense.

(10) The panel laughed the proposal off the table.
       Elena sneezed the foam off the cappuccino.
(11) Whenever I breathe I breathe them down.
       Feels like you're combing me baldheaded.
       Mommy, I poured you. (You poured me?) Yeah, with water.

4. Guidelines for a Theory of Syntax-Aided Verb Learning

In summary, sentence structures can provide information about the semantic structure of a verb in a particular sentence—such as how many participants the event described by the verb requires. This could help to solve the perspective problem with which I began: The semantic structure of a verb encompasses just the differences in perspective which make verb learning so mysterious. With information about this structure, the child is more likely to understand a sentence as its speaker intended, and to derive appropriate semantic content—"rolling" or "spinning" or "arm-waving"—from observation of events. According to the syntactic bootstrapping theory, children make use of the restricted but powerful relation between syntactic and semantic structures to interpret sentences, as adults also must, and therefore to learn verbs.

Given this general outline of relations between verb syntax and semantics, what possible mechanisms could permit the structures of sentences to influence young children's interpretations of sentences? In section II.C, I begin with one mechanism that has often been assumed, at least informally, in discussions of syntactic bootstrapping (Grimshaw, 1994; Pinker, 1994), and argue that this proposed mechanism leads to a strong prediction that has turned out to be false. In subsequent sections I describe a different possible mechanism for the use of sentence structure in verb learning, the structural alignment procedure previewed in the Introduction.

C. THEMATIC ROLES: SENTENCE STRUCTURE AS CAST LIST?

One procedure whereby children could infer aspects of verb meaning from sentences appeals to rules linking thematic roles and syntactic positions. Thematic roles are categories of participant roles in semantic structures, representing the abstract similarity among the *agents* (or causers) of various causal acts, the *themes* (objects that move or change) of various motions, states, and changes of state, the *experiencers* of diverse mental states, and so on. Innate rules linking such relational concepts to grammatical functions like subject and object have been proposed to explain striking cross-linguistic regularities in the assignments of semantic roles to sentence positions. Causal agents, for example, overwhelmingly appear as grammatical subjects across languages (e.g., Keenan, 1976, and many others). Various treatments of thematic roles differ significantly in their inventories of roles and how these roles map onto syntax; nevertheless, thematic roles are a primary device in linguistic theory for expressing relations between verb syntax and semantics (e.g., Dowty, 1991; Fillmore, 1977; Grimshaw, 1990; Jackendoff, 1987, 1990; Ladusaw & Dowty, 1988; Rappaport Hovav & Levin, 1988).

Rules linking thematic roles and grammatical functions play a central part in the semantic bootstrapping theory of syntax acquisition, in which children are assumed to rely on these rules to acquire phrase structure rules (Grimshaw, 1981; Pinker, 1984, 1989). A partial list of the linking rules given by Pinker (1989, p. 74) is shown in (12). The use of these links to determine the phrase structure of input sentences depends primarily on prior knowledge of the semantic structures of verbs. For example, if a child (a) already knows what *hit* means and (b) knows that Tom is the *agent* of hitting in the scenario the speaker intends to describe, the child could apply the first rule in (12) to infer from a sentence like "Tom hit Jerry" that the subject noun phrase goes first in English. The central claim of semantic boot-strapping is that children learn language-specific syntactic facts like word order by understanding the meanings of sentences and applying innate rules which univer-sally link those meanings to their syntactic expressions.

(12) agent → subject
       patient → direct object
       theme → subject, or if subject is already linked, direct object

In principle, the same rules could explain children's structure-sensitive inter-pretation of verbs: By applying the rules in reverse, from syntax to semantics, the child could interpret sentence subjects as agents or themes and objects as patients or themes. This conjecture leads to a clear prediction (Fisher, 1996a): In order to use these rules to gain sentence structure cues to verb meaning, the child must fig-ure out who the sentence designates as the grammatical subject or object. Apply-ing a linking rule, the child might then assume that the subject of the sentence is most likely to be the agent in the event, and therefore interpret a new verb as re-ferring to the current actions of the participant named by the subject noun phrase. On this view, identifying the referent of nouns in particular grammatical positions should be required to infer meaning from sentence structure.

Children do make inferences about verb meaning based on properties of the ob-served events; such observational biases will be discussed in section II.F.1. The ar-gument here concerns the effect of the sentence on verb interpretation, in addition to any biases in the observation of events. We have already seen, for example, that children can be influenced to interpret *the same scene* as one of "chasing after" rather than "running away from" depending on the sentence in which a new verb is presented (Fisher et al., 1994). If children achieve this sensitivity to sentence structure through linking rules like those in (12), then any influence of the sentence itself on verb interpretation must be mediated by information about the referents of the subject versus object noun phrases.

However, several experimental findings disconfirm this prediction, suggesting that some other mechanism must be at work: Children's interpretation of novel verbs can be influenced by sentence structure even when children are prevented from identifying the referents of the subject and object noun phrases. In several studies, 3- and 5-year-olds (Fisher, 1996a) and 28- to 32-month-olds (Fisher, 1999) were taught novel transitive or intransitive verbs for unfamiliar agent–patient events. An example is shown in (13). The identities of the subject and object were hidden by using ambiguous pronouns, yielding sentences that differed only in their number of arguments. Children's interpretation of a novel verb in its sentence context was assessed by asking them to choose the participant in each event whose role the verb described ("Which one is pilking her over there?" vs. "Which one is pilking over there?"). The children interpreted the verbs differently depending on the sentence structure, though neither sentence explicitly identified one participant in the event as the subject. In each study, children were more likely to choose causal agents as the subjects of transitive than intransitive verbs.

(13) Event: One person rolls another on a wheeled dolly by pulling with a crow-bar.
    TRANSITIVE: She's pilking her over there.
    INTRANSITIVE: She's pilking over there.

In previous studies of the role of syntax in verb learning, the linguistic contexts of novel verbs always specified the identity of the arguments of the verbs (e.g., The *duck* is blicking the *bunny*). Given this information based on the order of familiar words in the sentence, the linking rule procedure sketched above could account for all findings. This procedure could not explain children's success in the ambiguous pronoun task, however. The context sentences in this task specified only how many noun phases each verb occurred with (one or two), not which of the participants in the event was named by the subject noun phrase. The structure of the sentence must have provided children with information about the possible meanings of verbs in a way not mediated by identity of the subject versus the object of the sentence—and thus not based directly on linking rules like those expressed in (12). This finding gives strong support to the notion that sentence structures themselves are meaningful to children as well as adults, in a way not reducible to links between thematic roles and grammatical functions (e.g., Fisher, 1996a; Fisher et al., 1994; Goldberg, 1995).

D. SENTENCE STRUCTURE AS AN ANALOG OF SEMANTIC STRUCTURE

How could sentence structures provide information about the meaning of verbs without the aid of linking rules like those described above? The approach taken here capitalizes on the intrinsically structural nature of sentences, conceptual representations, and verb meanings (e.g., L. Bloom, 1970; Braine, 1992; Fisher, 1996a; Fisher et al., 1994; Gentner, 1982; Landau & Gleitman, 1985). In common with most recent work in verb semantics, I assume that the semantic structures of verbs are fundamentally of the same kind as the nonlinguistic conceptual structures by which people represent events (e.g., Grimshaw, 1990; Jackendoff, 1987, 1990; Pinker, 1989; Rappaport Hovav & Levin, 1988). Both verb semantic structures and conceptual representations of events demand a distinction between conceptual predicates and arguments, or in other words between relation, act, or state concepts and the objects or entities that embody them (Bierwisch & Schreuder,

1992; L. Bloom, 1970; Braine, 1992; Fodor, 1979). For example, I have a concept of an action for which I have no verb—a physical trick in which two people stand back to back with arms linked at the elbows, and one person bends forward so that the other is lifted off the ground. My concept of this action, though unlabeled, includes the information that two human participants are required for the action to take place, as well as relational information about the roles the two participants will play. Though these types of information could presumably be represented in many different ways, at some level of analysis we need to think of both concepts of events or states and the semantics of the verbs we use to name them as involving both conceptual objects or entities, and relations among them.

The two parts of this assumption—that conceptual representations of events are structured, and that their structures are fundamentally of the same kind as verb semantic structures—have important consequences for verb learning. First, when children interpret a sentence they map one structure onto another: A sentence can be represented as a structure relating a set of noun phrases, and the child's conceptual representation of an event can be represented as a structure relating a set of event participants. To the extent that these two distinct representations—syntactic and conceptual—have similar structures, a sentence could provide a partial analogy for its interpretation in conceptual terms (e.g., Gentner, 1983). Second, assuming that conceptual and semantic structures are of like kind, the result of this structural alignment will be, roughly, a semantic structure for the sentence.

To illustrate, even prior to the identification of subject and object, sentences still contain some *number* of noun phrase arguments. This simple structural fact could be informative. Transitive verbs, with two noun phrase arguments, describe semantic relations between the two named entities. Intransitive verbs, with only one argument, denote a state, activity, or property of the named entity. Once children can identify some nouns, they could assign different meanings to transitive and intransitive verbs by aligning a sentence containing two noun phrases with a conceptual structure including the two named entities in the current scene, and a sentence containing one noun phrase with a conceptual predicate characterizing the single named entity in the current scene. The result would be a rough semantic structure for the sentence, with semantic content derived from the specifics of the observed situation.

The semantic information gleaned from syntax via this procedure will necessarily be very abstract. As discussed in section II.B.1, the interpretive information that could be inferred from a sentence structure could be described as relevant to the semantic structure of a sentence rather than its semantic content (e.g., Grimshaw, 1993). Transitive verbs include words as diverse as *fear, like, drop,* and *see;* intransitive verbs include *dance* and *sigh.* These sets share, not the specifics of the acts or states they describe, but similar formal structure: *Dancing* and *sighing,* different as they are, require only one participant.

The basic requirement of the structural alignment view is that, in the ordinary process of analyzing both sentence and scene, representations emerge which are abstract enough to reveal their structural similarity. Several phenomena in infant cognition reflect detection of the similarity between representations in different modalities. For example, there is some evidence that infants detect numerical similarity between visible and audible stimuli (e.g., Starkey, Spelke, & Gelman, 1983), and recognize the visible shape of an object previously explored through touch (e.g., Streri, Spelke, & Rameix, 1993). The structural alignment of sentence and scene described here would also require a cross-modal mapping, based on similarity between quite distinct representations. The proposed structural alignment, like cross-modal mapping in young infants, is presumably not a conscious, explicit analogy, but rather an implicit detection of similarity between representations of sentence and scene.

The structural alignment procedure allows children to map entire sentence structures onto possible semantic structures derived from observation of events, without requiring identification of the referent of the subject noun phrase as such, and thus could account for the findings from the pronoun-disambiguation task described above (Fisher, 1996, 1999). Via structural alignment, merely counting the nouns within a representation of a sentence could give the hearer a clue as to the intended perspective on an event. This modest structural hint would increase the probability that the child could interpret verbs in sentences correctly despite the unpredictability of a verb's perspective on an event.

E. ADVANTAGES AND PITFALLS OF STRUCTURAL ALIGNMENT

The number of nouns in a sentence is a structural cue in the sense that number must be defined over some type of smaller unit—the recognizable nouns—within a larger unit—the sentence or utterance itself. In section III.B, I will return to the question of how this larger unit might be defined. The number of nouns in a sentence, however, will not always reflect the number of syntactic arguments associated with the main verb in the sentence. For example, intransitive sentences can contain more than one noun, as in "John and Mary danced" or "Bill looked at Fred." Given the inevitable mismatches between number of nouns in a sentence and number of arguments of a verb, the structural alignment procedure described above yields a number of interesting consequences for learning, predicting both useful consequences and errors which the learner will need to overcome.

1. Presyntactic Structural Cues

A primary advantage of the structural alignment route from sentence structure to meaning is that it can be used without identifying which noun is the subject and which the object. To begin mapping two-noun-phrase sentences onto two-participant conceptual relations, the child need only have begun to recognize some nouns.

If children can draw this inference, then simple structural properties of sentences could influence interpretations before much language-specific syntactic knowledge is acquired. Structural cues like the number of nouns in a sentence could provide a crucial presyntactic bootstrap for acquiring information about the lexical items and syntax of a language.

The notion that sentence structural cues could be useful in advance of language-specific syntax learning generates some novel predictions about errors that very young children might make. If children can conclude something about the meaning of a verb in a sentence merely by "counting the nouns," then intransitive sentences containing two nouns should be systematically misinterpreted. Some evidence supports this prediction. Hirsh-Pasek and Golinkoff (1996) found that 24-month-old boys (not girls) spent more time watching a causal than a noncausal event when told "Big Bird is glorping with Cookie Monster." The girls looked longer at the noncausal video, implying understanding of the function of *with* in this sentence. For the boys, however, presumably slightly less far along in linguistic development (e.g., Fenson et al., 1994), the presence of two nouns in the sentence seemed to influence verb interpretation before sufficient syntactic or lexical knowledge was available to interpret the sentence correctly. Similarly, Hirsh-Pasek and Golinkoff found that children at 19, 24, and 28 months misinterpreted sentences like "Find Big Bird and Cookie Monster glorping." Naigles (1990) showed that 25-month-olds could understand these sentences when given additional morphological pointers to their structure ("Big Bird and Cookie Monster are glorping"). Apparently, without multiple clues that the unfamiliar verb is intransitive, children can be fooled by a mismatch between number of arguments of a new verb and number of nouns. These findings are in accord with the predictions of the structural alignment account.

2. *Verbs, Prepositions, and Adjectives*

A second advantage of structural alignment is that it could guide the interpretation of any argument-taking predicate term. Words that occur with noun phrase arguments include not only verbs, but also prepositions and predicate adjectives. Prepositions encode spatial relations, as in (14), and adjectives encode attributes or states, as in (15). Although these types form distinct grammatical categories, all take noun phrase arguments and all encode a semantic relation between the two noun phrase arguments in the sentence or a state or property of a single noun phrase argument. These classes of words should therefore initially be interpretable in the same way as transitive and intransitive verbs—by mapping the relational term(s) onto a conceptual predicate involving the participants named in the sentence.

(14) The cat is on the bookcase.

Your keys are under the newspaper.

(15) I'm so happy for you.

John is noisy.

The similar treatment of all predicate terms follows from the general properties of syntax/semantics links reviewed in section II.B. The syntactic structure in which a relational term occurs is systematically related to its semantic structure—its number and type of conceptual participants. A structural alignment based on partial sentence structures provides no initial mechanism for distinguishing between different classes of argument-taking words like verbs, adjectives, and prepositions. This lack of specificity is consistent with the fact that not all languages have distinct categories of prepositions and predicate adjectives, but may instead use main verbs to convey spatial or attribute meanings (e.g., Croft, 1990; Maratsos, 1990). Maratsos (1990; see also Braine, 1987, 1992; Osgood, 1980) has suggested that children might approach language acquisition expecting a basic grammatical division between nouns and relational words, analogous to the semantic distinction between arguments and predicates. This variability across languages also provides another problem for the innate linking rules described in section II.C: Significant variation in the inventory of grammatical categories, or the alignment of grammatical categories with semantic categories, raises grave difficulties for the statement of specific universal correspondences between syntax and semantics. I return to this issue in section IV.

The notion that children can interpret sentence structure as a general analog of predicate-argument semantics could also help to explain how the child identifies argument-taking terms in the first place. Landau and Stecker (1990) found that young children interpreted an unfamiliar word as a relational term if it appeared with noun phrase arguments, and as a referential term if it did not. They taught 3-year-olds a novel word that the experimenter introduced while she placed an unfamiliar object on top of a box. The word was presented either as a noun ("This is a corp") or as a preposition ("This is acorp my box"). Children who heard the word presented as a noun considered that an object in any location relative to the box could be "a corp," but resisted changes in the object's shape. Children who heard the word presented as a preposition accepted shape changes but maintained that only objects in certain locations could be "acorp the box." Having arguments, "is acorp" was taken to refer to a relation between the referents of its subject ("this") and its complement ("my box."). Given the situation in which the word was presented, this relation was taken to be a spatial one.

The various types of predicate terms in English must eventually form separate grammatical categories. One suggestion consistent with the structural alignment account is that children could accomplish this separation as they begin to detect the various function morphemes associated with each category (e.g., Cartwright & Brent, 1997; Maratsos, 1982, 1990). For example, prepositions and adjectives will always occur with a form of the verb *to be,* and verbs can occur with tense markers. Even quite young children show some sensitivity to the distribution of function morphemes, suggesting that these might begin to differentiate the various categories of relational words for children from an early age (Gerken & McIntosh, 1993). The cur-

rent proposal suggests only that any argument-taking word can initially be interpreted as a relational term by structural alignment of the sentence structure in which
it appears with a conceptual representation that shares its basic structure.

The set of noun phrase arguments in a sentence can tell the child how many and
which participants are involved in the view of an event encoded by a new verb.
This clue should increase the probability that the child will adopt the verb's perspective, and therefore focus on relevant aspects of a scene. However, it cannot al-
leviate all of the verb perspective problem with which I began. A verb with two arguments could take the perspective of either in describing a scene, leaving an
enormous number of ways to characterize the relationship between the two participants in any event. For example, suppose a child hears an utterance containing
the two recognizable referential terms "Mommy" and "baby." In the scene described by this utterance, the mother might be standing beside the baby, touching
and looking at the baby, and so on; the baby could be kicking the mother and smiling at her. These are all two-participant relations that could be salient in a child's
representation of the scene. Thus, the problem of word mapping still applies,
though a structural clue has reduced the hypothesis space. In the following sections I review evidence for two further sources of information: (a) biases that lead
children to find some aspects of events more salient than others and (b) the choice
of subject noun phrase in a sentence.

1. Event-Based Preferences in Verb Interpretation

In practice, given an array of possibilities, children appear to find some relations
more salient than others. Any such tendencies should affect children's interpretations of sentences by influencing what aspects of world events the children are likely to attend to and consider worthy of mention. To the extent that these observational tendencies are similar in children and adults, they will tend to lead children
toward correct rather than incorrect interpretations. One preference that is well
documented in observers of many ages is a tendency to attend to *causal* relationships between a verb's arguments. Children are generally more likely to take the
agent in a causal scene to be the subject of a novel transitive verb (Fisher, 1996a;
Fisher et al., 1994; Naigles & Kako, 1993). This tendency could be due to a basic
predisposition to attend to first movers in causal events. Even prelinguistic infants
appear to be subject to this predisposition (e.g., Cohen & Oakes, 1993; Leslie,
1982). Children tend to show the same preference in interpreting a novel verb with
no explicit arguments (e.g., "Blicking!"; Fisher, 1996a; Fisher et al., 1994; Naigles
& Kako, 1993). This preference could be due both to the salience of causation and
to the tendency of even young children to consider transitive verbs prototypical
(Corrigan, 1988).

The tendency to attend to causal action is not a simple one, however. Observers' tendency to attend to causality and their interpretations of the locus of causality are intricately determined by knowledge and by the context in which they see the event. For example, an infant's interpretation of an event depends both on what is salient within the event and on its relationship to prior events (e.g., Baillargeon, 1994). Infants, like adults, are perplexed when a magician pulls a rabbit out of a hat, but only if the magician demonstrated that the hat was empty to begin with. The same context-dependence of event perception is found in studies of verb learning in preschoolers. In one study, children were more likely to focus on the patient's role in interpreting a novel verb for a causal event if the patient was human rather than nonhuman, suggesting that the salience of sentient experiencers can influence the representation of events (Fisher, 1996a). Similarly, embedding the same two agent–patient events in different series of other events changed children's interpretations of transitive and intransitive verbs applied to the agent–patient events (Fisher, 1996a).

Other studies of verb learning reveal related influences of the salience of various aspects of events in context. For example, Braine, Brody, Fisch, Weisberger, and Blum (1990) demonstrated novel actions for 2- and 4-year-olds, and described these events using novel verbs presented either transitively ("I'm wugging the ball"), intransitively ("The ball is wugging" and "I'm making the ball wug"), or neutrally ("Wugging!"). Uses of the novel verbs were elicited by asking children, "What am I doing?" or "What is the (object) doing?" while demonstrating the same action with a new object. Both the introducing context and the syntax of the question affected children's responses, as any structural view of verb learning would predict. Of further interest here, however, is a manipulation concerning the actions themselves: Some had transient effects on the patient (e.g., flipping a spoon by hitting it on one end), and others had enduring effects which continued beyond the launching action (e.g., setting a toy on a spring in motion). Across introducing contexts for the novel verbs, intransitive descriptions of the patient's role in a causal event were more frequent when the patient's motion was enduring. Apparently patients that underwent enduring motions were more likely to seem the more central participant in the event.

It has also been suggested that children have a tendency to interpret verbs as describing actions, and therefore as involving manner of motion rather than a change of state. For example, *stir* describes an action, but not a particular result, and *mix* implies a change of state (becoming mixed), but not necessarily a particular action. Gentner (1978) asked children whether they could describe a variety of events as cases of *stirring* or *mixing,* and found that 5-year-olds overapplied *mixing* to events in which no state change occurred, treating it as an action verb like *stir.* Gropen et al. (1991b) also found signs of a preference for manner-of-action interpretations in preschoolers' comprehension of familiar locative verbs like *fill* and *pour. Pour* is an action verb, while *fill* requires that an appropriate end state (full) be achieved in any manner. Children between 2 and 5 selected picture sequences in answer to the question "Which of these two sets of pictures is 'pouring' (or 'filling')?" Although children did show sensitivity to the change-of-state requirements of locative verbs like *fill,* the youngest children chose correct picture sequences more often than expected by chance only for the action (*pour*) verbs.

Like the tendency to attend to causal action, however, children's observed tendency to attend to manner of action is not an overwhelming preference, but rather can be altered by the details of events. That is, it is possible to lead children toward verb interpretations that include the manner of motion or that specify an end state of action by manipulating the physical salience of those two aspects. Gropen et al. (1991a) taught preschoolers, school-aged children, and adults two nonsense verbs describing novel events in which an object was moved into some location (e.g., moving pennies to a cloth supported by its edges). The distinctiveness of manner of motion (e.g., hopping versus straight path) and result change (e.g., the cloth collapses under the pennies) was manipulated within each event. The verbs were presented in an uninformative gerund context ("This is pilking"), and interpretations were assessed by eliciting uses of the verbs in sentences. All age groups were more likely to encode a moving object as the direct object of the verb ("pilking the pennies onto the cloth") when the manner was made especially distinctive and were more likely to encode a goal object as the direct object ("pilking the cloth with pennies") if the goal object underwent a striking change of state.

Successive uses of a verb to describe events varying on one feature or another can also influence which features children and adults will consider relevant to the meaning of a verb: Forbes and Farrar (1995) found that training with variable events made 3-year-olds, older children, and adults more likely to generalize verbs to label modified test events. This finding suggests a straightforward process of cross-situational analysis, which interacts with young children's verb interpretation biases.

In summary, observers tend to prefer some interpretations of verbs over others. Such preferences are intricately determined by the details of individual events in context, and will tend to increase the probability that children will select the view of an event intended by a speaker who shares both these observational tendencies and the same context. Each bias is fairly weak, however, leaving the observer a considerable amount of flexibility in the interpretation of verbs (e.g., Forbes & Farrar, 1995; Gropen et al., 1991a). Braine et al. (1990), for example, found that preschoolers spontaneously arrived at transitive action interpretations of novel verbs accompanying actions on objects only 58% of the time, and adults did so 68% of the time. Similarly, the effect of the transience of the patient's motion was significant but small (54% transitive uses for enduring effects, 69% for transient effects).

This flexibility is important, given that languages vary significantly in their choices of perspective options (e.g., Grimshaw, 1994; Talmy, 1985). A relevant example is cited by Bowerman (1990): In English the patient of *hit* (the thing hit) is nearly always its direct object, and an instrument can be added as an optional adjunct phrase ("John hit Tom with a stick"). In the language Chechen-Ingush, the nearest translation of *hit* differs in argument structure from its English counterpart—it must take three arguments, and places the instrument in direct object position (as in "John hit a stick against Tom"). Given the regular links between sentence and semantic structures, these verbs should have subtly different meanings even though they refer to the same kinds of events (e.g., Fisher, 1994; Goldberg, 1995; Rappaport Hovav & Levin, 1998). The Chechen-Ingush verb appears to analyze hitting as a motion event in which some object (e.g., a fist, a stick) moves toward and reaches a goal. English *hit* treats hitting as the action of an agent on a patient. This is a perspective difference like the one that characterizes the meaning of *fill* relative to *pour* (e.g., Gropen et al., 1991b). Uniform tendencies to attend to some aspects of events rather than others cannot account for cross-linguistic variation in syntactic and semantic structure. We have already seen, however, that these tendencies are not the only influences on verb learning. Rather, children's perceptions of what about world events is encoded by a verb will also be influenced by the sentence structure to be mapped.

2. *The Subject–Object Asymmetry as a Cue to Verb Meaning*

Can sentence structures provide more information about meaning than simply what participants are involved? Once the child can identify the subject and object of a sentence, this structural information should further narrow interpretations of a verb in a sentence. Several findings demonstrate that young children assign meaning appropriately to the difference between subjects and objects in interpreting new and familiar verbs. Very young children can use word order in sentences containing familiar action verbs to tell them who is doing what to whom. Hirsh-Pasek and Golinkoff (1991) found that 16- to 18-month-olds who heard "Big Bird is tickling Cookie Monster" looked longer at a video screen depicting this event than its opposite. Fisher et al. (1994) found that reversing the position of familiar nouns in transitive sentences used to describe a single event changed preschoolers' interpretations of a novel verb (e.g., from *getting a piggyback ride* to *giving a ride*). On what basis might very young children use the subject and object different to guide their interpretations of verbs? The structural alignment proposal and a linking-rule-based view of syntax-semantics links in verb acquisition offer different consequences for what meaning should be assigned to the formal asymmetry between subject and object.

a. Thematic roles and the subject–object asymmetry. Based on linking rules like those discussed in section II.C, the grammatical asymmetry between subject and object does not have a unified meaning. The interpretation of each grammatical role is based on multiple possible linking rules, so via these linking rules the subject can be agent, theme, possessor, or experiencer in different semantic structures. This flexibility follows from the mapping of many thematic roles onto very few possible grammatical positions: Different verbs have subjects that play an enormous variety of semantic roles, from the animate agent in (16) to the inanimate cause in (17). The many-to-one mapping of thematic roles onto grammatical roles has raised questions about how useful even a fully parsed sentence could be in the interpretation of a novel verb: If being the subject or object of a sentence has no particular meaning, how could sentence structures guide verb interpretation (e.g., Pinker, 1994)?

(16) John built a fire.
(17) Thunderstorms scare Bill.

    b. A prominence-based interpretation of subject versus object.   Many linguists have suggested, however, that the grammatical asymmetry between subject and object has semantic consequences that are not well described as differences in traditional thematic roles (e.g., Dowty, 1991; Gleitman, Gleitman, Miller, & Ostrin, 1996; Talmy, 1983). In addition, several analyses of relations between syntax and semantics have uncovered persistent problems with linking rules like those discussed in section II.C, and responded to them by altering notions of the semantic structures which are linked with syntactic structure (e.g., Dowty, 1991; Grimshaw, 1990). These approaches vary in important ways, and a full explanation of their properties and their differences in semantic and syntactic assumptions is far beyond the scope of this chapter. However, several such attempts share a property useful for verb acquisition based on sentence structure cues. That is, they propose a general notion of semantic *prominence,* and argue that semantic prominence, rather than the more detailed traditional thematic roles, predicts which argument will be the sentence subject.

    One example is the view developed by Grimshaw (1990). She argues that (a) a verb's arguments vary in prominence in its semantic structure, (b) relative prominence determines the assignment of argument roles to syntactic positions, and (c) the semantic prominence of arguments is based on two partly independent dimensions of semantic structure. The first of these dimensions is a hierarchy of thematic roles much like the classic set: agent, experiencer, goal/path, theme. Arguments whose roles are higher in this hierarchy are more likely to be sentence subjects than those lower in the hierarchy: Agents are more prominent than the themes of motion events, for example. The second of the two dimensions is a structure representing the timing of the event, in which participants whose roles are implicated in early parts of the event are more prominent (and thus more likely to be sentence subjects) than those whose roles emerge later. Thus, there are multiple respects in which one argument can be more prominent than another. Nevertheless, this analysis suggests that being subject versus object of a sentence may have a unified meaning, though an abstract one, in terms of semantic prominence.

    Another approach, differing in many important features but capturing the same notion of the generalized semantic prominence of grammatical subjects, has been to reduce the list of thematic roles to two universal *prototype* roles associated with subject and object positions in sentences. Dowty (1991) proposed a Proto-Agent/ Proto-Patient continuum, in which the argument of a transitive verb with more of the semantic properties of a Proto-Agent is linked to subject position. Properties contributing to Proto-Agency include volition, sentience, causation, movement, and existence independent of the event named by the verb. Again, there are multiple respects in which one argument can be more prominent (more agent-like) than the other. However, the Proto-Role position embodies a claim that the difference between subjects and objects shares semantic coherence—that the various ways in which one argument can be semantically more prominent than another form a natural category.

Finally, in an analysis of spatial descriptions, Talmy (1983) has described the subject as expressing the conceptual Figure, of which the location or motion relative to a reference or Ground object is the main issue of the sentence (see Osgood, 1980, for a similar take on a subject–object semantic asymmetry). Several suggestions that subjects are more "in perspective" than objects (e.g., E. Clark, 1990; Fillmore, 1977; Kuno, 1987) appeal to a related general notion of semantic prominence. For example, *give* and *receive* differ, not in the event participants required by the two verbs (both require a giver, a receiver, and an object given), but in which role the verb makes more prominent and thus in which role is assigned to subject position. Figure–ground and verb perspective can both be considered metaphorical descriptions of the difference in semantic prominence between subjects and objects of sentences.

As mentioned above, these three accounts differ in their assumptions about syntax, semantics, and relations between them. They all share, however, an abstract notion of semantic prominence, aligned with the syntactic distinction between subject and object. Whether the difference in semantic prominence is described as conceptual Figure versus Ground (Talmy), Proto-Agent versus Proto-Patient (Dowty), or a prominence ranking based on two semantic dimensions (Grimshaw), the intuition that the subject–object asymmetry signals some abstract semantic prominence asymmetry is widespread.

c. Asymmetrical interpretations by structural alignment: empirical evidence. Do children make use of this more general interpretation of subjects—as the more prominent argument in some semantic structure—in their interpretations of sentences? If so, then once children can identify which noun phrase in a sentence is the subject, they will know not only which participants the verb relates, but which participant's role is more prominent.

The structural alignment procedure sketched above provides a possible route for this inference. Pervasive differences in the interpretation of subjects and objects are to be expected if sentences provide a structural analogy for their meanings.

Simply, transitive sentences are asymmetrical: The subject has traditionally been described as higher than the object in a hierarchical structure (e.g., Chomsky, 1981). Although this picture is not a simple or uncontested one, the assumptions that subject and object can be structurally defined and that the subject is higher than the object in a hierarchical structure remain deeply embedded in mainstream modern theories of syntax (e.g., Baker, 1997; Grimshaw, 1990; Newmeyer, 1992). The structural asymmetry between subjects and objects has a wide variety of correlates in the surface appearance of subjects and objects in sentences, including a powerful tendency for subjects to appear before objects across languages, and for subjects and objects to have different distributions of pronouns (e.g., Keenan, 1976). On the structural alignment view, once a child has learned to identify subjects as "higher than" objects in a grammatical hierarchy, an interpretation that gives a semantically prominent role to the subject referent should be preferred.

The empirical strategy described here is to explore two complementary consequences of the hypothesis that listeners interpret sentence subjects as encoding the semantically more prominent argument. First, properties of events that make one participant role more prominent than another in a conceptual representation should influence the plausibility of various sentence descriptions: Some participants will make better conceptual figures than others (Talmy, 1983), lend themselves to semantic structures in which they are highly ranked in two dimensions of semantic prominence (Grimshaw, 1990), or have more of the properties that suggest proto-agency (Dowty, 1991). These factors should affect sentence interpretation by influencing what conceptual structures are readily available, and could be mapped onto a sentence. Second, however, if the subject–object asymmetry provides information about semantic prominence, specifying a sentence subject should override event-derived preferences in interpretation. A grammatical subject clearly identified in a sentence should lead the hearer to select a semantic relation in which the subject argument is the most prominent.

Both predictions are clearly upheld for adult listeners, who interpret the subject and object of a sentence asymmetrically even where they play the same role in the scene (Gleitman et al., 1996). For example, the verbs in (18–19) denote symmetrical relationships. Two objects are equally near each other, and two people meet to the same degree. Talmy (1983) suggested that the general notion of figure versus ground, aligned with subject versus object, could explain why it nevertheless typically makes more sense to say the (a) than the (b) sentence of each pair. In the ordinary scheme of things, a bicycle is more mobile than a house, and ordinary people are more likely to go to meet world leaders than the reverse.

(18) a. The bicycle is near the house.

     b. The house is near the bicycle.

(19) a. My cousin met the President.

     b. The President met my cousin.

Gleitman et al. (1996) documented preferences of just this type in adults who judged sentences like those in (18–19). Judges thought the first of each pair was more natural, preferring subject nouns that were smaller, more mobile, or less famous. Nevertheless, adults also acknowledged conceivable uses for the less preferred member of each pair. The result of changing the order of noun phrases in such sentences was to invite the listener to take the subject noun's referent as the conceptual figure. That is, (18b) could describe a small house trailer temporarily located near a large sculpture of a bicycle, and (19b) could be said if the speaker's cousin were admired by all, including the President. This pattern suggests that adults interpret the subject–object asymmetry in terms of semantic prominence, or figure and ground.

d. Children's preference for dynamic subjects. Some evidence indicates that the two complementary tendencies documented above for adults—(a) to prefer sentences with a semantically prominent participant role as subject and (b) to interpret the subject as information about the semantic prominence relations encoded by the verb—occur in young children as well. First, the event-based preferences in verb interpretation described in section II.F.1 suggest that young children assume the more dynamic participant in an event, or better conceptual figure, makes a better sentence subject. The tendency of causal agents, which move independently of their patients (e.g., Dowty, 1991; Keenan, 1976), to be subjects could be interpreted as a special case of a more general preference for dynamic subjects. Consistent with this, when the patients' motion is enduring, patient–subject intransitive interpretations of a novel verb are more likely (Braine et al., 1990), suggesting that the more mobile and active participant in a scene has some claim on subject position in default descriptions no matter what its traditional thematic role.

The well-established tendency of animate objects to occur as surface subjects is also consistent with the general figure–ground or perspective interpretation of the subject role. Bock et al. (1992; see also L. Bloom, Miller, & Hood, 1975; McDonald et al., 1993) invoked the related notion of predicability, suggesting that nouns referring to animate entities are likely sentence subjects because they can serve as the logical subjects of many conceptual predicates. Only animate entities can think, walk, see, or initiate actions. Young children have access to some information about the difference in predicability between animate and inanimate participants: 3-year-olds judge that only animate creatures can go up a hill under their own power (Massey & Gelman, 1988); 2-year-olds believe that only animate characters can possess objects (Golinkoff & Markessini, 1980), and react with surprise when inanimate objects begin to move on their own (Golinkoff, Harding, Carlson, & Sexton, 1984). In accord with the conceptual centrality of animacy, nouns naming animate objects appear as sentence subjects in adults' speech more often than nouns naming inanimate objects do (e.g., Bock et al., 1992; H. H. Clark & Begun, 1971; McDonald et al., 1993). This tendency appears in children's speech as well: A tendency to favor animate subject referents can be seen in children's earliest sentences (e.g., L. Bloom, 1970; Bowerman, 1973; Brown, 1973).

Effects of animacy can also be found in comprehension, and appear to depend on the fit of an animate referent with roles that could be assigned by a verb. Sentences with animate rather than inanimate subject referents are rated as more natural by adults, and this tendency varies with verb choice (e.g., Corrigan, 1986). Two-year-olds were more accurate in identifying the actor in pictures described by transitive sentences when the subjects of action verbs referred to animate entities (Corrigan, 1988; Corrigan & Odya-Weis, 1985). As for adults, the children's preference for animate subject referents varied with the verb: Inanimate referents of the subjects of verbs like *hurt* were identified as easily as animate subject referents. Trueswell et al. (1994) found that animacy influenced adults' parsing decisions. That is, a sentence beginning with a noun phrase followed by a verb will typically be interpreted as a subject and main verb (e.g., *The lawyer examined . . .*). However, similar sequences that named an inanimate referent (*The report examined . . .*) were more likely to be interpreted as the beginning of a relative clause (e.g., *The report (that was) examined by the lawyer . . .*). This animacy effect depended on the plausibility of particular noun–verb combinations: a prior study included many nouns that named inanimate referents but could plausibly be subjects of the immediately following verb (e.g., *The car towed . . .*) and did not yield the same influence of animacy on parsing decisions (Ferreira & Clifton, 1986). Taken together, these findings suggest that animate entities tend to be named as subjects in production, and are easily interpreted as subjects in comprehension, not because of a direct link between animacy and subject position, but because of the potential of animate entities to take on more dynamic roles and thus to serve as the logical subjects of many conceptual predicates (Bock et al., 1992).

The same preference for dynamic subjects appears in children's interpretations of novel verbs (Fisher, 1996b). Three-year-olds viewed videotaped displays in which the animacy and mobility of two participants varied independently. These events involved no causal action, but only the motion or location of one object or animal relative to another. Children were taught novel transitive verbs with ambiguous pronoun arguments (e.g., "It pilks it") and were asked to point to the subject referent in each scene ("Which one pilked the other one?"). Children and adults systematically chose dynamic—moving or animate—participants in events over others as subject referents, in the absence of information from a familiar verb or from the placement of a familiar noun in subject position. The tendency to choose moving or animate objects consistently in these displays did not appear when the children were merely asked to choose one of the objects in each display, without presentation of any verb to be interpreted. This finding suggests that the transitive sentence drew observers' attention to aspects of each video that were not obvious without a sentence—a situation involving the two participants, in which the dynamic participant's role is more central. Given no sentence to interpret, the choice of participants depended not on the salience of possible roles, but on the visual salience of objects in the display.

In summary, children find it easier to assign dynamic entities—good conceptual figures—to the subject role. This tendency is true of their spontaneous productions (e.g., L. Bloom, 1970; Bowerman, 1973; Brown, 1973; Lempert, 1984; Tomasello, 1992), their comprehension of sentences with familiar verbs (e.g., Corrigan, 1988; Corrigan & Odya-Weis, 1985), and their interpretation of novel verbs (Fisher, 1996b). This preference is consistent with the proposed prominence-based interpretation of the distinction between sentence subject and object.

e. The countervailing effects of subject choice.   If the preference for dynamic subjects were unfettered by other cues to the relative prominence of the arguments of a verb, then children should systematically misinterpret stative verbs as action words. But it is clear from their early productions that they do not. Nonactional verbs like *want, see, hear,* or *have* appear among the first verbs used by many children (e.g., Bowerman, 1990; Landau & Gleitman, 1985; Macnamara, 1982; Tomasello, 1992). Action verbs tend to predominate in children's early productions (e.g., L. Bloom, 1970; L. Bloom, Lightbown, & Hood, 1975), as predicted by the preference for active, dynamic subject choices. However, the apparent ease of acquisition of nonactional verbs like *want* and *see,* in the presence of this tendency toward action interpretations, suggests that additional powerful cues lead children away from action meanings when necessary. The cue proposed here is subject choice in a sentence.

Several findings suggest that preschoolers can use placement in subject position to determine the perspective of a novel verb on a scene even when that perspective is a less salient interpretation of a scene. For example, Naigles and Kako (1993) showed 2-year-olds videotaped composite events that paired a simple contact event (e.g., a duck touches a bunny on the head) with a very salient synchronous action performed by the two participants (e.g., both duck and bunny wheel their free arms in the air). These composite scenes were described with a nonsense verb presented either transitively ("The duck is kradding the bunny"), intransitively ("The duck and the bunny are kradding"), or as a bare gerund ("Look, kradding!"). The two events were then separated onto two video screens, and children were instructed to "Find kradding." Across conditions, children showed a general tendency to look at the screen showing arm-wheeling; these movements were also judged by adults to be larger in physical extent than the contact actions. However, the children in the transitive sentence condition looked significantly longer at the contact action screen than children in either the intransitive or the gerund condition. Similarly, Fisher et al. (1994) found that when novel verbs were presented in isolation, some perspectives were preferred over others. Three- and 4-year-olds and adults tended to view one scene as involving *chasing* or *scaring* rather than *running away*, and another as *giving a ride* rather than *getting a ride.*

Choice of subject in a transitive sentence, however, could reverse these preferences. In both cases the placement of a familiar noun in subject position altered
preschoolers' interpretations of new verbs.

Although children in both of these studies apparently considered one type of
role in each event more prominent than another, both roles involved action, and
thus neither subject choice was greatly at odds with the preference for dynamic interpretations of verbs. Can subject choice actually lead children to generate a nonactional interpretation for a verb, even in the presence of a salient action? This
question was put to a challenging test by teaching 4-year-olds novel verbs referring to events in which one animate participant moved another in some novel way
(Fisher, 1996b). Novel transitive verbs with either the causal agent or the patient
participant in subject position were used to describe each scene. For example, for
one event in which a bunny is seen turning a pig on a tall swiveling stool, one group
of children heard "The bunny pilks the pig" and the other group heard "The pig
pilks the bunny." The children were able to learn which participant each verb assigned to subject position, and to apply this knowledge to a new use of the verb in
an ambiguous sentence ("She pilks her"). They did this even when this assignment
was in conflict with the very strong bias to assume the more dynamic participant
in the event would be named as subject. Children's paraphrases of the novel verbs
revealed the effect this argument assignment had on their interpretations of the new
transitive verbs. When a plausible causal agent appeared in subject position, children assumed that the verb gave a fairly literal description of the causal event itself. When the patient of the salient causal act was named in subject position, however, children searched for an interpretation that treated that participant's role in
the event as more prominent. This led many children to consider more abstract inferences about the scene in view, including the participants' covert goals (e.g.,
"She's helping her," "She didn't want her to pull").

These findings suggest that children, like adults, can interpret a sentence subject roughly as the more prominent role in a conceptual representation (Gleitman
et al., 1996; Talmy, 1983). Other things being equal, interpretations that cast dynamic participants in subject position are more plausible. When an unambiguous
choice of subject is made, however, that choice leads the listener to interpret the
subject as the conceptual figure of the sentence.

The structural alignment view suggests a route whereby children might arrive
at a general prominence-based interpretation of the difference between subjects
and objects. Once children can identify the subject in a sentence, an appropriate
interpretation could be established by aligning the asymmetrical representation of
a sentence with a similar asymmetrical representation of an event.

An important additional piece of evidence favoring the structural alignment basis of the semantic difference between subject and object is that a very similar syntactic and semantic asymmetry holds between direct and oblique (or preposition-
al) objects. Direct objects are usually represented as higher than indirect objects

in a grammatical hierarchy, much as subjects are higher than objects (e.g., Croft, 1990). Accordingly, an asymmetry in semantic prominence similar to the difference between subjects and objects holds between direct and oblique objects, as in (20) (Fillmore, 1977; Fisher, 1994; Gleitman et al., 1996; Gropen et al., 1991a; Talmy, 1983).

Across content classes of verbs, the choice of different direct and oblique objects indicates a difference in the perspective of the verb on the same class of event. A direct object plays a semantically more prominent role in the action described by the verb than an oblique object does (e.g., Levin & Rappaport Hovav, 1991; Pinker, 1989). For example, in (20a) *spraying* is what happened to the paint rather than the wall; thus, it has often been noted that the wall can seem less covered by paint than in (20b) (e.g., Anderson, 1971; Dowty, 1991; Fillmore, 1977; Fisher, 1994; Pinker, 1989). Preschoolers could be biased to produce sentences like (20a) or (20b) by variations in the salience of the manner of motion and the effect on the goal in events (Gropen et al., 1991a), just as differences in the dynamic salience of participants' roles affect the choice of subject and object (Braine et al., 1990; Fisher, 1996b). Via structural alignment, any observable asymmetry in a sentence should be aligned with a corresponding asymmetry in a conceptual representation. Thus, the structural alignment procedure provides a unified account of the strikingly similar semantic distinction between subjects and objects, and between objects and obliques.

(20) a. Judy sprayed paint onto the wall.
      b. Judy sprayed the wall with paint.

G. AN ALTERNATIVE: SYNTACTIC BOOTSTRAPPING BASED ON LEARNED GENERALIZATIONS

A familiar alternative explanation for the use of sentence structure in comprehension could be offered, however. Even young 2-year-olds who succeed in interpreting novel verbs in accord with sentence structure (Hirsh-Pasek & Golinkoff, 1996; Naigles, 1990) already know some verbs, which occur in a variety of sentence structures. The children could have detected a correlation between these entire structures and varieties of verb meaning, for example, forming the generalization that transitive verbs denote certain conceptual relations between two participants and that intransitive verbs describe actions, states, or properties of one object. Children's inferences in syntactic bootstrapping experiments could be based on arbitrary, learned correspondences rather than on the structural alignment of sentence and conceptual structures.

Although many versions of a learned correspondence account could be constructed, some guidelines can be drawn from existing evidence. Children must at some point acquire correspondences between entire sentence structures and their relational meanings, allowing them to interpret transitive and intransitive sentences differently even when unable to identify the referent of the subject noun phrase (Fisher, 1996a). To permit these differential interpretations, a learned correspondence account would require abstract representations of sentences and scenes very much like those required for structural alignment. In order to form and apply a generalization concerning the different semantics of transitive and intransitive sentences, for example, new sentences must be represented abstractly enough to identify their structural similarity to previous sentences containing different words, and events must be represented abstractly enough to reveal the structural similarity among scenes involving different participants. The learned correspondence and structural alignment views thus differ only in the source of the correspondence between sentence and scene representations: based on structural alignment, the structural similarity of scene and sentence representations could be detected without prior verb learning. On the learned correspondence view, children could come to use sentence structural evidence only after forming links between sentence structures and semantic structures based on prior examples.

Some evidence has been interpreted as support for the learned correspondence account. Experiments based on a preferential looking measure of comprehension have failed to obtain effects of sentence structure on novel verb interpretation by children under 24 months (Hirsh-Pasek & Golinkoff, 1996). Children under 24 months do learn verbs; therefore, Hirsh-Pasek and Golinkoff concluded that they do so without assistance from sentence structure. However, as mentioned above, the sentences used in these studies required knowledge of the word order and closed-class items of the language being learned. For example, in these studies of children's understanding of transitive versus intransitive sentences, two nouns were placed in subject position of the intransitive sentences (e.g., "Big Bird and Cookie Monster are glorping!"; Hirsh-Pasek & Golinkoff, 1996). Any account that relies on presyntactic structural cues would not predict early success in interpreting such sentences. The presence of two nouns in these sentences should be a powerful cue to interpret the verb as encoding a relation between the two named participants. In order to interpret sentences like these as intransitive, children must use language-specific syntactic knowledge, such as the word order of English or the use of the plural auxiliary verb "are."

This discussion should make clear that new data are needed to decide between these two possibilities. Sensitivity to simple structural properties of sentences in children under 2 has not been studied, as needed to test the unique predictions of the structural alignment and learned correspondence accounts. However, the foregoing discussions provide two reasons to consider the structural alignment account a plausible one. First, the learned correspondence view provides no explanation for how the set of verb meanings needed to support the required generalization is acquired in the first place. As discussed in section I, a verb does not simply label an event, but takes a particular perspective on the event. For example, every event has a cause, but a speaker is free to mention it or not. Observations of events without linguistic hints give the child no way to decide whether a causal or noncausal view of the same event is intended. The sentence structure, on the other hand, gives powerful information about the perspective on an event encoded by a verb. Second, both the learned correspondence and structural alignment accounts require relatively abstract representations of sentences and scenes. For the correspondences between syntax and semantics to be learned, representations of sentences and scenes must at some point be abstract enough to permit generalizations from previous sentences to new sentences, and from prior scenes to novel scenes. The only step added in structural alignment is the detection of the structural similarity between representations of a sentence and a scene.

H. SUMMARY: THE STRUCTURAL ALIGNMENT PROCEDURE

Thus far I have suggested that the inevitable relational similarity between sentence structures and conceptual structures could allow children to make a rough interpretation of sentences by aligning these structures. Two lines of support have been offered for this hypothesis. First, experimental examinations of word learning reveal that children can infer something about which perspective on a single event is encoded by a verb based on only the number of available participants mentioned in the sentence (Fisher, 1996a). Thus, structural properties of sentences without explicit identification of subject versus object referents can guide sentence interpretation, raising the possibility that even partial or presyntactic representations of sentences could guide their interpretation. This reduction of the syntactic knowledge needed to exhibit some sensitivity to sentence structure is important because it suggests the availability of early structural guides for interpretation and makes novel predictions about early errors.

Second, I have argued that event-based preferences in the interpretation of verbs can be uniformly attributed to the tendencies (a) to assume that more dynamic participants in events should be more prominent in an asymmetrical semantic structure than less dynamic participants and (b) to link the most prominent role in a semantic structure to subject position in a sentence. In accord with the prominence-based interpretation of the subject role, word order in a sentence is informative even when it conflicts with the preference for dynamic subjects. The specification of a less dynamic subject leads listeners toward nonactional interpretations of verbs.

Thus, according to the structural alignment account, once children can identify any nouns within an utterance, they can (a) align the utterance with a conceptual representation of the relevant scene that relates the referents of those nouns. As soon as one referential term can be identified as the subject, the choice of interpretations can be narrowed further, by (b) aligning the utterance with a conceptual relation in which the referent of the subject noun plays the most semantically prominent role. The selected relation will describe the role of the subject relative to other arguments in the sentence. At this point, the hearer will have been led to view the situation from the perspective encoded by the verb, and is therefore more likely to assign appropriate properties of a specific situation to the relation encoded by a novel verb. This procedure is consistent with the general guidelines for a syntax-aided verb-learning procedure summarized above: sentence structures provide information only about the semantic structure of a verb in a sentence. The semantic content of the verb—the specific nature of the role of the subject relative to other arguments—must be filled in by observation of the situation.

III. The Construction of Partial Sentence Structures

The next step is to examine the structural requirements of the structural alignment procedure more closely. Sentence structures are not transparently represented in the world any more than word meanings are. Thus, we need to consider what assumptions about the perception and representation of utterances are required for children to use the proposed structural cues.

The power of structural alignment depends on three basic suppositions about children's representations of sentences. First, the child must be able to identify the nouns in a sentence. Partial representations of sentences will initially be limited by children's vocabularies and their ability to recognize multiple words rapidly in continuous speech. Second, the recognized nouns must be represented as grouped together within a single utterance. The partial representations required for structural alignment require that the child be able to group words into larger structures. Third, in order to use assignment to subject position as a cue to the intended figure–ground relations, the child must at some point become able to represent sentences asymmetrically, identifying the subject noun phrase as structurally more prominent.

Thus far I have treated this third requirement as an explicitly syntactic one, requiring that the child has already learned enough language-specific syntax to identify grammatical subjects. If so, then the child's very first interpretations of sentences would be influenced only by the number of arguments in the sentences, and the structural asymmetry of sentences would become informative later. However, there is another possibility. Subject and object noun phrases differ not only in their abstract grammatical properties, but also in several observable surface properties that are strongly correlated with the subject–object distinction across languages (e.g., Keenan, 1976). Below I will examine the possibility that some of these observable differences between subjects and objects could bias children toward an appropriately asymmetrical representation of sentences. This representation would allow the child to gain information about the intended semantic prominence relations of a sentence based on a partially represented sentence structure, before subject and object noun phrases can be identified by language-specific grammatical means.

In the following sections I examine available evidence on these three aspects of very young children's representation of sentences. Not surprisingly, one clear conclusion from this survey will be that we need to know much more about the factors that limit and facilitate children's representations of sentences. The notion of peripheral limitations on sentence production is a familiar one in the study of language acquisition (e.g., L. Bloom, Lightbown, & Hood, 1975; P. Bloom, 1990). But this idea is less familiar in comprehension, where conclusions about acquisition procedures are often based on the idealization that children fully represent sentences as word strings from the start. To differentiate the predictions of different accounts of syntactic bootstrapping, we need to know exactly what children can represent about sentences at various points in development.

A. LOCATING ARGUMENTS WITHIN UTTERANCES

If a child's representation of an input sentence is missing nouns, then this representation will of course provide less constraint on its alignment with conceptual structure than a sentence represented with its arguments intact. The ability to identify and comprehend multiple words within an utterance should be an initial limiting factor in the comprehension of sentences and therefore in the acquisition of verb meanings.

Adult listeners identify and comprehend familiar words rapidly and with apparent ease, and retain those words in memory long enough to understand a sentence. However, skilled word recognition takes a long time to develop. Even young school-aged children perform less well than adults in tests of spoken word recognition (see Nittrouer & Boothroyd, 1990, and Gerken, Murphy, & Aslin, 1995, for reviews). Toddlers and preschoolers make some startling errors, such as often failing to differentiate a nonsense word from a known word (e.g., Gerken et al., 1995; Hallé & de Boysson-Bardies, 1996; Stager & Werker, 1997). The difficulty of identifying and comprehending familiar words is also influenced by the position of the words in a sentence. For example, Fernald (1994) presented utterances containing familiar nouns to 15-month-olds, with the nouns either utterance-final or utterance-medial. Fernald assessed comprehension by measuring the difference in time spent looking at a slide of the named object versus a distracter during a brief period following the offset of the target word. The infants were more likely to show comprehension by this measure when the target word was utterance-final. Thus, identifying a spoken word and retrieving its meaning is a demanding task for young children, and this difficulty is exacerbated for sentence-medial words. We cannot assume that toddlers and preschoolers can routinely construct, and retain in memory, an accurate representation of a multiword utterance.

However, at least two familiar factors might facilitate children's identification of words embedded in sentences—acoustic stress on nonfinal words and the tendency of unstressed nonfinal words to have been mentioned before.

First, the perceptual disadvantage of medial position (see also Echols, 1993;

Echols & Newport, 1992; Peters, 1985; Slobin, 1985) was mitigated by acoustic stress in Fernald's task: 15-month-olds comprehended medial words as readily as final words when the medial words were lengthened. Stressing a medial word thus helped the children to identify the stressed word itself. Given these and other findings, a plausible conclusion is that stress and position in a sentence partly determine which words or parts of words children first identify and have available to guide comprehension of the sentence (Echols, 1993; Echols & Newport, 1992; Gleitman, Gleitman, Landau, & Wanner, 1987).

Nonetheless, stress on nonfinal words cannot solve all of the child's sentence representational problems, because nonfinal words are unlikely to be greatly stressed in ordinary conversation. Across languages, speakers tend to position new words at the ends of utterances and previously mentioned ("given") words nearer the beginnings of utterances (e.g., Givon, 1976; Keenan, 1976; MacWhinney, 1977; Prince, 1992) and to shorten repeated words (e.g., Fowler & Housum, 1987). Both of these properties are true of speech to infants (Fisher & Tokura, 1995): Mothers described simple puppet events to their 14-month-olds and to an adult. In both listener contexts, speakers usually placed a target puppet name in utterance-final position when it was mentioned for the first time, and placed second uses in final position significantly less often. Repeated words were also significantly shorter, quieter, contained smaller pitch excursions, and appeared in longer sentences than newly introduced words. The relative effects of repetition on the acoustic realization of words did not differ in infant-directed and adult-directed speech, suggesting that mothers reduce repeated words in speech to novice listeners as well as to expert listeners (see also Bard & Anderson, 1982). Thus, nonfinal words are likely to be given in the conversational context, and will most often not receive the kind of acoustic emphasis that eased their identification by 15-month-olds (Fernald, 1994).

Second, however, unstressed old words have a perceptual advantage of their own: They have been heard before. The reduction of given words in speech is practicable in part because listeners who have heard a word once need less acoustic information to recognize it again (Fowler & Housum, 1987). If the same principle is true of infants and toddlers, then the ordinary presentation of words as new and then given could increase the likelihood that learners will recognize more than one word per utterance. Infants might recognize unstressed words that are repetitions, as well as words in utterance-final position and words with exaggerated stress (Fernald & Mazzie, 1991; Fisher & Tokura, 1995).

The perceptual/memory phenomenon needed to allow this benefit from repetition is simply repetition priming of a kind readily found in auditory perception tasks with adults (e.g., Church & Schacter, 1994). Like adults, young children show long-term auditory word priming (Church & Fisher, 1998). Children 2, 2.5, and 3 years old heard a list of familiar words, participated in a brief distracter task, and then tried to repeat words that had been mildly low-pass filtered to make them slightly harder to identify. Children at all three ages more accurately repeated words from the study list than other familiar words. Merriman and Marazita (1995) also found evidence for the short-term priming of phonological units smaller than a word. They asked 2-year-olds to interpret nonsense nouns by choosing either a familiar object (e.g., a bottle) or an unfamiliar object (e.g., a scale). Each trial immediately followed a short story, which either included words sharing sound elements of the nonsense word, or did not include such words. Many studies have revealed that children tend to choose an unfamiliar object as the referent of an unfamiliar word (e.g., Markman, 1989). The 2-year-olds in this study were more likely to conform to this pattern when the preceding story primed elements of the nonsense word than when it did not.

Many observers have noted the frequency of partial self-repetitions in maternal speech (e.g., Broen, 1972; Fernald & Simon, 1984; Hoff-Ginsberg, 1985; Stern, Spieker, Barnett, & MacKain, 1983). The extreme repetitiveness of speech to young children may help children to recognize multiple words in utterances, through the priming of words that subsequently appear in a reduced form.

In this section I have made two main points. First, identifying multiple words within sentences is apparently a challenging information-processing feat for young children. Whenever children cannot identify the set of nouns in a sentence, they will have little or no information about the meaning of the sentence. The child's ability to create partial sentence structures, containing the set of nouns provided in the sentence, will initially limit the utility of sentence structures as guides for verb learning. Second, however, commonplace perceptual and memory factors should support children's recognition of words in sentences, and thereby support their creation of partial sentence structures. These factors include acoustic stress on new words and the priming of words that are repeated in a discourse.

B. GROUPING ARGUMENTS WITHIN UTTERANCES

Partial representations of sentences can serve as analogs of relational concepts only if the recognizable nouns are perceived as grouped within an utterance. Research on infant-directed speech suggests that utterance boundaries are marked by robust acoustic cues that could support the perceptual grouping of words into utterances; this argument is a part of what has been called the prosodic bootstrapping hypothesis (e.g., Gleitman et al., 1987; Jusczyk et al., 1992; Morgan, 1986; Morgan, Meier & Newport, 1987). Furthermore, recent evidence suggests that young infants are sensitive to the acoustic cues that signal prosodic groupings in their languages and use these cues to guide their representation of utterances.

In adult-directed English, utterance-final words tend to be lengthened relative to nonfinal words (e.g., Cooper & Paccia-Cooper, 1980; Scott, 1982), pitch tends to fall precipitously near the end of an utterance (e.g., Cooper & Sorenson, 1977), and pauses are longer at utterance boundaries than elsewhere (Cooper & Paccia-

Cooper, 1980; Scott, 1982). The same cues have been found in infant-directed speech as well, in an exaggerated form (Bernstein Ratner, 1986; Morgan, 1986). Infant-directed speech in several languages is characterized by smoothed and expanded pitch contours separated by long pauses, in contrast to the choppier contours of adult-directed speech (e.g., Fernald & Simon, 1984; Grieser & Kuhl, 1988; Masataka, 1992). These features, if universally available, could help utterances cohere as perceptual units.

Notable cross-linguistic similarities have been found in the acoustic shape of utterances, particularly in the use of rising or falling pitch contours in similar communicative contexts (e.g., Bolinger, 1978; Fernald, 1990; Papousek, Papousek, & Symmes, 1991). However, this similarity is limited by significant cross-linguistic variation in prosodic patterns, suggesting a complication for the detection of acoustic utterance boundaries by infants. For example, English has relatively extreme word lengthening at sentence boundaries, while other languages including Swedish, Estonian (Lehiste & Fox, 1993), and Japanese (Takeda, Sagisaka, & Kuwabara, 1989) do not. Such variations might be related to differences in grammar and segmental phonology. For example, Japanese is a verb-final language, and thus many sentences end in tense markers (e.g., the past tense - *ta*) which, like other closed-class morphemes, tend to be short (e.g., Campbell, 1992). Furthermore, Lehiste and Fox (1993) have suggested that languages that have phonemic vowel length contrasts (like Swedish, Estonian and Japanese) generally have less sentence-final lengthening. Such differences in prosodic patterns across languages influence adult listeners' perceptions. English listeners give less weight to syllable duration as a cue to stress in utterance-final position than Swedish listeners, apparently due to differing expectations for the default length of an utterance-final syllable (Lehiste & Fox, 1993).

A study of spontaneous infant-directed speech in English and Japanese revealed both cross-linguistic similarities and differences in the acoustic markings of utterance boundaries (Fisher & Tokura, 1996a). Three English-speaking and three Japanese-speaking mothers were recorded in spontaneous interactions with their 13- to 14-month-old infants, and multiutterance samples of each mother's speech were digitized for acoustic analysis. Measurements of the duration, the range in pitch (peak F_0–valley F_0), and the average amplitude of the vowel in each syllable, as well as the length of any pause following each syllable, were compared across positions in grammatically distinct utterances, determined from transcripts, to examine whether utterance-final syllables differed from others in their acoustic properties in the two languages.

Japanese and English revealed one very powerful segmentation cue that operated in exactly the same way across languages. As previously found by Broen (1972) for English and by Fernald and Simon (1984) for German, nearly all (96%) of the long pauses (≥ 260 ms) in both the English and Japanese samples occurred at the boundaries of grammatically distinct utterances. A majority of the grammatically distinct utterances in these samples—58% for English and 69% for Japanese—were followed by a long pause. Furthermore, in both languages these pauses were preceded by very long vowels and an increase in pitch range. Prepausal vowels were about twice as long and covered pitch excursions twice as great as vowels not preceding pauses. The similarity in these patterns is consistent with suggestions that final lengthening and a fall in pitch appear widely across languages because they follow from a natural tendency toward relaxation of the vocal apparatus preceding a pause (e.g., Hauser & Fowler, 1992; MacNeilage & Ladefoged, 1976; Martin, 1972). A prepausal reduction in amplitude also found for Japanese fits this view as well, and its absence in English is not surprising given the tendency of stressed (therefore louder) words to appear utterance-finally in infant-directed English (Fernald & Mazzie, 1991; Fisher & Tokura, 1995). The languages differed, however, in the magnitude of final lengthening. Prepausal vowels were lengthened significantly more in English than in Japanese.

Differences across languages in the extent of final lengthening confirm a role for learning in the perceptual identification of utterance-boundary cues by young infants. The reliability of pauses as markers of utterance boundaries in infant-directed speech, however, suggests a simple mechanism for this language-specific tuning. Infants might become accustomed to the characteristic melodies and rhythmic patterns that predict upcoming pauses, and begin to use them to anticipate utterance ends before they occur (e.g., Hauser & Fowler, 1992), as well as to perceive subjective pauses even where no silent pause is present, as adults do (e.g., Duez, 1993).

Thus the integrity of the utterance in infant-directed speech has a good acoustic basis. Infant-directed speech across languages consists largely of short utterances with smoothed, connected pitch contours, separated by very long pauses e.g., Fernald & Simon, 1984; Grieser & Kuhl, 1988; Masataka, 1992; Papousek & Hwang, 1991). The precise shape of these pitch contours and the rhythm of syllables within them differ in accord with the phonological system of each language. Prosodic patterns are to some extent language-specific, and their details must be acquired. The reliable separation of utterances by pauses, however, suggests an initial strong grouping cue that could support the early acquisition of language-specific prosodic melodies.

Quite young infants are sensitive to the acoustic properties of utterance boundaries. In a selective listening task, 6-month-old infants listened longer to samples of child-directed speech with pauses artificially inserted at sentence boundaries than with pauses inserted within utterances (Hirsh-Pasek et al., 1987; Kemler-Nelson, Hirsh-Pasek, Jusczyk, & Wright Cassidy, 1989). This difference was obtained even when the speech samples were low-pass filtered to remove lexical and segmental information. These findings have been interpreted as evidence that infants detect pitch and duration cues that predict upcoming pauses, and that pauses not heralded by these cues sound unnatural to them (but see Fernald & McRoberts,

1996, for an alternative view). Other evidence suggests, further, that children use the prosodic shape of utterances to group speech information in memory. In a habituation task, 2-month-olds were better able to remember the phonetic content and the order of words produced as a single utterance than of the same words produced in a list or as two sentence fragments (Mandel, Jusczyk, & Kemler-Nelson, 1994; Mandel, Kemler-Nelson, & Jusczyk, 1996). These findings suggest that the familiar melody of utterances helps infants to organize speech in memory, grouping words into a coherent perceptual structure.

C. REPRESENTING THE SUBJECT–OBJECT ASYMMETRY

Thus far I have suggested two ways in which the properties of child-directed speech could aid children in constructing partial sentence structures of the kind needed to support the structure-sensitive interpretation of verbs. The tendency for unstressed nonfinal words to have been previously mentioned, along with the repetitive nature of child-directed speech, should increase the probability that children can recognize multiple words within an utterance. The separation of utterances by long pauses, with characteristic pitch and temporal changes preceding pauses, could teach children to represent utterances as bounded sequences in the speech stream. Children could then use the set of recognizable referential terms within a bounded utterance to guide their interpretation by structural alignment. In this section I consider the possibility that observable differences between sentence subjects and objects could lead children to represent sentences asymmetrically and therefore to use even partial sentence structures as a source of information about the asymmetrical semantic structure of a sentence.

1. Acoustic Cues to Within-Utterance Phrase Boundaries

One possibility is that acoustic properties similar to those examined in section III.B for utterance boundaries could also tend to occur at phrase boundaries within sentences, helping to establish a boundary between the subject and verb phrase. Morgan et al. (1987; Morgan, 1986) have argued that grammars are unlearnable unless they provide some perceptible markers correlated with the boundaries of major phrases. The evidence for clear prosodic cues to phrase boundaries in child-directed speech is less strong than the evidence for utterance boundary cues, however. One robust property of speech to children is that the utterances are short (e.g., Broen, 1972; Fernald & Simon, 1984; Newport, Gleitman, & Gleitman, 1977; Snow, 1972; Stern et al., 1983), and short utterances are less likely to contain audible prosodic breaks at major phrase boundaries (Ferreira, 1993; Gee & Grosjean, 1983). Certainly, pauses within the clause are vanishingly rare in speech to infants and young children (e.g., Broen, 1972; Fernald & Simon, 1984; Fisher & Tokura, 1996a).

Nevertheless, 9-month-old infants in a selective listening task listened longer to samples of spontaneous child-directed English with pauses artificially inserted at the subject–verb boundary than to samples in which pauses did not coincide with a major phrase boundary (Jusczyk et al., 1992). This result suggests that at least some sentences in these spontaneous speech samples had internal acoustic properties that made a pause following the subject sound more natural than a pause elsewhere. In a subsequent study, Gerken, Jusczyk, and Mandel (1994) used as stimuli special sets of sentences read aloud, in order to determine what sentence types were likely to contain perceptible acoustic changes marking the subject–verb phrase boundary. In this study, pauses after the subject phrase were preferred only in sentences that had lexical noun phrase subjects rather than pronoun subjects ("Sammy likes to play baseball" versus "He likes to play baseball") and in yes–no questions, in which an unstressed auxiliary precedes a pronoun subject ("Do you like to play baseball?"). Gerken et al. found consistent local changes in the duration and pitch of syllables preceding the subject–verb boundary, but not preceding the verb–complement boundary, in both the lexical-subject and yes–no question samples.

Similar local acoustic changes preceding sentence-internal phrase boundaries were also found in samples of spontaneous speech to 14-month-olds in English and Japanese (Fisher & Tokura, 1996a). In English, phrase-final syllables were reliably longer than the immediately preceding syllable within the same utterance, but nonfinal syllables did not tend to be longer than their preceding syllables. No tendency toward slowing at the end of the subject phrase occurred in Japanese; however, phrase-final syllables were lower pitched than preceding nonfinal syllables, to a greater degree than the ordinary decline in pitch throughout the sentence. These findings are preliminary, because few sentences in the samples were amenable to these analyses. In the Japanese speech to 14-month-olds, most utterances did not contain an internal phrase boundary; this lack is due simply to the frequency of phrase deletion in Japanese (e.g., Rispoli, 1989). In the English samples, the vast majority of the sentences—84% across speakers—had pronoun subjects (see also Broen, 1972). These characteristics of casual speech to infants left few opportunities for clear acoustic markings of the boundary between subjects and verb phrases. Where such opportunities existed, however, some acoustic markings of phrase boundaries were reliable enough to be detected amid the variability of spontaneous speech.

Two conclusions from these perceptual and acoustic findings seem warranted. First, the variability of spontaneous speech to infants does not entirely overwhelm smaller within-sentence acoustic regularities. These patterns can create a perceptible discontinuity within utterances at the region of a phrase boundary when they occur, suggesting to the listener that an utterance contains distinct parts (e.g., Gerken et al., 1994). Second, however, distributional factors—the deletion and pronominalization of phrases—guarantee that few sentences in spontaneous speech to infants contain these types of cues. The rarity of within-utterance acoustic cues to phrase boundaries suggests that other distributional supports for the asymmetrical internal structure of sentences are needed (e.g., Fisher & Tokura, 1995, 1996a, 1996b; Gerken et al., 1994; Morgan, 1996).

2. *Word Order in Partial Sentence Structures*

Lacking knowledge of the syntax of a particular language, children could observe a number of surface asymmetries between subjects and objects that appear across languages (e.g., Croft, 1990; Keenan, 1976). One of the most striking of these asymmetries is order. In the vast majority of languages, the subject precedes the object (e.g., Croft, 1990; Tomlin, 1986), preserving the prominence of the subject noun phrase even in a partial representation of a sentence. In an analysis of a free word-order language (Finnish), the subject-first order was statistically more frequent than object-first order, due to the strong correlation between grammatical subject and discourse topic (Karttunen & Kay, 1985). The overwhelming preference for subject-first orders in the world's languages is a strong hint that children readily interpret a word-order asymmetry as meaningful, and that they agree on what it should mean (see Bowerman, 1993).

In addition, studies of adults' processing of sentences suggest that the typical ordering of subjects before objects could automatically trigger an appropriately asymmetrical representation. The first noun phrase in an utterance has a privileged place in memory, more readily recalled and constituting a better prompt for the rest of the sentence than other noun phrases (MacWhinney, 1977), even if it is not the grammatical subject, as in (21) (Gernsbacher & Hargreaves, 1988). This finding suggests that order itself, independent of a syntactic analysis, affects the representation of utterances in memory and could cause sentences to be represented asymmetrically. MacWhinney (1977) argued that the first referential term in a sentence is taken as a conceptual starting point for understanding the sentence, which is exactly the effect required to achieve a perspective-based interpretation of the subject-object asymmetry.

(21) Because of *Lisa,* Tina was evicted from her apartment.

3. *Subjects as Old Information*

Another set of powerful asymmetries between subjects and objects concerns the likelihood that transitive subjects make reference to entities already mentioned in the discourse (e.g., Bates, 1976; Bates & MacWhinney, 1982; Keenan, 1976; Prince, 1992). A referent mentioned again may have already been represented by the listener, and this history should tend to influence the interpretation of subsequent utterances just as it aids identification of the repeated word.

Adult listeners expect recently mentioned referents to be maintained across utterances (e.g., H. H. Clark & Havilland, 1977; Grosz & Sidner, 1986; Johnson-Laird, 1983; Kintsch & van Dijk, 1978). In accord with this expectation, passages are easier to comprehend when successive sentences share referents (e.g., Ehrlich & Johnson-Laird, 1982) and when words referring to old referents are shortened (Fowler & Housum, 1987), deleted, or pronominalized (e.g., Cloitre & Bever, 1988; Fillmore, 1968; Keenan, 1976; Marslen-Wilson, Levy, & Tyler, 1982; Prince, 1992). When the subject of a sentence has the same referent as the subject of the preceding sentence, the noun is not repeated in its original form, but is shortened, pronominalized, or omitted altogether. In comprehension, adults appear to assume that unreduced nouns introduce new referents, and are briefly misled if a full noun phrase is used to refer to a continuing subject. For example, comprehension is slowed when an unreduced noun phrase appears in subject position where a pronoun would suffice (e.g., "Bruno was the bully of the neighborhood. *Bruno/He* chased Tommy all the way home"; Gordon, Grosz, & Gilliom, 1993).

Speech to young children displays strong forms of the same features that facilitate comprehension for adults. Child-directed speech is repetitive, containing many sequences of utterances with partial phrasal overlap (e.g., Broen, 1972; Fernald & Simon, 1984; Hoff-Ginsberg, 1985; Newport et al., 1977; Snow, 1972; Stern et al., 1983). Mothers addressing young children shorten repeated words (Fisher & Tokura, 1995), use pronoun subjects most of the time (e.g., Fisher & Tokura, 1996a, 1996b), and readily omit subjects in languages that permit it, such as Japanese, Italian, and Chinese (e.g., Rispoli, 1989; Valian, 1990; Wang, Lillo-Martin, Best, & Levitt, 1992). Subjects are more often deleted than objects even in languages that allow both to be dropped (e.g., Japanese and Chinese; Rispoli, 1989; Wang et al., 1992). Also, in addressing infants, mothers emphasize new words by stressing them and placing them at the ends of sentences (Fernald & Mazzie, 1991; Fisher & Tokura, 1995). Thus subjects and objects are very distinct in the speech addressed to children; subjects are much more likely to refer to already-mentioned elements, and correspondingly likely to be realized as pronouns or omitted from the sentence altogether.

Both experimental and observational studies of children's own language production support the hypothesis that children, like adults, are disposed to maintain arguments from sentence to sentence, and have early knowledge of the strong tendency of sentence subjects to express given information.

First, young children profit from the repetitiveness of child-directed speech much as adults would. Two-year-olds whose mothers repeated themselves often, deleting, moving, or pronominalizing elements of sentences, showed greater increases in verb use over a 2-month period than children whose mothers repeated themselves less (Hoff-Ginsberg, 1985). This finding shows that children are affected by the repetition of phrases or of referents across adjacent sentences in a discourse.

Second, many researchers have found that young talkers quickly pick up patterns of information flow in their languages. MacWhinney and Bates (1978) elicited descriptions of pictures from 3-, 4-, and 5-year-old speakers of American English, Hungarian, and Italian, as well as adult speakers of each language. Though 3-year-olds were in many respects less systematic in their responses than older children or adults, they differed across languages in their choices of sentential devices to describe new and repeated elements of the pictures. For example, Italian-speaking 3-year-olds tended to omit sentence subjects when the subject referred to an element repeated from a previous picture, while under the same circumstances English-speaking 3-year-olds were more likely to pronominalize sentence subjects. Language-specific rules for marking given and new elements in sentences seem to be acquired at an early age. Similarly, when Korean and Japanese 3- and 4-year-olds were asked to repeat sentences with two conjoined clauses containing repeated noun phrases, as in (22), they altered the majority of such sentences by reducing the second, redundant noun phrase to a pronoun (as in (23); O'Grady, Suzuki-wei, & Cho, 1986). When imitating stimulus sentences that already displayed this pattern, as in (23), the children very rarely altered the pattern of pronominalization in their repetitions. Very young children's spontaneous productions also show adult-like tendencies to omit or pronominalize given elements rather than new elements, to avoid sentences containing more than one new nominal element, and to avoid placing new nominal elements in the subject position of transitive sentences (e.g., Allen, 1998). All of these findings support the hypothesis that children are sensitive to patterns of repetition in conversations, and to grammatical devices for expressing given and new information.

(22) Because Hannah was thirsty, Hannah drank juice.
(23) Because Hannah was thirsty, she drank juice.

   The asymmetry in the physical realization of new and given nouns may also be informative to young children. Adults interpret shortened nouns and pronouns as indications that a referent has been mentioned before (e.g., Cloitre & Bever, 1988; Fowler & Housum, 1987). Levinsky and Gerken (1994) reported intriguing evidence that young children may understand the significance of acoustic reduction in much the same way. They asked 2.5-year-olds to imitate sentences like "The cow pushes the horse," presented either with a neutral stress pattern or with focal stress on the verb or object noun phrase. Children sometimes substituted a pronoun for the subject noun phrase, especially when the verb or the object received focal stress. Although Levinsky and Gerken did not conduct acoustic analyses of the sentences, applying focal stress to the verb or the object in these sentences probably resulted in de-stressing the subject. Stressing the verb or object of the sentence draws attention toward it; the subject is relegated to the background and thus is likely to be pronominalized. Furthermore, these children rarely if ever replaced an object noun phrase with a pronoun, again suggesting that young English speakers are sensitive to the correlation between subject position, continuing topic, and pronouns.

A tendency for the nominal elements of one sentence to influence the representation and interpretation of the next could help to explain how language acquisition works at all, given the frequency of pronoun use and argument omission in causal speech (e.g., Rispoli, 1995). In languages like Chinese, Korean, and Japanese, which permit the deletion of many constituents, many sentences considered in isolation are quite uninformative, both about their meanings and about the syntactic requirements of their lexical items. For example, in a study of Japanese speech to 2-year-olds, Rispoli (1989) estimated that only 13% of transitive verbs occurred with both of their arguments within the utterance. On average, a child would have to hear a transitive verb eight times before hearing it once with both of its arguments present in a single sentence. A likely conclusion is that any complete theory of comprehension, by learners or by adults, must assign a central role to effects of the structure and content of one utterance on the next.

For present purposes, the prevalence of observable subject–object asymmetries across languages could lead children to represent sentences asymmetrically. Across languages, subjects tend to be reduced, pronominalized, or deleted. Superficially, these tendencies might seem to make subjects less rather than more prominent in a representation of a sentence. However, the pervasive asymmetry in the realization of subjects and objects exists *because the subjects have been mentioned before.* Thus, the repeated form need not be as intelligible as the first use. The suggestion advanced here is that subject referents, whether named in a current sentence or not, could be represented as the more prominent "starting point" of the sentence, based on their tendency to precede objects both within and across utterances in a discourse. An asymmetrical representation of a sentence would provide cues to the two aspects of verb perspective with which I began— identifying the set of participants involved in the semantic relation encoded by the verb, and identifying which of them is the conceptual figure whose role the verb describes.

As mentioned above, two views have been advanced on the use of subject choice as a cue in interpreting transitive verbs. First, subject choice might be an explicitly syntactic cue. Once a child can identify subjects of sentences as such, he or she could achieve an appropriately asymmetrical interpretation of transitive sentences. This cue, unlike the number of arguments assigned to a verb, would become useful in verb learning only after some basic syntax acquisition. Second, however, subject choice could serve as a presyntactic cue to the interpretation of transitive verbs, available even in partial sentence structures. As summarized in this section, some simple properties of sentences, correlated with grammatical subjects across languages, might bias children to adopt the verb's perspective on a two-participant scene. These properties include word order, pronominalization, and the strong tendency of subject referents to have been mentioned before. The evidence reviewed in this section supports the plausibility of the second, presyntactic view. In the final section I describe some evidence concerning cross-lin-

guistic variation in grammar that also supports a presyntactic view of structural
cues to verb learning.

IV. Conclusions: Verb Learning and Thematic Roles Revisited

Clearly, much further research is needed to establish under what circumstances
and at what ages children can achieve the simple representations of sentences required for structural alignment to work, when children can use the proposed simple structural cues, and whether the early misinterpretations predicted by the
structural alignment of partial sentence structures reliably occur. However, the
evidence reviewed here makes an initial case that presyntactic structural cues to
verb meaning arise from the structural similarity of sentences and conceptual representations.

I have suggested that children use structural alignment to map noun phrases in
a sentence onto roles in a conceptual representation of an event. In this process of
alignment, the child seeks a conceptual relation that (a) includes the participants
mentioned in the sentence and (b) takes the subject as a conceptual figure, describing its role relative to other arguments. The result of this process could be an
interpretation in quite specific terms. For example, hearing "The car hit the lamp-
post" the child might interpret the arguments of *hit* essentially as "hitter" and "hit-
tee." Semantic roles of such narrow scope have been described as *individual thematic roles,* which categorize event participants only abstractly enough to capture
the similarity among various uses of the same word (e.g., Dowty, 1989; Ladusaw
& Dowty, 1988). The structural alignment account would allow the event-specific information attached to a new verb to be arbitrarily specific; however, its de-
pendence on structural alignment guarantees that only the gross structure of the
selected interpretation will affect argument linking. This view offers two potential
advantages over a verb-learning procedure that depends on the links between
thematic role types (like agent and patient) and syntactic functions (like subject
and object), that have dominated discussions of verb syntax and semantics (e.g.,
Dowty, 1991; Grimshaw, 1994; Pinker, 1989).

First, and most crucially, the structural alignment view readily permits limited
variation in verb syntax and semantics within and across languages. Like an account based on linking rules, structural alignment predicts strong cross-linguistic
regularities in the event content of various grammatical positions in sentences.
However, it does so based only on the conceptual salience or predicability (e.g.,
Bock et al., 1992; Gleitman et al., 1996; McDonald et al., 1993; Talmy, 1983) of
certain participant roles in events, rather than on innate links between the subject
role and one position in each of an innate set of semantic structures. Mobile, ac-

tive, or animate event participants are very salient; thus, conceptual relations with these as central figures will often be readily available to be mapped onto sentences. The sentence itself, via structural alignment, can modify the salience of aspects of an event, allowing the child to select a conceptual representation that shares the relational structure of the sentence. This structure-guided mapping would permit verbs to be learned despite the partial arbitrariness of the linguistic encoding of scenes.

One example of a cross-language difference in the semantic and syntactic structure of a verb with similar event content was given in section II.F.1—the case of *hit* as an agent–patient verb in English, and a locative action verb in Chechen-Ingush (Bowerman, 1990). Such variability in the linguistic expression of world events is not an isolated rarity. For example, languages provide a rich vocabulary for talking about human reactions to stimuli—*fear, scare, like, please, admire, embarrass, upset,* and so on. Such verbs can take the stimulus as the subject and describe its effect on a human experiencer (as in "Thunderstorms scare John"), or take the experiencer as the subject and encode the reaction to a stimulus (as in "John likes thunderstorms"). Most languages have some verbs displaying each pattern, but tend to favor one or the other (Bowerman, 1990; Talmy, 1985). Viewed in terms of traditional thematic role types, these two argument assignments are contradictory (e.g., Grimshaw, 1990): Both classes of verbs have the same two thematic roles (stimulus and experiencer), but neither is uniformly selected as subject. Structural alignment can explain how children learn the apparently contradictory argument assignments of *scare* and *like:* Via structural alignment, each verb describes the role of the subject relative to the object, whether influencing it or reacting to it. If children are sensitive to sentence structures, then they can learn the verbs their language provides, even though verbs vary within and across languages in their perspectives on the same events. Simply detecting the structural similarity between representations of scene and sentence provides an appropriately flexible constraint on relations between syntax and semantics.

Second, the structural alignment view naturally permits a grammatical phenomenon that is quite intractable on many other theories—the acquisition of the "ergative" pattern of grammatical markings (e.g., Dixon, 1994). In essence, languages must distinguish three major grammatical roles: The single argument of an intransitive sentence, and the two arguments of a transitive sentence. Most languages group these three roles into two major grammatical roles, but not all do so in the same way. In discussing these three roles, linguists typically label intransitive subjects 'S,' transitive subjects 'A,' and transitive objects 'O,' as shown in (24). The 'A' in this nomenclature is short for Agent, despite the fact that only a subset of transitive subjects are agents in the usual sense of animate causers of events. Most languages, including English, display the nominative pattern, in which the subject of an intransitive sentence (S) is treated like the A argument of a transitive sentence. In English, S and A arguments both appear in preverbal position, and pronouns in that position are in nominative case, as in (24). The grouping of arguments S and A defines the familiar category "subject" of nominative syntax.

(24)   <u>She</u> looked around.
       S

       <u>She</u> saw <u>her</u>.
       A   O

In contrast, in languages with the ergative pattern, the O and S arguments receive the same grammatical case and the A argument of a transitive verb is assigned a different case (Dixon, 1994; Marantz, 1984). Ergative languages are sometimes described as having patient subjects rather than agent subjects (e.g., Fillmore, 1977; Marantz, 1984). If "subject" is defined based on grammatical markings shared with the intransitive subject S, then the patient arguments of prototypical transitive sentences are surface subjects in ergative languages. This conclusion would violate a central assumption of an acquisition theory based on innate thematic role linking rules (e.g., Dowty, 1991; Pinker, 1989): If languages exist in which agents are not subjects, then an innate link between agent and subject cannot play a basic role in the acquisition of grammar.

However, others would argue that the claim that ergative languages have patient subjects does not describe the linguistic phenomena very well. No language is entirely ergative: All languages that have some ergative properties also use the nominative pattern in some linguistic contexts (Dixon, 1994). Thus, on the patient–subject analysis, a transitive verb would differ in the argument (A or O) that is the "subject," depending on such factors as whether the arguments are nouns or pronouns (Blake, 1976) and the tense of the verb (Dixon, 1994). Ergative languages therefore cast doubt not only on the innate linking of a universal set of semantic roles like agent and patient with grammatical roles like subject and object, but also on the basic premise that a single primitive syntactic category of subject applies to both transitive and intransitive sentences across languages.

Problems defining subjects are not new. The lack of a set of semantic or syntactic criteria that pick out a single subject category across languages constitutes a long-standing problem in linguistic theory (e.g., Keenan, 1976). The point here, however, is that because the structural alignment account does not depend on linking rules or true syntactic categories, it readily permits this kind of variation across languages while preserving some simple biases concerning the relationship between syntax and semantics.

The number of nouns in a sentence should be as informative to children learning an ergative language as it is to those learning the more common nominative pattern. Children interpret transitive and intransitive sentences differently based on the differing number of arguments (Fisher, 1996a, 1999); therefore, they will not initially be required to treat either argument of a transitive verb as being the same as the subject of an intransitive verb. Children can separately acquire the surface markings of the arguments of transitive and intransitive verbs, based on their initial, structure-sensitive interpretation of verbs in sentences.

In addition, I argued that children might gain access to a useful interpretation of the subject–object asymmetry in transitive sentences in terms of verb perspective. In section III.C I suggested two possible routes for this interpretation, one requiring identification of the syntactic role subject, and one based on the tendency of subject nouns to come first, within sentences (most of the world's languages have a subject–object order) but especially across sentences (subject nouns are more likely to be repeated). Ergative languages show the same asymmetry in the distribution of repeated and new nouns that other languages do (Dixon, 1994; du Bois, 1987): The A argument of a transitive sentence is much more likely to refer to an entity already mentioned in the conversation than the O argument is. If, as suggested above, children interpret this repetition as a cue to the verb's perspective on an event, then they will interpret verbs correctly based on presyntactic structural cues in either ergative or nominative languages.

These two consequences of the structural alignment view concern the basic problem that the syntactic bootstrapping view was developed to solve: The syntax and semantics of verbs varies across languages, and children must have the capacity to learn the verbs and structures their language provides. Bowerman (1985, 1990; Choi & Bowerman, 1991) described children's early sensitivity to orthogonal categorizations imposed by different languages and suggested that a basic responsiveness to the structure of the language the child hears must play a primary role in language acquisition. Similarly, Jackendoff (1990) noted some arbitrariness in the syntactic properties of verbs within languages. Grimshaw (1979) also argued that the semantic predictability of syntactic complement type is imperfect, requiring lexical entries for verbs to include specifically syntactic as well as semantic information.

By assuming a circumscribed form of one-to-one mapping in sentence interpretation, based only on the relational similarity between sentences and their meanings, the structural alignment procedure allows children to learn these partly arbitrary patterns. In the process of structural alignment, the semantic content of a verb (e.g., hitting vs. dropping) is obtained from world observations as mapped onto the sentence structure. In this way children could find the structure of their language intrinsically meaningful, and the variety of different characterizations of events within and across languages would be limited only by the structures of the verbs the learner hears, and by the learner's ability to represent a conceptual relation congruent with the sentence.

ACKNOWLEDGMENTS

The research reported in this article was supported by National Science Foundation grant BNS 9113580, National Institute of Child Health and Human Development grant HD/OD34715-01, and by the University of Illinois. I thank Renée Baillargeon, Judy DeLoache, Susan Garnsey, Lila Gleitman, and Henry Gleitman, for many helpful comments.

REFERENCES

Allen, S. E. M. (1998, June). *Learning about argument realization in Inuktitut and English: Gradual development in the use of non-ellipsed forms.* Paper presented in the Argument Structure Workshop, Max Planck Institute for Psycholinguistics, Nijmegen, NL.

Anderson, S. R. (1971). On the role of deep structure in sentence interpretation. *Foundations of Language, 6,* 197–219.

Baillargeon, R. (1994). Physical reasoning in young infants: Seeking explanations for impossible events. *British Journal of Developmental Psychology, 12,* 9–33.

Baker, M. (1997). Thematic roles and syntactic structure. In L. Haegeman (Ed.), *Elements of grammar: Handbook of generative syntax* (pp. 73–137). Dordrecht: Kluwer.

Baldwin, D. A. (1993). Early referential understanding: Infants' ability to recognize referential acts for what they are. *Developmental Psychology, 29*(5), 832–843.

Bard, E., & Anderson, A. (1982). The unintelligibility of speech to children. *Journal of Child Language, 10,* 265–292.

Bates, E. (1976). *Language and context: The acquisition of pragmatics.* New York: Academic Press.

Bates, E., & MacWhinney, B. (1982). Functionalist approaches to grammar. In E. Wanner & L. R. Gleitman (Eds.), *Language acquisition: The state of the art* (pp. 173–218). New York: Cambridge University Press.

Behrend, D. (1995). Processes involved in the initial mapping of verb meanings. In M. Tomasello & W. E. Merriman (Eds.), *Beyond names for things: Young children's acquisition of verb meaning* (pp. 251–276). Hillsdale, NJ: Erlbaum.

Bernstein Ratner, N. (1986). Durational cues which mark clause boundaries in mother-child speech. *Journal of Phonetics, 14,* 1303–1309.

Bierwisch, M., & Schreuder, R. (1992). From concepts to lexical items. *Cognition, 42,* 23–60.

Blake, B. J. (1976). On ergativity and the notion of subject: Some Australian cases. *Lingua, 39,* 281–300.

Bloom, L. (1970). *Language development: Form and function in emerging grammars.* Cambridge, MA: MIT Press.

Bloom, L., Lifter, K., & Hafitz, J. (1980). The semantics of verbs and the development of verb inflections in child language. *Language, 56,* 386–412.

Bloom, L., Lightbown, P., & Hood, L. (1975). Structure and variation in child language. *Monographs of the Society for Research in Child Development, 40*(2, Serial No. 160).

Bloom, L., Miller, P., & Hood, L. (1975). Variation and reduction as aspects of competence in language development. In A. Pick (Ed.), *Minnesota Symposia on Child Psychology* (Vol. 1, pp. 3–55). Minneapolis: University of Minnesota Press.

Bloom, P. (1990). Syntactic distinctions in child language. *Journal of Child Language, 17*(2), 343–355.

Bock, J. K. (1987). An effect of the accessibility of word forms on sentence structures. *Journal of Memory and Language, 26,* 119–137.

Bock, J. K., Loebell, H., & Morey, R. (1992). From conceptual roles to structural relations: Bridging the syntactic cleft. *Psychological Review, 99,* 150–171.

Bolinger, D. (1978). Intonation across languages. In J. H. Greenberg (Ed.), *Universals of human language: Vol. 2. Phonology* (pp. 471–524). Stanford, CA: Stanford University Press.

Bowerman, M. (1973). Structural relations in children's utterances: Syntactic or semantic? In T. E. Moore (Ed.), *Cognitive development and the acquisition of language* (pp. 197–213). New York: Academic Press.

Bowerman, M. (1982). Reorganizational processes in lexical and syntactic development. In E. Wanner & L. R. Gleitman (Eds.), *Language acquisition: The state of the art* (pp. 319–346). New York: Cambridge University Press.

Bowerman, M. (1985). What shapes children's grammars? In D. I. Slobin (Ed.), *The cross-linguistic study of language acquisition* (Vol. 2, pp. 1257–1319). Hillsdale, NJ: Erlbaum.

Bowerman, M. (1990). Mapping thematic roles onto syntactic functions: Are children helped by innate linking rules? *Linguistics, 28,* 1253–1289.

Bowerman, M. (1993, April). *Typological perspectives on language acquisition: Do cross-linguistic patterns predict development?* Paper presented at the 25th annual meeting of the Child Language Research Forum, Stanford, CA.

Braine, M. D. S. (1987). What is learned in acquiring word classes—a step toward an acquisition theory. In B. MacWhinney (Ed.), *Mechanisms of language acquisition* (pp. 65–87). Hillsdale, NJ: Erlbaum.

Braine, M. D. S. (1992). What sort of innate structure is needed to "bootstrap" into syntax? *Cognition, 45,* 77–100.

Braine, M. D. S., Brody, R. E., Fisch, S. M., Weisberger, M. J., & Blum, M. (1990). Can children use a verb without exposure to its argument structure? *Journal of Child Language, 17,* 313–342.

Broen, P. (1972). *The verbal environment of the language-learning child* (ASHA Monographs, No. 17). Washington, DC: American Speech and Hearing Society.

Brown, R. (1973). *A first language.* Cambridge, MA: Harvard University Press.

Campbell, N. (1992). Segmental elasticity and timing in Japanese speech. In Y. Tokhura, E. Vatikiotis-Bateson, & Y. Sagisaka (Eds.), *Speech perception, production, and linguistic structure* (pp. 403–418). Amsterdam. IOS Press.

Carlson, G. N., & Tanenhuas, M. K. (1988). Thematic roles and language comprehension. In W. Wilkins (Ed.), *Syntax and semantics: Thematic relations,* (pp. 263–288). Orlando, FL: Academic Press.

Cartwright, T. A., & Brent, M. R. (1997). Syntactic categorization in early language acquisition: Formalizing the role of distributional analysis. *Cognition, 63,* 121–170.

Choi, S., & Bowerman, M. (1991). Learning to express motion events in English and Korean: The influence of language-specific lexicalization patterns. *Cognition, 41,* 83–121.

Chomsky, N. (1981). *Lectures on government and binding.* Dordrecht: Foris.

Church, B. A., & Fisher, C. (1998). Long-term auditory word priming in preschoolers: Implicit memory support for language acquisition. *Journal of Memory and Language, 39,* 523–542.

Church, B. A., & Schacter, D. L. (1994). Perceptual specificity of auditory priming: Implicit memory for voice intonation and fundamental frequency. *Journal of Experimental Psychology: Learning, Memory, and Cognition, 20,* 521–533.

Clark, E. (1990). Speaker perspective in language acquisition. *Linguistics, 28,* 1201–1220.

Clark, H. H., & Begun, J. S. (1971). The semantics of sentence subjects. *Language and Speech, 14,* 34–46.

Clark, H. H., & Havilland, S. E. (1977). Comprehension and the given-new contract. In R. O. Freedle (Ed.), *Discourse production and comprehension* (pp. 1–40). Norwood, NJ: Ablex.

Cloitre, M., & Bever, T. G. (1988). Linguistic anaphors, levels of representation, and discourse. *Language and Cognitive Processes, 3,* 293–322.

Cohen, L., & Oakes, L. (1993). How infants perceive a simple causal event. *Developmental Psychology, 29*, 421–433.

Cooper, W., & Paccia-Cooper, J. (1980). *Syntax and speech.* Cambridge, MA: Harvard University Press.

Cooper, W., & Sorenson, J. M. (1977). Fundamental frequency contours at syntactic boundaries. *Journal of the Acoustical Society of America, 62*, 683–692.

Corrigan, R. (1986). The internal structure of English transitive sentences. *Memory & Cognition, 14*, 420–431.

Corrigan, R. (1988). Children's identification of actors and patients in prototypical and nonprototypical sentence types. *Cognitive Development, 3*, 285–297.

Corrigan, R., & Odya-Weis, C. (1985). The comprehension of semantic relations by two-year-olds: An exploratory study. *Journal of Child Language, 12*, 47–59.

Croft, W. (1990). *Typology and universals.* New York: Cambridge University Press.

Dixon, R. M. W. (1994). *Ergativity.* New York: Cambridge University Press.

Dowty, D. (1989). On the semantic content of the notion of 'thematic role.' In G. Chierchia, B. Partee, & R. Turner (Eds.), *Properties, types and meaning* (pp. 69–129). Dordrecht: Kluwer.

Dowty, D. (1991). Thematic proto-roles and argument selection. *Language, 67*, 547–619.

du Bois, J. (1987). The discourse basis of ergativity. *Language, 63*, 805–855.

Duez, D. (1993). Acoustic correlates of subjective pauses. *Journal of Psycholinguistic Research, 22*, 21–39.

Echols, C. H. (1993). A perceptually-based model of children's earliest productions. *Cognition, 46*, 245–296.

Echols, C. H., & Newport, E. (1992). The role of stress and position in determining first words. *Language Acquisition, 2*(3), 189–220.

Ehrlich, K., & Johnson-Laird, P. N. (1982). Spatial descriptions and referential continuity. *Journal of Verbal Learning and Verbal Behavior, 21*, 296–306.

Fenson, L., Dale, P. S., Reznick, J. S., Bates, E., Thal., D. J., & Pethick, S. J. (1994). Variability in early communicative development. *Monographs of the Society for Research on Child Development, 59*(5, Serial No. 242).

Fernald, A. (1990). Intonation and communicative intent in mothers' speech to infants: Is the melody the message? *Child Development, 60*, 1497–1510.

Fernald, A. (1994, January). *Infants' sensitivity to word order.* Paper presented at the meeting of the Linguistic Society of America, Boston.

Fernald, A., & Mazzie, C. (1991). Prosody and focus in speech to infants and adults. *Developmental Psychology, 27*, 209–221.

Fernald, A., & McRoberts, G. (1996). Prosodic bootstrapping: A critical analysis of the argument and the evidence. In J. L. Morgan & K. Demuth (Eds.), *Signal to syntax: Bootstrapping from speech to syntax in early acquisition* (pp. 365–388). Hillsdale, NJ: Erlbaum.

Fernald, A., & Simon, T. (1984). Expanded intonation contours in mothers' speech to newborns. *Developmental Psychology, 20*, 104–113.

Ferreira, F. (1993). Creation of prosody during sentence production. *Psychological Review, 100*, 233–253.

Ferreira, F., & Clifton, C. (1986). The independence of syntactic processing. *Journal of Memory and Language, 25*, 348–368.

Ferreira, F., & Henderson, J. M. (1990). Use of verb information in syntactic parsing: Evidence from eye movements and word-by-word self-paced reading. *Journal of Experimental Psychology: Learning, Memory, and Cognition, 16*, 555–568.

Fillmore, C. J. (1968). The case for case. In E. Bach & R. T. Harms (Eds.), *Universals in linguistic theory* (pp. 1–88). New York: Holt, Rinehart & Winston.

Fillmore, C. J. (1977). The case for case reopened. In P. Cole & J. M. Sadock (Eds.), *Syntax and semantics: Vol. 8. Grammatical relations* (pp. 59–81). New York: Academic Press.

Fisher, C. (1994). Structure and meaning in the verb lexicon: Input for a syntax-aided verb learning procedure. *Language and Cognitive Processes, 9,* 473–518.

Fisher, C. (1996a). Structural limits on verb mapping: The role of analogy in children's interpretation of sentences. *Cognitive Psychology, 31,* 41–81.

Fisher, C. (1996b). *Who's the subject? Sentence structures as analogs of verb meaning.* Unpublished manuscript, University of Illinois, Urbana.

Fisher, C. (1999). *Structural limits on verb mapping: 2.5-year olds interpret verbs based on their number of arguments.* Manuscript in preparation.

Fisher, C., Gleitman, H., & Gleitman, L. R. (1991). On the semantic content of subcategorization frames. *Cognitive Psychology, 23,* 331–392.

Fisher, C., Hall, G. D., Rakowitz, S., & Gleitman, L. R. (1994). When it is better to receive than to give: Syntactic and conceptual constraints on vocabulary growth. *Lingua, 92,* 333–375.

Fisher, C., & Tokura, H. (1995). The given/new contract in speech to infants. *Journal of Memory and Language, 34,* 287–310.

Fisher, C., & Tokura, H. (1996a). Acoustic cues to linguistic structure in speech to infants: Cross-linguistic evidence. *Child Development, 67,* 3192–3218.

Fisher, C., & Tokura, H. (1996b). Prosody in speech to infants: Direct and indirect acoustic cues to syntactic structure. In J. L. Morgan & K. Demuth (Eds.), *Signal to syntax: Bootstrapping from speech to syntax in early acquisition* (pp. 343–363). Hillsdale, NJ: Erlbaum.

Fodor, J. A. (1979). *The language of thought.* Cambridge, MA: Harvard University Press.

Forbes, J. N., & Farrar, M. J. (1995). Learning to represent word meaning: What initial training events reveal about children's developing action verb concepts. *Cognitive Development, 10,* 1–20.

Forrest, L. (1996). Discourse goals and attentional processes in sentence production: The dynamic construal of events. In A. Goldberg (Ed.), *Conceptual structure, discourse, and language* (pp. 149–162). Stanford, CA: CSLI Publications.

Fowler, C., & Housum, J. (1987). Talkers' signaling of "new" and "old" words in speech and listeners' perception and use of the distinction. *Journal of Memory and Language, 26,* 489–504.

Gee, J., & Grosjean, F. (1983). Performance structures: A psycholinguistic and linguistic appraisal. *Cognitive Psychology, 15,* 411–458.

Gentner, D. (1978). On relational meaning: The acquisition of verb meaning. *Child Development, 49,* 988–998.

Gentner, D. (1982). Why nouns are learned before verbs: Linguistic relativity versus natural partitioning. In S. A. Kuczaj (Ed.), *Language development: Vol. 2. Language, thought and culture* (pp. 301–334). Hillsdale, NJ: Erlbaum.

Gentner, D. (1983). Structure-mapping: A theoretical framework for analogy. *Cognitive Science, 7,* 155–170.

Gerken, L., Jusczyk, P. W., & Mandel, D. (1994). When prosody fails to cue syntactic structure: Nine-month-olds' sensitivity to phonological vs syntactic phrases. *Cognition, 51,* 237–265.

Gerken, L., & McIntosh, B. J. (1993). Interplay of function morphemes and prosody in early language. *Developmental Psychology, 29,* 448–457.

Gerken, L. Murphy, W. D., & Aslin, R. N. (1995). Three- and four-year-olds' perceptual confusions of spoken words. *Perception & Psychophysics, 57,* 475–486.

Gernsbacher, M. A., & Hargreaves, D. J. (1988). Accessing sentence participants: The advantage of first mention. *Journal of Memory and Language, 27,* 699–717.

Geyer, H., Gleitman, L. R., & Gleitman, H. (1991). *Semantic/syntactic linkages in the Hebrew verb lexicon.* Unpublished manuscript, University of Pennsylvania, Philadelphia.

Givon, T. (1976). Topic, pronoun, and grammatical agreement. In C. N. Li (Ed.), *Subject and topic* (pp. 149–188). New York: Academic Press.

Gleitman, L. R. (1990). The structural sources of verb meanings. *Language Acquisition, 1,* 3–55.

Gleitman, L. R., Gleitman, H., Landau, B., & Wanner, E. (1987). Where learning begins: Initial representations for language learning. In F. Newmeyer (Ed.), *Linguistics: The Cambridge Survey: Vol. 3. Psychological and biological aspects* (pp. 150–193). New York: Cambridge University Press.

Gleitman, L. R., Gleitman, H., Miller, C., & Ostrin, R. (1996). Similar, and similar concepts. *Cognition, 58,* 321–365.

Goldberg, A. (1995). *Constructions: A Construction Grammar approach to argument structure.* Chicago: University of Chicago Press.

Golinkoff, R., Harding, C. G., Carlson, V., & Sexton, M. E. (1984). The infant's perception of causal events: The distinction between animate and inanimate objects. In L. P. Lipsitt & C. Rovee-Collier (Eds.), *Advances in infancy research* (Vol. 3, pp. 145–151). Norwood, NJ: Ablex.

Golinkoff, R., & Markessini, J. (1980). "Mommy sock": The child's understanding of possession as expressed in two-noun phrases. *Journal of Child Language, 7,* 119–136.

Gordon, P. C., Grosz, B. J., & Gilliom, L. A. (1993). Pronouns, names, and the centering of attention in discourse. *Cognitive Science, 17,* 311–347.

Grieser, D. L., & Kuhl, P. K. (1988). Maternal speech to infants in a tonal language: Support for universal prosodic features in motherese. *Developmental Psychology, 24,* 14–20.

Grimshaw, J. (1979). Complement selection and the lexicon. *Linguistic Inquiry, 10,* 270–326.

Grimshaw, J. (1981). Form, function, and the language acquisition device. In C. L. Baker & J. J. McCarthy (Eds.), *The logical problem of language acquisition* (pp. 165–182). Cambridge, MA: MIT Press.

Grimshaw, J. (1990). *Argument structure.* Cambridge, MA: MIT Press.

Grimshaw, J. (1993, April). *Semantic structure and semantic content: A preliminary note.* Paper presented at the conference on Early Cognition and the Transition to Language, University of Texas at Austin.

Grimshaw, J. (1994). Lexical reconciliation. *Lingua, 92,* 411–432.

Gropen, J., Pinker, S., Hollander, M., & Goldberg, R. (1991a). Affectedness and direct objects: The role of lexical semantics in the acquisition of verb argument structure. *Cognition, 41,* 153–195.

Gropen, J., Pinker, S., Hollander, M., & Goldberg, R. (1991b). Syntax and semantics in the acquisition of locative verbs. *Journal of Child Language, 18,* 115–151.

Grosz, B. J., & Sidner, C. L. (1986). Attention, intentions, and the structure of discourse. *Computational Linguistics, 12,* 175–204.

Hallé, P., & de Boysson-Bardies, B. (1996). The format of representation of recognized words in infants' early receptive lexicon. *Infant Behavior and Development, 19,* 463–481.

Hauser, M., & Fowler, C. (1992). Fundamental frequency declination is not unique to human speech: Evidence from non-human primates. *Journal of the Acoustical Society of America, 91,* 363–369.

Hirsh-Pasek, K., & Golinkoff, R. (1991). Language comprehension: A new look at some old themes. In N. Krasnegor, D. Rumbaugh, M. Studdert-Kennedy, & R. Schiefelbusch (Eds.), *Biological and behavioral aspects of language acquisition* (pp. 301–320). Hillsdale, NJ: Erlbaum.

Hirsh-Pasek, K., & Golinkoff, R. (1996). *The origins of grammar.* Cambridge, MA: MIT Press.

Hirsh-Pasek, K., Kemler-Nelson, D., Jusczyk, P., Cassidy, K., Druss, B., & Kennedy, L. (1987). Clauses are perceptual units for young infants. *Cognition, 26,* 269–286.

Hoff-Ginsberg, E. (1985). Some contributions of mothers' speech to their children's syntactic growth. *Journal of Child Language, 12,* 167–185.

Jackendoff, R. (1987). The status of thematic relations in linguistic theory. *Linguistic Inquiry, 18,* 369–411.

Jackendoff, R. (1990). *Semantic structures.* Cambridge, MA: MIT Press.

Johnson-Laird, P. N. (1983). *Mental models: Toward a cognitive science of language, inference and consciousness.* Cambridge, MA: Harvard University Press.

Jusczyk, P. W., Hirsh-Pasek, K., Kemler Nelson, D., Kennedy, L., Woodward, A., & Piwoz, J. (1992). Perception of acoustic correlates of major phrasal units by young infants. *Cognitive Psychology, 24,* 252–293.

Karttunen, L., & Kay, M. (1985). Parsing in a free word order language. In D. Dowty, L. Karttunen, & A. Zwicky (Eds.), *Natural language parsing: Psychological, computational, and theoretical perspectives* (pp. 279–306). New York: Cambridge University Press.

Keenan, E. L. (1976). Towards a universal definition of "subject." In C. N. Li (Ed.), *Subject and topic* (pp. 303–334). New York: Academic Press.

Kemler-Nelson, D., Hirsh-Pasek, K., Jusczyk, P. W., & Wright Cassidy, K. (1989). How the prosodic cues in motherese might assist language learning. *Journal of Child Language, 16,* 55–68.

Kintsch, W., & van Dijk, T. A. (1978). Toward a model of text comprehension and production. *Psychological Review, 85,* 363–394.

Kuno, S. (1987). *Functional syntax.* Chicago: University of Chicago Press.

Ladusaw, W. A., & Dowty, D. R. (1988). Toward a non-grammatical account of thematic roles. In W. Wilkins (Ed.), *Syntax and semantics: Vol. 21. Thematic relations* (pp. 61–73). Orlando, FL: Academic Press.

Landau, B., & Gleitman, L. R. (1985). *Language and experience: Evidence from the blind child.* Cambridge, MA: Harvard University Press.

Landau, B., & Stecker, D. (1990). Objects and places: Geometric and syntactic representations in early lexical learning. *Cognitive Development, 5,* 387–312.

Lehiste, I., & Fox, R. A. (1993). Influence of duration and amplitude on the perception of prominence by Swedish listeners. *Speech Communication, 13,* 149–154.

Lempert, H. (1984). Topic as a starting point for syntax. *Monographs of the Society for Research in Child Development, 49*(5, Serial No. 209).

Leslie, A. M. (1982). The perception of causality in infants. *Perception, 11,* 15–30.

Levin, B., & Rappaport Hovav, M. (1991). Wiping the slate clean: A lexical semantic exploration. *Cognition, 41,* 123–151.

Levinsky, S., & Gerken, L. (1994, April). *Children's knowledge of pronoun usage in discourse.* Paper presented at the 26th annual meeting of the Child Language Research Forum, Stanford, CA.

Macnamara, J. (1982). *Names for things: A study of human learning.* Cambridge, MA: MIT Press.

MacNeilage, P., & Ladefoged, P. (1976). The production of speech and language. In E. Carterette & M. Friedman (Eds.), *Handbook of perception: Vol. 7. Language and speech* (pp. 75–120). New York: Academic Press.

MacWhinney, B. (1977). Starting points. *Language, 53,* 152–168.

MacWhinney, B., & Bates, E. (1978). Sentential devices for conveying givenness and newness: A cross-cultural developmental study. *Journal of Verbal Learning and Verbal Behavior, 17,* 529–558.

Mandel, D. R., Jusczyk, P. W., & Kemler-Nelson, D. G. (1994). Does sentential prosody help infants organize and remember speech information? *Cognition, 53,* 155–180.

Mandel, D. R., Kemler-Nelson, D. G., & Jusczyk, P. W. (1996). Infants remember the order of words in a spoken sentence. *Cognitive Development, 11,* 181–192.

Marantz, A. (1984). *On the nature of grammatical relations.* Cambridge, MA: MIT Press.

Maratsos, M. (1982). The child's construction of grammatical categories. In E. Wanner & L. R. Gleitman (Eds.), *Language acquisition: The state of the art* (pp. 240–266). New York: Cambridge University Press.

Maratsos, M. (1990). Are actions to verbs as objects are to nouns? On the differential semantic bases of form, class, category. *Linguistics, 28,* 1351–1379.

Markman, E. (1989). *Categorization and naming in children: Problems of induction.* Cambridge, MA: MIT Press.

Marslen-Wilson, W., Levy, W., & Tyler, L. K. (1982). Producing interpretable discourse: The establishment and maintenance of reference. In R. Jarvella & W. Klein (Eds.), *Speech, place, and action* (pp. 339–378). New York: Wiley.

Martin, J. G. (1972). Rhythmic (hierarchical) versus serial structure in speech and other behavior. *Psychological Review, 79,* 487–509.

Masataka, N. (1992). Early ontogeny of vocal behavior of Japanese infants in response to maternal speech. *Child Development, 62,* 1177–1185.

Massey, C., & Gelman, R. (1988). Preschoolers' ability to decide whether a photographed unfamiliar object can move itself. *Developmental Psychology, 24,* 307–317.

McDonald, J., Bock, K., & Kelly, M. (1993). Word and world order: Semantic, phonological, and metrical determinants of serial position. *Cognitive Psychology, 25,* 188–230.

Merriman, W. E., & Marazita, J. M. (1995). The effect of hearing similar-sounding words on young 2-year-olds' disambiguation of novel noun reference. *Developmental Psychology, 31,* 973–984.

Morgan, J. L. (1986). *From simple input to complex grammar.* Cambridge, MA: MIT Press.

Morgan, J. L. (1996). Prosody and the roots of parsing. *Language and Cognitive Processes, 11,* 69–91.

Morgan, J. L., Meier, R. P., & Newport, E. L. (1987). Structural packaging in the input to language learning: Contributions of prosodic and morphological marking of phrases to the acquisition of language. *Cognitive Psychology, 19,* 498–550.

Naigles, L. (1990). Children use syntax to learn verb meanings. *Journal of Child Language, 17,* 357–374.

Naigles, L., & Kako, E. (1993). First contact in verb acquisition: Defining a role for syntax. *Child Development, 64,* 1665–1687.

Newmeyer, F. (1992). Iconicity and generative grammar. *Language, 68,* 756–796.

Newport, E., Gleitman, H., & Gleitman, L. R. (1977). Mother I'd rather do it myself: Some effects and non-effects of maternal speech style. In C. E. Snow & C. A. Ferguson (Eds.), *Talking to children: Language input and acquisition* (pp. 109–149). New York: Cambridge University Press.

Nittrouer, S., & Boothroyd, A. (1990). Context effects in phoneme and word recognition by young children and older adults. *Journal of the Acoustical Society of America, 87,* 2705–2715.

O'Grady, W., Suzuki-wei, Y., & Cho, S. W. (1986). Directionality preferences in the interpretation of anaphora: Data from Korean and Japanese. *Journal of Child Language, 13,* 409–420.

Olguin, R., & Tomasello, M. (1993). Two-year-olds do not have a grammatical category of verb. *Cognitive Development, 8,* 245–272.

Osgood, C. E. (1980). *Lectures on language performance.* New York: Springer-Verlag.

Papousek, M., & Hwang, S. C. (1991). Tone and intonation in Mandarin babytalk to presyllabic infants: Comparison with registers of adult conversation and foreign language instruction. *Applied Psycholinguistics, 12,* 481–504.

Papousek, M., Papousek, H., & Symmes, D. (1991). The meanings of melodies in motherese in tone and stress languages. *Infant Behavior and Development, 14,* 415–440.

Peters, A. (1985). Language segmentation: Operating principles for the perception and analysis of language. In D. I. Slobin (Ed.), *The crosslinguistic study of language acquisition: Vol. 2. Theoretical issues* (pp. 1029–1068). Hillsdale, NJ: Erlbaum.

Pinker, S. (1984). *Language learnability and language development.* Cambridge, MA: Harvard University Press.

Pinker, S. (1989). *Learnability and cognition.* Cambridge, MA: MIT Press.

Pinker, S. (1994). How could a child use verb syntax to learn verb semantics? *Lingua, 92,* 377–410.

Prince, E. (1992). Subjects, definiteness and information status. In W. C. Mann & S. A. Thompson (Eds.), *Discourse description: Diverse linguistic analyses of a fund-raising text* (pp. 294–325). Philadelphia: John Benjamins.

Rappaport Hovav, M., & Levin, B. (1988). What to do with theta-roles. In W. Wilkins (Ed.), *Syntax and semantics: Vol. 21. Thematic relations* (pp. 7–36). New York: Academic Press.

Rappaport Hovav, M., & Levin, B. (1998). Building verb meanings. In M. Butt & W. Geuder (Eds.), *The projection of arguments: Lexical and compositional factors* (pp. 97–134). Stanford, CA: CSLI Publications.

Rispoli, M. (1989). Encounters with Japanese verbs: Caregiver sentences and the categorization of transitive and intransitive action verbs. *First Language, 9,* 57–80.

Rispoli, M. (1995). Missing arguments and the acquisition of predicate meanings. In M. Tomasello and W. E. Merriman (Eds.), *Beyond names for things: Young children's acquisition of verbs* (pp. 331–352). Hillsdale, NJ: Erlbaum.

Ritter, E., & Rosen, S. (1993). Deriving causation. *Natural Language and Linguistic Theory, 11,* 519–555.

Scott, D. (1982). Duration as a cue to the perception of a phrase boundary. *Journal of the Acoustical Society of America, 71,* 996–1007.

Slobin, D. I. (1985). Crosslinguistic evidence for the language-making capacity. In D. I. Slobin (Ed.), *The cross-linguistic study of language acquisition* (Vol. 2, pp. 1157–1249). Hillsdale, NJ: Erlbaum.

Snow, C. (1972). Mothers' speech to children learning language. *Child Development, 43,* 549–565.

Stager, C. L., & Werker, J. F. (1997). Infants listen for more phonetic detail in speech perception than in word-learning tasks. *Nature, 388,* 381–382.

Starkey, P., Spelke, E., & Gelman, R. (1983). Detection of intermodal numerical correspondences by human infants. *Science, 222,* 179–181.

Stern, D. N., Spieker, S., Barnett, R. K., & MacKain, K. (1983). The prosody of maternal speech: Infant age and context related changes. *Journal of Child Language, 10,* 1–15.

Streri, A., Spelke, E., & Rameix, E. (1993). Modality-specific and amodal aspects of object perception in infancy: The case of active touch. *Cognition, 47,* 251–279.

Takeda, K., Sagisaka, Y., & Kuwabara, H. (1989). On sentence-level factors governing segmental duration in Japanese. *Journal of the Acoustical Society of America, 86,* 2081–2087.

Talmy, L. (1983). How language structures space. In H. Pick & L. Acredolo (Eds.), *Spatial orientation: Theory, research, and application* (pp. 225–282). New York: Plenum.

Talmy, L. (1985). Lexicalization patterns. In T. Shopen (Ed.), *Language typology and syntactic description: Vol. 3. Grammatical categories and the lexicon* (pp. 57–149). Cambridge, England: Cambridge University Press.

Tomasello, M. (1992). *First verbs: A case study of grammatical development.* New York: Cambridge University Press.

Tomasello, M., & Akhtar, N. (1995). Two-year-olds use pragmatic cues to differentiate reference to objects and actions. *Cognitive Development, 10,* 201–224.

Tomlin, R. (1986). *Basic word order: Functional principles.* London: Croom Helm.

Trueswell, J. C., Tanenhaus, M., & Garnsey, S. M. (1994). Semantic influences on parsing: Use of thematic role information in syntactic ambiguity resolution. *Journal of Memory and Language, 33,* 285–318.

Valian, V. (1990). Null subjects: A problem for parameter-setting models of language acquisition. *Cognition, 35,* 105–122.

Wang, Q., Lillo-Martin, D., Best, C. T., & Levitt, A. (1992). Null subject versus null object: Some evidence from the acquisition of Chinese and English. *Language Acquisition, 2,* 221–254.

THE ROLE OF ESSENTIALISM IN CHILDREN'S CONCEPTS

Susan A. Gelman

DEPARTMENT OF PSYCHOLOGY
UNIVERSITY OF MICHIGAN
ANN ARBOR, MICHIGAN 48109

[Essence is] the very being of anything, whereby it is what it is. And thus the real internal, but generally . . . unknown constitution of things, whereon their discoverable qualities depend, may be called their essence.
—Locke (1894/1959, Book III, p. 26)

There is no property ABSOLUTELY *essential to any one thing*. . . . [However,] the notion that there is no one quality genuinely, absolutely, and exclusively essential to any-

ADVANCES IN CHILD DEVELOPMENT
AND BEHAVIOR, VOL. 27

thing is almost unthinkable. . . . we are so stuck in our prejudices, so petrified intellec-
tually, that to our vulgarest names . . . we ascribe an eternal and exclusive worth.
—James (1890/1983, pp. 959–960)

Essentialism . . . dominated the thinking of the western world to a degree that is still not
yet fully appreciated by the historians of ideas. . . . It took more than two thousand years
for biology, under the influence of Darwin, to escape the paralyzing grip of essentialism.
—E. Mayr (1982, pp. 38, 87)

People act as if things (e.g., objects) have essences or underlying natures that make them
the thing that they are. Furthermore, the essence constrains or generates properties that
may vary in their centrality. One of the things that theories do is to embody or provide
causal linkages from deeper properties to more superficial or surface properties.
—D. Medin (1989, p. 1476)

I. Introduction

Philosophers have long suggested that members of a category share a nonobvious, immutable core (or "essence") that confers identity and predicts a vast array of
other properties. Although "essence" has at times been used to refer to defining
properties (also known as a "sortal essence"; e.g., for "bear" this essence might include such characteristics as being a carnivore and being ferocious), our focus is on
what is sometimes referred to as a "causal essence" (Hirschfeld, 1996), that is, properties that are responsible for the observable characteristics and identity of an item
(e.g., for "bear" this might include DNA). On this view all humans, for example,
have something deep and hidden in common that makes them human. Specific essentialist construals can be found in concepts as divergent as *soul* and *DNA,* though
essentialism may also be an unarticulated, placeholder notion—a belief *that* a category has a core, without knowing *what* that core is. Essentialism is surprisingly
pervasive across history, extending back at least to Plato in the 4th century B.C. (E.
Mayr, 1982). Yet paradoxically, it runs counter to reality. One can neither see nor
feel an animal's essence: It is theorized rather than directly encountered. Moreover,
essentialism may not accurately characterize even biological species (Hirschfeld,
1996; R. Mayr, 1991; Sober, 1994), let alone socially constructed categories such
as race (e.g., Brace, 1964; Hirschfeld, 1996; Templeton, 1998). James (1890/1983)
may thus be right to have derided essentialism as a prejudice.

The present chapter concerns "essentialism" as a folk psychological understanding. I distinguish between essentialism as a philosophical position and essentialism as a folk belief. The former addresses the nature of reality (a metaphysical question); the latter addresses the nature of people's ordinary belief
systems (a psychological question). The question that frames this research is where
essentializing comes from. How deeply engrained is it in our language and conceptual systems? At this point the possible roots of an essentialist assumption have

been much disputed. Essentialism could be the by-product of Western philosophy or cultural traditions, as some have argued (Fuss, 1989; Guillaumin, 1980; Rorty, 1979). Or maybe we are essentialists at this point in history because we can view the scientific enterprise fairly close-up and know about unobservable entities such as DNA and molecules. In contrast to both of these positions, I argue in this chapter that people are deep-down essentialists even without the benefit of science. The study of adults in this culture cannot provide evidence on the issue, because with adults the effects of schooling and scientific training cannot be teased apart. Children, however, provide an excellent test case, because they have had little exposure to or knowledge of either Western philosophy or scientific theories. Children also enable a strong test of the centrality of essence-like constructs, given children's well-documented focus on object appearances (e.g., Inhelder & Piaget, 1964; Jones & Smith, 1993).

The rest of the chapter has three parts. First, I review evidence that an essentialist bias emerges early in development—at least by $2\frac{1}{2}$ years of age and perhaps earlier. I discuss an array of commonsense beliefs about categories and their structure that seem similar or parallel to the philosophical notion ("psychological essentialism"; D. L. Medin & Ortony, 1989). I draw heavily from work in my own laboratory, but also other work that is relevant. Then, I open up to a discussion of origins: how do children come to have this expectation about the structure of categories? Although more speculative, the section on origins contains a review of ongoing research on the role of parental input and language. This section is followed by a brief consideration of questions and controversies raised by an essentialist framework.

II. Evidence for an Early Essentialist Bias

A. PRELIMINARY POINTS

An important preliminary point is that direct evidence of essentialism would be at best difficult to obtain. As noted earlier, essentialism does not entail that people know what the essence is. D. L. Medin and Ortony (1989) referred to this unknown-yet-believed-in-entity as an "essence placeholder." People may implicitly assume, for example, that some as-yet-unknown quality that bears have in common confers category identity and causes their identifiable surface features, and they may use this belief to guide inductive inferences and produce explanations—without being able to identify any feature or trait as the bear essence. This belief can be considered an unarticulated heuristic rather than a detailed, well-worked-out theory.

Furthermore, an essence would rarely be consulted to determine category membership, for the simple reason that people often do not know (or cannot readily access) the relevant information (S. A. Gelman & Medin, 1993). In such instances, people use other features instead. Gender provides a useful example: Although we typically assess someone's gender based on outward (clothed) appearance and voice, even young children acknowledge that genital information is more diagnostic (Bem, 1989), and in our technological society we even use chromosomal information in certain contexts (e.g., amniocentesis; Olympic Games committees). Thus, evidence that people use salient observable cues for categorization cannot be taken as evidence against essentialism.

These initial points of clarification imply that essentialism is difficult (perhaps impossible) to study *directly.* Psychological essentialism means that people believe in the existence of essences, not that people have detailed knowledge regarding the content of essences, nor that the world is organized in accord with essences. Studies demonstrating that people classify instances based on nonessential features, or that people cannot specify an essence, or that people's representation of a concept does not match that of science (e.g., Dupré, 1993) are not evidence against psychological essentialism. They are valuable for examining what kinds of information are used on certain tasks, but they do not constitute tests of psychological essentialism as a folk psychological theory of concepts. Accordingly, my collaborators and I have relied on indirect, converging methods. The evidence comes from three related lines of research: (a) inductive potential, (b) robustness over transformations, and (c) causal explanations. Together, these studies provide evidence that young children's categories are richly structured and extend beyond surface features, incorporating nonvisible properties and causal features. In section IV, I return to the question of whether these features jointly comprise an essentialist framework.

B. INDUCTIVE POTENTIAL

1. Category-Based Induction

Inductive inferences extend beyond what is already known or what could be known with logical certainty (as opposed to deductive inferences). For a number of years, my collaborators and I have examined "category-based induction," or the inferences people make from one category member to another, especially for hidden, unobservable properties. Most theoretical accounts of categories, though not specifically excluding the possibility of such inferences, do not provide a means of explaining them. For example, an assumption in defining-features theories of categories is that category-relevant features are finite and known; and an assumption in prototype theories is that the relevant properties have been detected and observed (even when learning is automatic and nondeliberate). Nonetheless, children draw many rich inferences from one member of a category to another, even when the instances appear very different on the surface and even when only the label tells children that they are the same kind of thing. For example, Ellen Markman and I presented 4-year-olds triads such as a blackbird, a bat, and a flamingo (S. A.

Gelman & Markman, 1986). An experimenter named all the items (e.g., "bird," "bat," "bird") and taught the children a new biological fact about one instance (e.g., that the blackbird fed its young mashed-up food). The children were then asked to generalize the property. The children inferred that the flamingo, but not the bat, feeds its young the same kind of food as the blackbird, even though the flamingo is superficially less similar than the bat to the blackbird. My collaborators and I have replicated this finding with hundreds of children between 2 and 7 years of age, and the effect is very robust (Davidson & Gelman, 1990; S. A. Gelman, 1988; S. A. Gelman & Coley, 1990, 1991; S. A. Gelman, Collman, & Maccoby, 1986; S. A. Gelman & Markman, 1987; S. A. Gelman & O'Reilly, 1988).

We have also conducted numerous control experiments to rule out the possibility of task demands such as that children drew inferences from the label simply because the experimenter provided a label and they were attempting to please the experimenter. The control studies revealed that children do not blindly follow the experimenter's labels and that labels are not even *necessary* for obtaining category-based inferences. (a) Children do not draw inferences when the property-to-be-inferred is fortuitous (e.g., "fell on the floor this morning"; S. A. Gelman, 1988) or inconsequential (e.g., which color chip to place on a picture; S. A. Gelman & Markman, 1986). (b) Children do not draw inferences when the animal is labeled with an adjective describing a transient state (e.g., labeling animals from contrasting categories as "sleepy" and "wide awake" instead of "bird" and "dinosaur"; S. A. Gelman & Coley, 1990). (c) Children do not draw inferences from nonce words (e.g., "fep") when the categories to which they refer are perceptually heterogeneous (Davidson & Gelman, 1990). (d) Even when labels are *not* provided, children draw category-based inferences when pictures include sufficient cues to detect category membership (e.g., they draw an inference from a beetle to a leaf-insect, despite the leafy appearance of the latter, apparently because it has eyes and antennae; S. A. Gelman & Markman, 1987).

The studies of category-based induction demonstrate two distinct points: (a) Children readily use categories as the basis for inductive inferences regarding nonobvious properties, and (b) language can be a vehicle for identifying these categories (see also Markman, 1989). In other words, knowing the category label helps children draw important property inferences. When these data first appeared, they were surprising, in that they seemed to conflict with research on children's well-known reliance on perceptual properties on many cognitive tasks. Children are highly attentive to perceptual information (Inhelder & Piaget, 1964; Smith, 1995). Nonetheless, even $2\frac{1}{2}$-year-old children can overlook such cues when provided with labels for familiar, richly structured categories.

2. Developmental Change

My collaborators and I have also examined developmental *changes* in children's category-based inductions. Specifically, children appear to overgeneralize the importance of categories for promoting inferences, generalizing to the entire category from just a single instance. In one set of experiments (Lopez, Gelman, Gutheil, & Smith, 1992), we found that children readily draw category-based inferences from a single exemplar, but unlike adults they fail to modulate their inferences in response to more detailed information concerning the number or heterogeneity of training exemplars (information that adults use). For example, in one condition the research participants saw a single bird and learned that it has property X; in a second condition they saw five birds of the same type (homogeneous set); and in a third condition they saw five different kinds of birds (heterogeneous set). Five-year-olds, eight-year-olds, and adults were tested. Only the adults consistently used information regarding number and heterogeneity. We replicated the effect with a simpler task and basic-level (rather than superordinate) categories (Gutheil & Gelman, 1997). Again, children rarely made use of information regarding number of exemplars or diversity of exemplars, thus suggesting the power of a category to promote broad generalizations from even a single instance. This conclusion is also consistent with evidence that covariation or statistical information is insufficient to account for the concepts of both children (Kalish & Gelman, 1992) and adults (Ahn, Kalish, Medin, & Gelman, 1995).

3. Property-to-Category-Label Inferences

We have suggested that, typically, children more readily draw property inferences based on knowing the category label than the reverse (i.e., inferring the category label based on knowing category properties) (S. A. Gelman et al., 1986). That is, the category label seems to have special status for young children. However Gil Diesendruck, Kim Lebowitz, and I have also found that preschool children can use essential properties as an index to naming (Diesendruck, Gelman, & Lebowitz, 1998). We conducted a series of studies on a well-known word-learning error often referred to as the "mutual exclusivity" assumption (Markman, 1989; Merriman & Bowman, 1989), or the "novel name–nameless category" principle (Golinkoff, Mervis, & Hirsh-Pasek, 1994). Children have a powerful tendency to assume that words refer to nonoverlapping sets or, more simply put, children tend to assume that each object has only one label. For example, children who know that a poodle is a "dog" will typically deny that it is a "poodle" or an "animal." We predicted that children would overcome this mutual exclusivity tendency if they learned that dogs and poodles, for example, share internal properties.

Three-, four-, and five-year-olds were taught new words for a series of animals or artifacts, then were tested on their interpretations of the new words. For example, children were shown two distinct kinds of squirrels (a typical squirrel and a flying squirrel) and were told: "This one [the flying squirrel] is a squirrel; it's a mef. This one [the typical squirrel] is a squirrel; it's not a mef." Before teaching the new word, the experimenter described how the two instances were alike. In the Insides condition, the experimenter described internal properties (e.g., that the two squirrels had "the same stuff inside . . . the same kind of bones, blood, muscles, and brain"). In the Control condition, the experimenter described superficial similarities (e.g., that the two squirrels were "the same size . . . [and live] in the same zoo in the same kind of cage"). The labeling phase alone provided all the information children needed to construct the hierarchy accurately. However, we knew from past work (e.g., S. A. Gelman, Wilcox, & Clark, 1989) that children tend to collapse such a hierarchy into two mutually exclusive sets. The question, then, was whether the brief description of internal similarities would be sufficient to alter the children's patterns of word learning.

The results demonstrated significant condition effects. In the Control condition, with superficial similarities, the children typically treated the two labels (e.g., "squirrel" and "mef") as mutually exclusive ($M = 5.29$ out of 10 trials) and rarely gave the correct, subordinate interpretations ($M = 2.86$). In contrast, in the Insides condition, in which the items were described as sharing internal similarities, children overcame the error and gave fewer mutual exclusivity interpretations ($M = 3.62$) and more subordinate interpretations ($M = 3.83$). Children showed no condition effects when learning new labels for *artifacts,* whether the information provided concerned internal properties or common function. Thus, the use of internal information to constrain word learning was specific to animal kinds.

Diesendruck (1996) replicated this finding in Brazil with Portuguese-speaking children of widely varying socioeconomic backgrounds. The results were in most respects very similar, with the same weakening of mutual exclusivity in the Insides condition. This finding illustrates the generality of the effect across languages and across variations in socioeconomic status.

4. Summary

Even for young children, nonobvious properties are central to children's category-based inferences and word learning. The properties children infer from one category member to another concern internal features and nonvisible functions, and children draw inferences even when category membership competes with perceptual similarity. Thus, these data are consistent with the notion that members of a category share essential features.

C. ROBUSTNESS OVER TRANSFORMATIONS

An underlying essence would allow individuals to undergo marked change yet retain their identity. This is not to say that every essentialized category remains constant over time; for example, one's age is constantly changing, yet age groupings (e.g., baby, adolescent) are essentialized (M. G. Taylor & Gelman, 1993). However, maintaining category identity over such changes constitutes compelling evidence for an understanding of sameness beyond observable properties. Adults in Western culture believe that radical changes, such as metamorphosis, are possible (Rips, 1989). Furthermore, as Keil (1989) has shown, second graders (though not preschoolers) realize that animals but not artifacts can maintain identity over such transformations.

1. Removal of Insides versus Outsides

Henry Wellman and I, working with younger children, demonstrated a similar kind of understanding (S. A. Gelman & Wellman, 1991). We used a paradigm very similar to that of Keil (1989), but with simpler transformations: Each item had either its "insides" or its "outsides" removed. Test items were selected to be clear-cut examples (for adults) of objects for which insides, but not outsides, are essential. For example, blood is more important than fur to a dog; the engine of a car is more important than the paint. As a control, we also selected a set of items for which the insides are not integral parts (e.g., a jar; a refrigerator).

We asked 4- and 5-year-old children to consider three transformations: (a) removal of insides (e.g., "What if you take out the stuff inside of the dog, you know, the blood and bones and things like that, and got rid of it and all you have left are the outsides?"), (b) removal of outsides (e.g., "What if you take off the stuff outside of the dog, you know, the fur, and got rid of it and all you have left are the insides?"), and (c) movement (e.g., "What if the dog stands up?") as a control. For each transformation, children were asked two questions: (a) identity ("Is it still a dog?") and (b) function ("Can it still bark and eat dog food?"). As predicted, the children correctly reported that the identity of the containers (e.g., refrigerator) would not change if the insides were removed. For the other items, the children said that if the *insides* are removed, the identity and function of an object change, but that if the *outsides* are removed, the identity and function do not change, even when removing the outsides would sharply change the appearance of the object.

2. Growth and Metamorphosis

In an additional series of studies, Rosengren, Gelman, Kalish, and McCormick (1991) examined children's understanding that identity is maintained over the natural biological transformation of growth. We reasoned that an important piece that may have been missing from prior research was consideration of the *mechanism* underlying transformations. In other words, children may be sensitive to whether the mechanism is a natural biological transformation or one that defies biological laws. The implication is that even though children report that some transformations lead to identity change, they may realize that natural transformations such as growth do not.

Rosengren et al. found that children as young as 3 years of age expect animals to undergo changes over time (via growth) without affecting identity, that children believe that such changes are strongly constrained (e.g., one can get bigger but not smaller over time), and that these changes are specific to the domain of living things. For example, 3-year-olds, 5-year-olds, and adults were shown a picture of an animal and were told, "Here is a picture of Sally when Sally was a baby. Now Sally is an adult." They were then shown two pictures, one identical to the original and one the same but larger, and were asked which was a picture of Sally "as an adult." In all age groups, the participants tended to choose the larger figure, showing that they expected the object to increase in size with growth.

By 5 years of age, children realize that animals can undergo metamorphosis without change in identity. In another condition children saw a picture of a juvenile of a species that undergoes radical metamorphosis (such as a caterpillar). They then saw a picture of the same creature, only smaller (e.g., a smaller caterpillar), and a picture of a larger animal differing in shape (e.g., a moth). Again, participants were asked to choose which picture represented the animal after it became an adult. Three-year-olds were at chance, but 5-year-olds chose the metamorphosized animal significantly above chance levels. By the age of 5 years, then, children believe that an individual can naturally undergo even substantial shape changes over time yet retain its underlying identity.

3. Brain Transplants

Thus, a variety of studies now demonstrate that children treat category identity and category-linked properties as remarkably robust. Various transformations, some yielding striking changes in appearance, are insufficient to alter children's predictions concerning what an animal is and how it behaves. Indeed, children even maintain constancy over one transformation that *should* (according to adults) alter identity—that of a brain transplant. If an animal receives a new brain, its thoughts, memories, and identity should also (hypothetically) be transformed. Nonetheless, Johnson (1990) found that preschool and kindergarten children maintain that an animal's species-characteristic behaviors and memories are preserved even after a brain transplant (e.g., a pig with a child's brain would still have memories of being a pig, not a child). To rephrase this result in the present framework, children appear to treat an animal's essence as unchanged even following a brain transplant.

Gail Gottfried and I have conducted further studies with very similar results (Gottfried, 1997; Gottfried, Gelman, & Schultz, in press). For example, we described a hypothetical scenario in which a horse received a cow's brain. The test questions concerned species-typical thoughts or memories (e.g., "What does this one [the horse] think about: does it think about *running fast* or does it think about *giving milk?*"). Although most third graders, like adults, reported that a brain transplant affects thinking and remembering, most kindergartners reported that a brain transplant leaves thinking and remembering unaffected (27% of kindergartners' responses vs. 71% of third-graders' responses indicated that the brain affected thoughts and memories).

Our data demonstrate that the developmental change from kindergarten to third grade was *not* due to younger children's ignorance about the brain: Even the kindergartners knew where the brain is located, what it is used for, and its necessity for mental functions such as thinking or remembering. Children's responses were also not due to information-processing demands of the task, as our procedure was methodologically simpler than Johnson's (1990) but yielded highly similar results. Furthermore, children performed very well on a structurally identical control task that did not test essential (i.e., identity-determining) properties. Specifically, in the control task the cross-species transformation concerned the animal's stomach (rather than brain), and the children were asked about the animal's stomach contents (rather than thoughts and memories). On this task, children readily accepted the transplant as effective. For example, an elephant with a cat's stomach was judged to have milk inside, not peanuts. Although stomach contents are highly associated with the animal, stomach contents are not central to identity. Altogether, these results again are consistent with the suggestion that kindergarten children view category-specific properties as unchanging, even in the face of powerful transformations.

4. Transformations and Constancy

The results reviewed above, on children's concepts of transformations, may seem contrary to several well-established lines of research on early concepts. The Piagetian conservation tasks demonstrate that preschoolers have considerable difficulty reasoning about transformations of physical quantities (e.g., volume, area, length). Similarly, on gender constancy tasks, preschoolers accept that even superficial changes can alter gender identity (e.g., a boy who grows his hair long would turn into a girl; Kohlberg, 1966; Liben & Signorella, 1987). Several factors seem to account for the discrepancy across measures, including task demands (e.g., Siegal & Robinson, 1987), age-related changes in knowledge base, and whether the transformations are natural or unnatural (Rosengren et al., 1991). In general, performance is best with familiar, highly practiced transformations (e.g., costumes) as opposed to unfamiliar transformations (e.g., appearance changes induced by injections). Performance is also better with natural transformations (e.g., growth), than with unnatural transformations (e.g., surgery) (Rosengren et al., 1991). However, by second grade, children maintain the constancy of identity over even unfamiliar transformations.

5. Nature–Nurture Studies

We next consider changes in rearing conditions, which may be considered a transformation of sorts. To the extent that innate features are crucial to category membership, changes in rearing conditions should be viewed as largely irrelevant to category identity or functioning. In order to examine these issues, researchers have used either an "adoption" task (S. A. Gelman & Wellman, 1991) or a "switched-at-birth" task (Hirschfeld, 1996). These tasks pose a nature–nurture conflict to children and ask them to choose which is more predictive. The basic idea is to describe an animal or child who at birth is either adopted by another family or is switched (accidentally) with another animal or child. The birth parents and the upbringing parents differ on some crucial dimension (e.g., race, species, personality trait). The question then is how the animal or child will turn out. If respondents predict that the animal or child will be like the birth parents, they are presumably using a nativist model. If instead they predict that the animal or child will be like the upbringing parents, they are presumably using an environmental model.

Henry Wellman and I found that nature wins out over nurture for 4-year-olds' judgments about infant animals and plant seeds (S. A. Gelman & Wellman, 1991). For example, respondents said that a baby kangaroo raised among goats will grow up to hop and have a pouch. (All properties were pretested to make sure that children knew the answer when no conflict was presented—for example, they said that kangaroos are good at hopping and have a pouch and that goats are good at climbing and do not have a pouch.) They very rarely appealed to the environment. Again we can think of this response as demonstrating robustness of the category despite external transformations.

Children were not simply displaying an overall bias to link categories with their associated properties (e.g., to say that kangaroos have kangaroo properties). We found a consistent difference between how children treated animal behaviors and how they treated physical features. Surprisingly, children thought physical features were somewhat more malleable than behaviors. For example, if a baby kangaroo was reared by goats, children were somewhat less consistent in predicting that it would develop a pouch, than that it would hop. This finding was not due to a knowledge difference, because children were just as knowledgeable about physical properties as behaviors, in the absence of a nature–nurture conflict. The major point here is that 4-year-olds assume that each living thing has innate potential, and that innate potential can overcome the environment.

Carey and her collaborators (Carey, 1995; Carey & Spelke, 1994; Solomon, Johnson, Zaitchik, & Carey, 1996) cautioned that a biological notion of innate potential is not required to account for these findings, and that at least some of them might be attributed to children's expectations that identity is maintained over time (i.e., because the animal was labeled as being a member of a particular species—such as a kangaroo—children may have assumed that it would continue to have kangaroo properties, without reasoning about the mechanism involved). In subsequent studies, however, Hirschfeld (1995, 1996) and Springer (1995) used a procedure in which subjects were *not* told the category identity of the infant. In one series of studies, Hirschfeld (1995) showed preschoolers pictures of two families, one dark-skinned and the other light-skinned, whose newborns were inadvertently switched in the hospital. Each family took home and raised the other's infant. Children were then shown pictures of two school-aged children, one dark-skinned and the other light-skinned, and asked which was the child when he or she grew up and began school. Three-year-olds chose at chance, but 4-year-olds relied over-

whelmingly on a nativist reasoning strategy, choosing the child who matched the
birth parents (not the adopted parents) on skin color. In a subsequent experiment,
Springer (1995) replicated this finding and extended it, demonstrating that 5-year-
olds believe that not only race but also a range of biological (though not psychological) properties are fixed at birth and immutable over the life span. Here again,
the data support the essentialist interpretation. Children reasoned that category
identity is determined at birth and impervious to environmental influences. Moreover, both sets of studies show that an essentialist notion of innate potential gov-
erns children's expectations about racial identity.

Various researchers have extended this work to other kinds of properties that
adults consider to be more environmentally determined, including gender-linked
characteristics (e.g., wanting to play with dolls), language (e.g., English, Portuguese), and traits (e.g., shy, smart). One intriguing result from these studies is
that children's essentialist interpretations are quite powerful, at a young age. Indeed, in some domains they may be even more essentialist for preschoolers than
for older children and adults. For example, Larry Hirschfeld and I conducted a
switched-at-birth experiment using language as the contrast (Hirschfeld & Gelman, 1997). Preschoolers were told about two couples, one who spoke English and
one who spoke Portuguese (with audiotaped speech samples provided to illustrate
the contrast). As in Hirschfeld's and Springer's studies, the children were told that
the newborn of each couple was switched with the infant of the other couple. Children were then played two audiotaped speech samples, one in English and the
other in Portuguese, and were asked to choose which was the language that the
switched-at-birth child spoke when it grew up. Although 3-year-olds performed at
chance, 5-year-olds consistently selected the language of the birth parents.

6. Nature–Nurture: Beliefs about Gender

Another example of more powerful expectations at a younger age comes from
the domain of gender. M. Taylor (1996) examined essentialist beliefs about gender in subjects ranging from preschool to college age. The task was again a nature–nurture task similar to those described above. Subjects were told about an infant boy who was raised from birth by his aunt on an island populated entirely by
girls and women. Another item concerned an infant girl who was raised from birth
by her uncle on an island containing only boys and men. Subjects were then asked
to infer various properties of the boy or girl when he or she was 10 years old (e.g.,
would he or she play with trucks or dolls?). The study yielded two notable findings: First, the youngest subjects (4-year-olds) inferred that gender-linked properties were inherent in the child and not determined by the environment (e.g., they
typically inferred that the boy raised with females would play with trucks and be
good at football). Second, the strongest evidence of essentializing was with the
youngest subjects; by roughly 9–10 years of age, subjects began to incorporate socialization and interactionist explanations.

7. Nature–Nurture: Beliefs about Traits

Thus by late preschool, children reliably use a nature over nurture premise in reasoning about race, language, and gender, suggesting that an essentialist bias for innate potential may shape children's expectations about a broad range of phenomena (see Rothbart & Taylor, 1990, for discussion of essentialist construals of social categories). Gail Heyman and I examined children's beliefs about the origins of traits (S. A. Gelman & Heyman, 1997; Heyman & Gelman, 1997). Because traits concern psychologically based categories of people, they do not receive the rich perceptual support that one finds with basic-level animal kinds (e.g., "shy people" do not all look alike). Furthermore, the models adults use are intriguingly complex. Magazines for parents provide free speculation about inborn personality characteristics in babies, yet at the same time provide advice on how to structure the environment so as to raise a calmer, more obedient, more intelligent child. At this point, very little is known about how beliefs about trait origins develop in children. Until recently, the major focus has been on how stable or consistent children think traits are over time. Because children often seemed not even to acknowledge or appreciate the existence of traits, no point was seen in asking more broadly about trait theories. However, some findings suggest that children do possess early trait understandings (Eder, 1989; Heyman & Gelman, 1998). Based on this research, the task of characterizing children's trait theories becomes timely.

The main method that Heyman and I have been using to examine these issues is again a switched-at-birth task. The literature includes a few studies in which the switched-at-birth task was used to study traits or other personal characteristics (e.g., Solomon et al., 1996; Springer, 1995). However, in all these studies, personal characteristics were included as control items. The studies are therefore inconclusive about trait beliefs for two reasons. First, the kinds of properties were quite varied and differed from one another in how central they were to a person's identity (ranging from traits to preferences or beliefs), yet they were not analyzed separately. Second, the personal properties in these control studies were presented alongside other properties. So, for example, the same child would be asked to reason about traits, beliefs, and physical characteristics. The problem is that the context of the surrounding questions may prime children to think about traits in one way versus another.

In contrast to past research, Heyman and I conducted studies that focused primarily on traits. For example, in our studies we described nice people who pick up other people's trash, and mean people who throw rocks at dogs. A baby born to the nice people was raised by the mean people, and vice versa. The question was whether the baby would be nice, like the birth parents, or mean, like the upbringing parents. We conducted several studies with children as young as kindergarten age, up through fifth grade (and adults). Trait properties included shy/outgoing, active/inactive, smart/not smart, nice/mean. Physical characteristics included such things as ear shape and foot size. We systematically varied order: half the subjects at each age got a physical characteristic as their first item, and half did not. One supplementary issue was whether thinking about physical characteristics first primes a more nativist way of reasoning.

Two particularly noteworthy results were obtained. First, with age, traits were increasingly differentiated from physical properties. Nonetheless, even kindergarteners distinguished the two kinds of characteristics. They consistently treated physical characteristics as innately determined, but their views of traits were mixed.

Second, the youngest children exhibited large order-effects. Children who were asked about a physical characteristic first tended to judge properties as more biologically determined than children who were not asked about a physical characteristic first. In other words, if a child's first item was about hair texture, foot size, or ear shape, the child tended to focus on the birth parents for all the items. In contrast, if the first item was a trait or belief, the child was much less likely to focus on the birth parents. This finding leads to an important methodological point. In some cells, children were not different from chance *overall,* but their performance varied substantially depending on how they were primed. This pattern, of null performance overall but strong order effects, might help explain why in past work some researchers found differences between biological and nonbiological properties and other researchers did not (Solomon et al., 1996; Springer, 1995). Another implication of the order effect is that young children's responses were malleable, suggesting that children were being primed to choose one or the other of two competing models.

A final point is that children were developing surprisingly rich conceptions of traits in elementary school. We saw this development in their open-ended justifications, which we elicited and coded in one of the switched-at-birth studies. A certain portion of the time, when children did select the birth parents, they expressed rather powerful nativist theories, especially at 9 to 11 years of age. Examples are the following explanations of why a child born to not-so-smart parents, but raised with smart parents, would be not-so-smart (with age group listed in parentheses):

(5–6 years old)   "He wasn't born to smart parents."

(6–8 years old)   "The family would try, but the baby would always stay not very smart."

(9–11 years old) "It will have trouble. It's in its genes."

(9–11 years old) "You can change the way you act but you can't change the brain. If the baby was born to not-so-smart people, it couldn't learn things as well because it has a low I.Q."

Another noteworthy point is that children's beliefs were sometimes more complicated than a simple "yes" or "no." For example, one subject predicted that a child born to active parents but raised by inactive ones would turn out to be inactive, explaining: "The way they were raised. The child would want to be active but would be forced into not being more active and would get used to it." In other words, even when children chose the environment, they sometimes expressed that the environment was working against a natural tendency in another direction. Conversely, sometimes children talked about an innate potential that took environmental support to emerge, as in the following example from a subject speculating about a child who was born to smart parents but raised by not-so-smart parents: "The baby will not be smart at first, but in school it will get smart. The baby learns well because of the original parents. The new parents will be proud of the child for doing better than they expected." Especially given that even adults appeal to a mixed model, the development of these theories in early childhood should be well worth exploring in greater detail.

8. Summary

Several studies with a variety of methodologies demonstrate that by 4 or 5 years of age, children treat a range of natural categories as resistant to transformation. These results need not imply a *biological* understanding of categories (see Solomon et al., 1996, for discussion), but they do suggest an essentialist one.

D. CAUSAL EXPLANATIONS

To this point we have been considering evidence that children treat categories as richly structured, inference-promoting, and capturing underlying, nonobvious properties. What is missing so far is the notion of nonobvious properties as having causal force. In other words, do children believe that the inner qualities shared by category members *cause* apparent properties? If a causal account is appropriate, then we should find evidence that children invoke internal or nonobvious properties especially for events and feature clusters that otherwise are in need of explanation. In other words, children should search for causes and impute essentialist ones to cover the gaps (S. A. Gelman & Kalish, 1993).

Gail Gottfried and I (S. A. Gelman & Gottfried, 1996) tested this hypothesis by showing children events with or without a clear external cause (e.g., an item self-propelling across a table). If internal or immanent properties are the result of causal determinism, children should invoke them when an external cause is not available. We varied the presence of external cause in two ways: by varying (a) the structure of the event (half occurred by means of a visible human agent, half did not) and (b) the ontological domain of the item undergoing movement (animal or artifact). Artifacts are created and controlled by external agents, even when they seem to be behaving "on their own" (e.g., the electric garage door is operated by a remote-control device). In contrast, animals are self-sufficient and self-sustaining (R. Gelman, Durgin, & Kaufman, 1995), even when they are being controlled by others (e.g., digestion and respiration are largely beyond the control of others).

In this task, 3- and 4-year-old children saw videotapes of actual items either moving alone across a flat surface or being transported by a person, and were asked to explain how they moved. All items were unfamiliar to the children, so that they could not simply rely on rote knowledge. We went to an exotic pet shop and video-taped, for example, a chinchilla hopping around its cage and a chameleon walking on a rug. We bought unusual artifacts such as a wind-up toy sushi. For those with wind-up mechanisms, we wound them up, let them go, and videotaped their movements. For those without wind-up mechanisms, we attached a clear plastic thread to each one and pulled on the thread; on the videotape, the object is seen as moving as if by magic.

By editing the videotapes, we made every item seem to start at a standstill, then to move on its own. Children watched the videotapes and, after each one, were asked how the item moved. Specifically, children received three causal questions per item. We were interested in whether children appealed to internal cause ("Did something inside this make it move?") or immanent cause ("Did this move by itself?"). Rochel Gelman has proposed that children maintain an "innards principle," according to which animals move on the basis of their own inner power (R. Gelman, 1990; R. Gelman et al., 1995). However, few data were available concerning whether children construed this principle as based literally on internal parts or more abstractly as self-generated causation. In addition, we included a control question concerning a *non*internal, *non*inherent mechanism: external cause ("Did a person make this move?").

The results are complicated, as can be seen in Figure 1. Significant effects of both domain (animal vs. artifact) and event structure (transported vs. alone) were obtained. First, we looked at the question about a *person* as cause. We had initially predicted that this question would serve as a control, tapping simply the structure of the event (i.e., yielding a main effect of event type, with no effect of domain). Surprisingly, however, children as young as 3 years of age imposed domain differences in their interpretations. Children often reported that a person did *not* make the animals move, even when the animals were visibly transported. In contrast, children often invoked a person as agent of the artifacts' movement, even when the artifacts were moving alone. So even the control questions yielded some evidence that children were taking into account the causal implications of the domain.

The question about *immanence* (Does it move by itself?) revealed that children were again responsive to both agency in the event and the implicit agency in the object. Motion was judged to be self-caused for animals, regardless of condition. Even when a person bodily carried the animal from one end of the screen to the other, children insisted that the animal itself was responsible. In contrast, for the artifacts, what mattered was whether or not an external agent was shown. We consider the immanence responses to be genuine explanations and not simply re-descriptions of the event, for two reasons: (a) the domains differ significantly in how frequently immanence was invoked, and (b) some children spontaneously referred to the self as the causal agent (e.g., "Itself made it move").

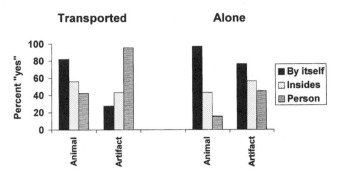

Fig. 1. *Mean percentage of causal attributions regarding "by itself," "insides," and "person" questions as a function of movement condition and domain. (From S. A. Gelman & Gottfried, 1996.)*

The next question is how children construe this inherent causal force, and specifically whether children think of it as a physical, internal part. As shown in Figure 1, the children's responses to the *insides* question were much less clear than their responses to the other two questions. The children did not appear to localize the cause in any concrete internal part. However, two small pieces of evidence suggest that children may link internal cause to external movement *for artifacts.* Both pieces of evidence came from the children's open-ended comments. First, when the children saw the artifacts moving, they sometimes talked about internal parts as potential causal mechanisms: "Hey, look! This is funny. It's moving by itself. Something's in it." "How does it move by itself? Some kind of electric?" The other piece of evidence has to do with how the children described the insides of the artifacts. After the children viewed each event and answered the yes/no questions, they were asked to describe the insides of each item. For animals, the insides were described the same regardless of condition: muscles, bones, blood, brains, and so forth. For artifacts, though, the children gave different kinds of descriptions in the two conditions. When people transported the artifacts, children often described the objects as being empty inside or as having nonfunctional parts, like wood. But when the artifacts moved on their own, children were significantly more likely to describe mechanical or electrical internal causes (e.g., gears, batteries, or electricity).

In summary, these initial data show that children *do* have a notion of immanent cause—a cause whose source is the object itself—but they do not think of it as an internal part. Maybe children possess a skeletal sense of self-generated cause *before* they have learned about specific internal causal mechanisms (R. Gelman, 1990; Simons & Keil, 1995). When they do make the link between internal cause and outer behavior, they may do so with artifacts first. More research is needed to examine the nature of this skeletal understanding and to uncover the developmental story of how cause functions in children's and adults' concepts (see S. A. Gelman & Kalish, 1993).

E. SUMMARY

In a variety of respects, categories promote inductive inferences about hidden
characteristics, privilege internal properties, and generate causal explanations.
This "essentialist" construal has powerful positive and negative implications for
how young children reason. On the positive side, it may be one impetus underlying a search for knowledge. The same impulse that leads children to treat certain
categories as possessing innately given similarities also leads them to search for
deeper regularities in nature (much like scientists). On the negative side, it seems
to foster stereotyping. For example, treating race classifications as discoverable
and real encourages the mistaken belief that deep and immutable differences are
linked to race. As the biologist Alan Templeton concluded on the basis of his analyses of millions of genetic sequences from mitochondrial DNA, "Race is a real cultural, political, and economic concept in society. But it is not a biological concept,
and that, unfortunately, is what many people wrongfully consider to be the essence
of race in humans—genetic differences" (McDonald, 1998, p. A19). We turn next
to the question of where these assumptions about categories come from.

III. Origins of Essentialist Reasoning

The preceding data are consistent with the argument that language learners have
an essentialist bias. Even if human categories do not correspond precisely to actual discontinuities in the world (but see Kornblith, 1993), an essentialist assumption makes them seem to do so. The question for this section is why children show
this pattern. Why do 3- and 4-year-olds expect categories to reveal hidden, unobservable qualities? And how do they distinguish between the kinds of categories
that have this structure (including animal kinds and social categories) and the kinds
of categories that do not (including simple artifacts)?

A. CONCEPTUALIZING THE QUESTION OF ORIGINS

A simple empiricist view might be something like: "Children learn whatever
they are told (or observe)." Yet surely this cannot be a full or satisfactory account.
For one thing, it begs the question of why adults would be telling children an essentialist story to begin with. But equally problematic is the fact that children can
be remarkably resistant to counter-evidence. (To be sure, they are also susceptible
to misleading suggestions or questions). A classic example of this resistance includes the Piagetian training studies that demonstrated repeatedly that children
cannot learn fundamental concepts (such as conservation of weight) simply by being told the correct answer. The stereotyping literature is also replete with examples of subjects (children and adults) twisting events in recall to fit prior biases

TABLE I

Possible Origins of Essentialist Beliefs

Starting point	Child	Others (World, Language, Culture)
Domain-general	"Essentialist assumption" (S. A. Gelman, Coley, & Gottfried, 1994)	Logic of count nouns (Carey, 1995; R. Mayr, 1991)
Domain-specific	Innate module (Atran, 1990; Pinker, 1994)	Biological knowledge; religious beliefs

(Liben & Signorella, 1987). Studies of folk theories likewise demonstrate powerful reasoning biases that contradict even direct instructions (Kaiser, McCloskey, & Proffitt, 1986). In summary, even young children can be active processors of information, and not merely passive recipients.

I illustrate this resistance to counter-evidence with a bit of essentialist reasoning from my daughter, Stephanie, when she was about $3\frac{1}{2}$ years old. She had been playing with a set of blocks that included a stylized dog and cat. Their faces were nearly identical, though only the cat had eyelashes. Later that day, Stephanie announced that "hes" don't have eyelashes; only "shes" have eyelashes. I then asked my husband to come into the room and take off his glasses. "Look at Daddy," I said. "Does he have eyelashes?" Stephanie looked right into his eye and said, "No. Daddy's a 'he', and 'hes' don't have eyelashes." Rather than change the theory to fit the evidence, my daughter ignored the evidence that disconfirmed the theory.

The problem of developmental origins is considerably complex, but as a starting-point it can be crudely conceptualized as a 2×2 matrix, as shown in Table I. One dimension concerns the extent to which essentialism originates with the child versus is imparted by others (either with cues found directly in the physical world, or with language and/or cultural practices). To address this question, input needs to be examined directly. Even on the most nativist accounts, input must play some role, because at the very least we have to learn which categories to essentialize, given that people in different cultures have different sorts of beliefs about categories such as caste or occupation. What do children hear about categories in books, on television, and from their parents? Is essentialism transmitted to children directly, or do children have beliefs that are not found in the input?

The second dimension concerns whether essentialism starts out as a domain-general or domain-specific assumption. At least two diverging possibilities can be identified. First, children may initially have a domain-general assumption. This hypothesis is consistent with related arguments by Carey (1995), Macnamara (1986), and R. Mayr (1991). On this view, children may start by thinking that *any* word tells you that something is a kind. Simply by naming something, we may confer kind status on it. If so, then the developmental task is to refine an overly broad assumption. Second, in contrast, children may start with a domain-specific assumption, perhaps as a component of an innate biology "module." This hypothesis is consistent with formulations put forth by Atran (1990) and Pinker (1994). On this view, children should start out treating only biological categories as having essences, and with age begin extending this mode to other domains, such as personality traits or social groupings. If so, then the developmental task is to extend a narrow assumption beyond the boundaries of biology.

As can be seen in Table I, currently viable theoretical accounts can be found in all the cells of the table. In the following subsections, I take up each dimension in turn, first examining the "horizontal" dimension of source of input, and next turning to the "vertical" dimension of domain specificity.

B. SOURCE OF INPUT

Formal schooling can be ruled out as a necessary precursor for richly structured categories because by age $2\frac{1}{2}$ years children appreciate the inductive potential of categories despite not yet having attended school (S. A. Gelman & Coley, 1990). What, then, are the developmental precedents for the appreciation that categories can be richly structured, but that only some categories have this form? In examining these issues, one must avoid dichotomizing explanations of category acquisition and development into "learned versus innate." Explanations do not lie along a unidimensional continuum (Marler, 1991). Indeed, parental input and child biases may work together toward a common goal (Markman, 1992), with children's interpretive biases and parents' structuring of the input acting in consistent and mutually reinforcing ways.

1. Parental Language

Clearly, parental naming patterns influence categorical structure by demarcating category boundaries. However, labels alone may not explain the rich structure evident in preschoolers' categories. A further examination of the informational content of parental speech and mismatches between parental speech and children's concepts is crucial to explaining how children's concepts come selectively to exhibit rich structure. Past research shows that parents do routinely provide information beyond labeling, although such information increases over the preschool years. DeLoache and DeMendoza (1987), in a study of 12-, 15-, and 18-month-old children, found that 74% of the information provided by mothers while reading an alphabet book to their children was, in their words, "simple" (that is, labels, sounds, or letter names). However, the amount of more "elaborated" information (including facts, dramatizations, and references to the child's experience) increased substantially across the ages studied (from 12 to 42%). The amount of elaborated information that parents provide continues to increase beyond 18 months. For example, Adams and Bullock (1986) found that parents of 3-year-olds provide categorical statements such as, "They [penguins] live at the South Pole and they swim and they catch fish." Callanan and Oakes (1992) found that parents of children as young as 3 years of age provide explanations prompted by children's questions regarding a range of biological, physical, and mental phenomena.

Callanan (1990) has examined directly the issue of what information about categories parents provide beyond labeling. In one study, parents were asked to teach a set of four basic-level and four superordinate-level concepts to their preschool children, one concept at a time. In a second study, parents were asked to teach four subordinate- and four basic-level concepts to their preschool children. For each concept to be taught, the mother was given a set of pictures of category instances that could be used or not used, at the mother's discretion. The researcher provided no further information to parents regarding how to teach these concepts, with the goal of examining the kinds of strategies parents might ordinarily use with their children.

Callanan found that the information parents provided varied with category level. Parents focused more on perceptual features and parts when teaching their children about basic- and subordinate-level categories, and focused more on functions when teaching their children superordinate-level categories. Parents also tended to talk more about typical features than idiosyncratic features. These findings suggest that parental input may help children focus on features that are important to the category being discussed (see also Mervis & Mervis, 1988, for evidence that parental language may help children's category development). More generally, parental input may help guide and limit the content of children's inferences (e.g., members of a basic-level category, such as *wrench,* tend to have similar perceptual features and parts; members of a superordinate-level category, such as *tool,* tend to have similar functions).

Callanan also proposed that parental descriptions may help children learn not just which features or kinds of features to associate with a particular category, but also which categories are coherent and can be expected to share many features. For example, when a parent describes vehicles as "things that move," the child may learn not only that movement is typical of vehicles, but also that vehicles as a class have common properties (even when the information is misleading, as in the example above). In other words, parental descriptions convey information both by their content (i.e., which features correspond to which categories) and by their form (i.e., making statements about the category as a whole vs. specific category members, thereby focusing on category coherence). In summary, parents focus on properties that are important for the category in question.

2. Essentialist Properties in Parental Speech

The studies reviewed above demonstrate that middle-class U.S. parents provide potentially rich category information in their informal conversations with children, and that this information extends beyond simple labeling routines. However, these studies were not designed to examine the extent to which parents might convey essential properties to children, or how parents distinguish categories for which essences are relevant (such as animal species) from categories for which essences are irrelevant (such as simple artifacts). These questions were the focus of a study that we conducted, examining parents' statements to their 20- and 35-month-old children (S. A. Gelman, Coley, Rosengren, Hartman, & Pappas, 1998). We were interested in two questions: First, do parents directly teach children the content of essentialist beliefs? Do they teach them, for example, that insides are more important than outsides; that characteristics are inherited; or that for some categories, all instances are alike? Second, do parents convey that certain categories have inductive potential? Do they focus on objects not as individuals but as members of a larger category?

Each mother–child pair came into the lab and looked through two picturebooks together, while we videotaped them. Each picturebook had nine pages, with several objects to a page. One picturebook was focused on animals; the other was focused on artifacts. We created the books so that each page displayed appearance–reality contrasts (e.g., one page in the animal book included two bats and a bird; one page in the artifact book included a Snoopy telephone, a standard telephone, and a Snoopy doll). The parents were simply told to look through the books with their children as they ordinarily would. We coded over 3,000 on-task utterances from the mothers (roughly 10 utterances per mother per page). Close to 40% of these utterances included information that went beyond labeling. We scrutinized the videotapes for possible clues in the input language and gestures. Our question was whether mothers provide explicit information that could directly teach children about essences. Based on studies by Keil (1989, 1994), Rochel Gelman (1990), Flavell, Flavell, and Green (1983), Springer (1992), Hirschfeld (1996), and in my laboratory, we knew that 4-year-olds make certain assumptions about animal categories: They assume that disparate members of an animal category are alike in nonobvious ways. They also have strong expectations about insides, kinship, origins, teleology, and the appearance-reality distinction. So if children are essentialists because their parents train them to be, we would expect to hear mothers say things like the following *hypothetical* examples:

"All":	"Did you know that all bats give milk to their babies?"
Insides:	"This dog has blood and bones inside. He needs them if he wants to stay strong and healthy."
Kinship:	"The kitty has stripes because her mommy and daddy have stripes."
Origins:	"That bird came from an egg that grew inside her mama."
Teleology:	"Polar bears are white because that helps them hide in the snow."
Appearance/reality:	"Birds and bats look the same on the outside, but inside they're different in ways you can't see."

Based on these a priori hypotheses, we coded the data. Here is a sampling of what the mothers actually said, for each of these coding categories. These are fairly typical, *actual* examples:

"All":	"I think . . . roosters all have that thing."
Insides:	"Batteries go in the car and the other car and the clock."
Kinship:	"There's the mother cat and there's the baby."
Origins:	"That's where we get our milk. The cows give us all the milk that we drink."
Teleology:	"Look at his nose. That's for eating ants."
Appearance/reality:	"These look like snakes, but they're called eels."

The actual examples mothers provided are substantially sketchier than the hypothetical examples. Even more important, these kinds of statements were extremely rare. Parents rarely talked about insides, and when they did, it was *exclusively* for artifacts (typically batteries). Likewise, even though children have a rich set of beliefs about kinship, origins, and teleology, parents provided almost no input about these topics. Appearance–reality statements were a bit more common, and were significantly more frequent for animals than artifacts. But parents never resolved appearance–reality contrasts in terms of internal parts, inheritance, or the like. Altogether, these explicit statements about essences accounted for less than 2% of parents' speech. So to the extent that mothers' input in our laboratory reflects their behavior with books at home, it seems implausible that children learn essentialism from this kind of direct statement.

3. Generic Noun Phrases

Although explicit reference to essences was rare, mothers much more frequently focused on categories by using *generic noun phrases* (e.g., *Bats* live in caves). Table II contains examples of generic noun phrases drawn from our database. Generic noun phrases refer to a category (e.g., bats) as an abstract whole, and refer to qualities that are relatively essential, enduring, and timeless (Carlson & Pelletier, 1995). Generics thus refer to kinds (see also Shipley, 1993; Wierzbicka, 1994, on kinds). Properties stated generically are not essential in the same sense as the nonobvious properties discussed earlier. However, they are *relatively* more essential than nongenericized properties. For example, although it is not essential that seals bounce balls (indeed neither all seals nor only seals bounce balls), it is a distinctive, nonaccidental property (cf. the property of being born on a Tuesday). In contrast, nongenerics (e.g., *These bats* live in a cave, *My cat* caught two mice, There are *some dinosaurs* in the museum) refer to accidental, transient, or contextually bound properties. Properties (e.g., "extinct") that refer to the category as a whole can be predicated only of generic noun phrases. Accordingly, we can say that *dinosaurs* are extinct, but we cannot say that a *particular* dinosaur or set of dinosaurs is extinct.

TABLE II

Examples of Statements Including Generic Noun Phrases[a]

Kitty cats love to unravel yarn.
Ants live underground.
A chipmunk's a little smaller than a squirrel.
Bats are little furry things that live in caves.
That's not the ocean, but they do live at—seals live in the ocean really.
Because I thinks seals like to bounce balls.
What do chipmunks like to eat?
Do you know what batteries are for?

[a]From S. A. Gelman, Coley, Rosengren, Hartman, & Pappas, 1998.

In our sample, 14 of the 16 mothers produced at least one generic statement, and most produced several (e.g., "*A wok* is how people in China cook. Well, actually, *a wok* is how people in America cook like Chinese people."). They talked about the category as a whole even when all they could see on the page was a single instance ("That's a chipmunk. And *they* eat the acorns."). Sometimes they shifted between singular and plural forms—as if one example can stand in for the larger category ("Did you know when *a pig* gets to be big, *they*'re called hogs?"). Mothers averaged approximately 3.37 generics per 100 utterances, with individual variation ranging from 0–8% of total utterances.

Although generics occurred in only a small percentage of mothers' speech, I argue that this frequency represents a substantial and potentially salient amount of input to children. Nouns can function in many different ways, including: generic reference, singular definite reference, general definite reference, nonreferring definite reference, distributive general reference, collective general reference, specific indefinite reference, and nonspecific indefinite reference (Lyons, 1977, pp. 177–197). Given this variety of functions, any given noun phrase type will constitute only a small fraction of speech. Accordingly, even the most salient of noun phrase types will occur in less than the majority of utterances. (Analogously, although food is a highly salient and important concept for young children, mention of food appears in much less than half of their utterances, because there are many competing topics of conversation.)

In order to determine the relative salience of generics, it is thus misleading to consider the *proportion* of speech containing generics, and more meaningful to consider the absolute frequency of such speech. As noted earlier, 87% of the mothers produced at least one generic in a 10- to 15-min session. (In contrast, only 56% of the mothers talked about numbers, and only 37% of the mothers referred to object shape.) During this brief session, each mother produced on average approximately 189 utterances, 3–4% of which were generics (i.e., 7.25). By extrapolation, this suggests that children would typically hear over 30 generics per hour, if placed in a comparable context, or hundreds of generics per day. Indeed, the rate of generics in maternal speech is comparable to the rate that mothers produce causal language (Hickling & Wellman, 1998) and exceeds the rate that children produce genuine psychological references to thoughts and beliefs at 6 years of age (Bartsch & Wellman, 1995). In our own sample, the rate of generic usage was greater than the rate at which mothers talked about object size (3.09% of utterances), color (1.96% of utterances), number (0.77% of utterances), shape (0.35% of utterances), or texture (0.22% of utterances). By contrast, truly rare linguistic forms, such as the dative passive, would be found much less frequently.

A striking feature of mothers' generics is that they were domain-specific, appearing significantly more frequently for animals than artifacts (M percentage of coded utterances containing a generic $= 5.15$ for animals and 1.44 for artifacts). The domain differences in generic usage cannot be attributed to familiarity of the category, similarity among category members, thematic relatedness among category members, or amount of maternal talk. We controlled for similarity and thematic relatedness by selecting the stimulus materials from a larger set of items that were pretested on adults, and we controlled for familiarity and amount of talk by conducting analyses that took into consideration the amount of talk and maternal ratings of child familiarity. The domain differences are also unlikely to be attributable to lack of sufficient knowledge about the artifacts. Mothers certainly knew several category-general properties true of each artifact depicted (including its parts, function, thematic associates, and appearance), and mentioned many of these properties in reference to *particular* objects and contexts. Importantly, though, mothers typically failed to mention these properties in generic form.

Why, then, did animals elicit so many more generics than artifacts? We interpret this result as reflecting conceptual differences between animal versus artifact categories. On the assumption that mothers construe animal kinds as more richly structured than artifact kinds (deeper similarities, greater coherence, etc.), they should more easily conceptualize animal categories as abstract wholes, and hence use generics. Support for this interpretation can be found in the divergence between maternal input patterns and the written texts of the books used in a replication study. The replication study used two commercially available picture books: one about farm animals and the other about trucks. Coding of the texts of these books revealed many generics in both the farm animal and truck domains ($Ms =$ 67 vs. 50 generics per 100 coded utterances, respectively), with no significant domain differences in generics found in the texts. The domain difference in the texts was slight relative to the domain difference in maternal speech, suggesting the importance of maternal conceptual biases. What is then relevant for the present discussion is that the domain difference in maternal generic usage is available to young children, and may inform children's acquisition of this very same conceptual distinction.

Although the present studies did not examine children's *comprehension* of generics, we hypothesize that generics serve two distinct functions for young children. First and most obviously, generics may teach children particular category-wide generalizations. From maternal generics, children can learn particular facts concerning animal vocalizations, habitat, diet, behaviors, and so forth. Because these properties are predicated of the kind as a whole, they may become more central to children's conceptual representations than if they had been stated nongenerically. Furthermore, because these facts are stated generically (rather than as universal quantifiers), they may be particularly robust against counter-evidence (e.g., "birds lay eggs" allows for male birds, whereas "all birds lay eggs" does not; Krifka et al., 1995; Lyons, 1977). Thus even erroneous properties stated generically, such as stereotypes concerning gender or race, may be more difficult to counter and erase than erroneous properties stated absolutely.

The second potential function of maternal generics may be to indicate to children that a category as a whole is an inference-promoting entity, even beyond the particular properties mentioned in the generic statements. In other words, hearing numerous generic statements about a category may lead children to treat this category as a "kind," of which indefinitely many category-wide generalizations could be made. In short, we suggest that hearing generics may lead children to make inferences regarding the structure of the category. If so, then generics may serve this function even when the information is relatively superficial (e.g., "Little rabbits are called kits"), or when little or no new information is provided (e.g., with questions, such as "How do they [bats] sleep?"), because the generic form itself implies that category members are importantly alike.

4. *Generics in Mandarin Chinese*

Generics in English are marked with specific formal devices such as bare plurals (e.g., bears) and definite singular noun phrases (e.g., the bear). Yet languages differ in the formal devices employed to express definiteness and plurality (Croft, 1990). What are the implications of these cross-linguistic differences for the expression of generics in languages other than English? Mandarin is a particularly revealing comparison language because it lacks articles and the singular–plural distinction on nouns. Thus, it contains sentences that could be translated into English using either generic or nongeneric forms (Krifka, 1995). For example, the following sentence:

xiao3	yalzi	yao2yao2bai3bai3	de	zou3	lu4
little	duck	waddlingly	DE	walk	road

could be translated into English as: (a) "The duck is waddling," (b) "The ducks are waddling," or (c) "Ducks waddle." Only (c) is generic.

A long-standing but untested claim is that these linguistic differences lead to corresponding conceptual differences in how speakers of Mandarin versus English think about abstract kinds (Moser, 1996). A. H. Bloom (1981, p. 36) stated the linguistic relativity hypothesis clearly:

> Perhaps the fact that English has a distinct way of marking the generic concept plays an important role in leading English speakers, by contrast to their Chinese counterparts, to develop schemas specifically designed for creating extracted theoretical entities, such as the theoretical buffalo, and hence for coming to view and use such entities as supplementary elements of their cognitive worlds.

However, Bloom's evidence for this position was insufficient, on his own admission (p. 36), and he cautioned that further research is needed.

Twila Tardif and I examined generics cross-linguistically (English and Mandarin), in child-directed speech from U.S. and Chinese caregivers interacting with their 20- to 23-month-old children (S. A. Gelman & Tardif, 1998). Examples of generics include: "Baby birds eat worms" [English]; and *da4 lao3shu3 yao3 bu4 yao3 ren2* ("Do big rats bite people or not?") [Mandarin]. As shown in the top panel in Figure 2, generic noun phrases were reliably identified in both languages, although they occurred less frequently in Mandarin than in English. In both languages, generic usage was domain specific, with generic noun phrases used most frequently to refer to animals. Nongeneric noun phrases, which were much more frequent, showed significantly different distributions across domains in both languages (see the bottom panel of Figure 2), thus suggesting that domain-specificity for generics cannot be attributed to the salience of the animal domain. In summary, we argue for universal properties of "kind" concepts that are expressed with linguistically different constructions. However, the frequency of expression may be modified by the manner in which generics are worded in the language.

5. Generic Noun Phrases in Children's Speech

The data on generics to this point are from parents. A central question concerns children's own production and interpretation of generic noun phrases. Athina Pappas and I conducted an initial study demonstrating that even preschool children (ages 2–4 years) make use of generics and distinguish between generic and nongeneric uses (Pappas & Gelman, 1998). Mother–child pairs were videotaped while looking through a book of animal pictures. Each page depicted either a single instance of a particular category (e.g., one crab) or 12–15 instances of a particular category (e.g., 12–15 crabs). The results indicated a substantial difference in how generics versus nongenerics were distributed in the speech of both the mothers and the children. The form of the nongeneric noun phrases was closely linked to the structure of the page: Singular noun phrases were used more often when a single instance was presented, and plural noun phrases were used more often when multiple instances were presented. In contrast, the form of the generic noun phrases was independent of the information depicted; for example, plural noun phrases were as frequent when only one instance was presented as when multiple instances

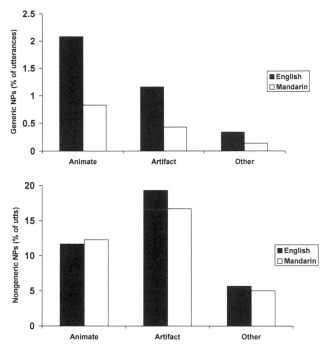

Fig. 2. Top panel. Generic noun phrases (mean percentage of utterances) in English and Mandarin as a function of domain. Bottom panel. Nongeneric noun phrases (mean percentage of utterances) in English and Mandarin as a function of domain. (From S. A. Gelman & Tardif, 1998.)

were presented. We interpreted the data as providing evidence that generic noun phrases differ in their semantics and conceptual organization from nongeneric noun phrases, both in the input to young children and in children's own speech. Thus, this simple linguistic device may provide input to and a reflection of children's early developing notion of "kinds."

C. DOMAIN SPECIFICITY

A further issue we have been exploring is the domain specificity or generality of children's early generics, in an ongoing project using the CHILDES database (S. A. Gelman, Rodriguez, Nguyen, & Koenig, 1997). Brian MacWhinney and Catherine Snow compiled and computerized the database, which includes longitudinal transcripts of natural speech from various researchers (MacWhinney, 1991). The participants in our study were eight children who had been followed longitudinally for 1 to 3 years beginning at 2 or 3 years of age, as shown in Table III. The corpus included a total of almost 200,000 utterances.

TABLE III

Children in the CHILDES Database Who Were Included in the S. A. Gelman, Rodriguez,
Nguyen, and Koenig (1997) Study

Child	Researcher	Age		
		2 years	3 years	4 years
Abe	Kuczaj (1976)	×	×	×
Adam	R. Brown (1973)	×	×	×
Ross	MacWhinney	×	×	×
Sarah	R. Brown (1973)	×	×	×
Peter	L. Bloom (1970)	×		
Naomi	Sachs (1983)	×	×	
Nathaniel	Snow	×	×	
Mark	MacWhinney		×	×

For comparisons across ages, we analyzed data from only the four children for whom we had data at all age levels. For analyses within an age group, we examined all children with data at that age. We first conducted a computerized search for all utterances containing plural nouns, mass nouns, or nouns preceded by the article *a* or *an,* as these are possible generic constructions. (Although a singular noun preceded by *the* can be generic (e.g., "The lion is a ferocious beast"), this construction is more formal and rarely used in parental speech to children (Gelman, Coley et al., 1998). Thus, by excluding such utterances we may be underestimating generic usage in children's speech.) Then we coded each noun phrase (a) as generic or nongeneric and (b) for domain. For domain, we made a three-way distinction between animals or animal parts (e.g., butterflies, people, firemans, elephants, ghosts, bones), artifacts (e.g., shoes, money, toys, cars, houses, pirate hats), and all other domains (e.g., yogurt, a rainbow, flowers, jokes, parties). The results presented in Figure 3 are based on initial analyses of a subset of the data and should be considered preliminary. However, the patterns are sufficiently clear to draw some tentative conclusions.

First, children as young as 2 years of age spontaneously produced generics in everyday conversations. Examples included the following (with generic noun phrases in italics): "That shirt's not for *girls*" (Ross, 2-7); "*Animals* eat *berries* and *they* eat *mushrooms*" (Abe, 2-9); "*Indians* live in Africa" (Adam, 3-3); "*Bad guys* have some guns" (Mark, 3-7); "Don't play with *guns*" (Sarah, 4-10). The eight children we studied produced over 3,000 generic noun phrases during the sessions recorded between ages 2 and 4 years. The children thus were not focused exclusively on the here-and-now, and readily talked about categories as abstract "kinds." All seven of the 2-year-olds we studied produced some generics, and for 4-year-olds generics constituted nearly 4% of their total utterances (including both

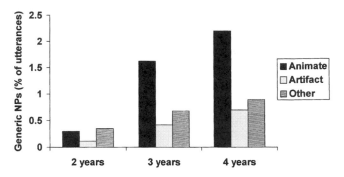

Fig. 3. Mean number of generic noun phrases per 100 utterances as a function of age and domain, in the CHILDES database. (From S. A. Gelman, Rodriguez, Nguyen, & Koenig, 1997.)

searched and unsearched utterances). Again, although the frequency of generic utterances is only a small fraction of children's total speech, this frequency is high when one considers the amount of speech produced, the variety of noun phrase types that are possible, and the comparable frequency of other salient and important topics (e.g., parental discussion of causality; Hickling & Wellman, 1998; see discussion of these issues in section III.B.5, Generic noun phrases).

Second, the use of generics increased from ages 2 to 4 years. We do not yet know why the developmental increase occurs. It may reflect a conceptual change in the early preschool years. Specifically, a developmental increase may occur in how readily children think about categories abstracted from context. Alternatively, the change might reflect increasing syntactic skills during this age range. Four-year-olds have better control over the syntactic devices needed to create generics, such as articles, plurality, and tense (R. Brown, 1973), which could account for the change.

Third, children's generics are domain-specific. At each age, children produced significantly more generics for animate kinds than for artifacts or all other domains (e.g., plants, food, rocks). The data were consistent across subjects: Seven of the eight children showed the domain difference at every age, and the eighth child showed this pattern at one of the two ages for which we had data. These results argue against the notion that children possess a domain-general essentializing tendency.

At this point no firm conclusions can be drawn about the basis of this early domain-specificity. Superficially, it might appear that children produce generics primarily for biological categories, because animals and people are biological entities, but this might not be the case, because *categories* of animals and people are not necessarily biological. Certainly a sizeable subset of the generics produced referred to nonbiological social kinds (e.g., teachers, poor people, cowboys, Italy people, strangers, good little girls, Naomis, bad people, carpenters). Thus, the data may argue that children produce more generics for the animate domain, rather than that children produce more generics for the biological domain.

D. SUMMARY

The question of origins is complex and has only begun to be addressed in systematic studies. However, initial evidence suggests several conclusions. Essentialism is neither the result of formal schooling (children essentialize even at preschool age) nor a direct reflection of the structure of the world (children essentialize nonbiological categories such as race). Mothers do not directly or explicitly teach their children about essences, although they may provide some subtle indications of the richness of category structure in the form of generic noun phrases. Thus, children's biases and maternal input may work together in the development of essentialized categories. A controversial issue concerns whether children's earliest essentialist construals are domain-general or domain-specific. However, the argument for a broad domain-general essentializing tendency in early childhood is seriously undermined by the evidence that children's spontaneous generic noun phrases exhibit clear-cut domain differences (animate vs. artifact) as early as 2 years of age. More research is needed to determine why these domain differences arise. (See also S. A. Gelman & Hirschfeld, 1999, for a discussion of the domain specificity of essentialism.)

IV. Questions and Controversies

In the preceding sections, I have summarized a variety of findings concerning children's categories, illustrating that certain of children's categories (especially their categories of animals and people) are richly structured and inference promoting. I interpreted these results as providing evidence for psychological essentialism in young children. In the present section I briefly review three questions and controversies raised by this framework: (a) Is the essentialist framework apt? If so, is it necessary? In other words, what does the notion of essentialism buy us? (b) What are the components of essentialism? How is an "essence" different from a "kind"? How is an "essence" different from a "theory"? (c) What is the role of language in the development of essentialized concepts?

A. IS THE ESSENTIALIST FRAMEWORK NECESSARY?

Although the data reviewed in this chapter are consistent with essentialism, we have not found any direct evidence for essentialism, nor any detailed set of beliefs we can point to as the content of the essences of children's categories. Do we need to invoke essences at all? At least two plausible arguments can be leveled *against* an essentialist framework, both of which we consider in this section. One argument is that nonobvious features cannot be essential to children's concepts, because concepts are highly context sensitive and grounded in perceptual knowledge. In other words, essentialism may not be compatible with other facts that are known about human concepts. The other argument is that essentialism as a covering framework is unnecessary. Even accepting the centrality of nonobvious features, a critic may argue that the essentialist framework is unnecessary because all the phenomena uncovered in these studies can be characterized by appealing to more localized components. We argue against both these positions below.

1. Context Sensitivity

An issue widely discussed in the 1990s is the seeming disparity between essentialism and approaches arguing for the context sensitivity of concepts (S. A. Gelman & Medin, 1993; Smith, Jones, & Landau, 1996). On the one hand, the research summarized here implies that theories determine the structure and function of categories, at times even overriding salient perceptual information, and that even children treat concepts as having essences (S. A. Gelman, Coley, & Gottfried, 1994; D. Medin, 1989). On the other hand, concepts are highly flexible, sensitive to context, variable depending on the task, and influenced by perceptually immediate (on-line) properties (Barsalou, 1993; Jones & Smith, 1993). These proposals would seem to be contradictory: One proposal is that essences are at the core of concepts; the other proposal is that perceptual features are core, or, in the extreme, that concepts have no core. Accordingly, a number of scholars have suggested that essentialism is incompatible with context sensitivity (Braisby, Franks, & Hampton, 1996; Malt, 1994; Smith & Heise, 1992).

In contrast, Gil Diesendruck and I have argued that the contradiction is only apparent: Psychological essentialism is compatible with the context sensitivity often noted by cognitive scientists (see S. A. Gelman & Diesendruck, 1999, for more extended discussion). The resolution rests on three main points: First, essentialism is a skeletal, guiding heuristic rather than a fixed definition. Thus, essentialism allows for flexible, open-ended conceptual structures. Relatedly, essentialism is not a claim that perceptual features are unimportant. Essences are often correlated with and predictive of perceptual features (e.g., according to a somewhat oversimplified folk portrayal, XY chromosomes *cause* the observable properties of a male). However, given that typically we do not have direct access to the essence, the correlated and observable properties become crucial to many tasks (Keil, 1989). This linkage between observable properties and the assumption of underlying causal (essential) properties can provide an account of why perceptual prototypes, though insufficient for characterizing many categorization decisions (see Keil, 1989; Rips, 1989), are so prevalent in on-line processing of concepts.

Second, different kinds of concepts require different theories to account for their structure. Although essentialism is an apt characterization of basic-level animal categories and concepts of human kinds, it is much less relevant to other kinds of concepts. The information a child uses will be limited by the information supplied. If the only information children receive concerns shape, texture, and size, then frequent use of shape is unsurprising. In contrast, when children are reasoning about real-world living kinds, issues of ontology, essence, and kind become important.

Third, the power of perceptual features often derives from their status as markers of theory-relevant information. Although shape can be an especially salient dimension to young children, its salience derives largely from its value as an index or predictor of other information (Ebeling, 1997; S. A. Gelman, Croft, Fu, Clausner, & Gottfried, 1998; S. A. Gelman & Diesendruck, 1999; D. Medin, 1989; Soja, Carey, & Spelke, 1992; Waxman & Braig, 1996). When ontological knowledge and theoretical beliefs are available, and when they conflict with shape, children often sort and name on the basis of these other factors.

2. Why Invoke Essentialism as an Overarching Framework?

A second potential argument against essentialism is that it is unnecessary because we could instead refer to the component phenomena discussed earlier: Categories have inductive potential, categories are stable over transformations, causal features are central to categories, and categories exhibit important domain differences in their structures. Moreover, several well-established developmental phenomena seem closely related, including the appearance–reality contrast (Flavell et al., 1983), the expectation that events have causes (A. L. Brown, 1990; Bullock, Gelman, & Baillargeon, 1982; Schultz, 1982), and the belief that unobservable entities can have massive effects (Au, Sidle, & Rollins, 1993; Gopnik & Wellman, 1994; Kalish, 1996). Nonetheless, two primary arguments favor going beyond the component phenomena and framing these results in terms of essentialism: (a) parsimony and (b) the existence of explicit essentialist formulations. The parsimony argument is straightforward: A range of phenomena that co-occur, developmentally and cross-culturally, seem instantiations of a single broader principle. Certainly these phenomena are distinct, but if one considered each phenomenon *exclusively* as distinct and unrelated to the others, one would then miss whatever broader generalizations can be reached by addressing their commonalities. More fine-grained developmental analysis will be needed to discover how tightly linked are these various phenomena in development. Second, *explicit* essence formulations are found in some cultures, and they seem continuous with the implicit, skeletal formulations examined in these studies. An example is the notion of a "soul" in Western philosophy, "kunam" among the Tamil (Daniel, 1984), "spirit" among some organ-transplant recipients (Sylvia & Novak, 1997), and "word magic" in Western and other cultures (Benveniste, 1971; Piaget, 1929). By treating people's implicit construals as essentialism, we have a framework that covers them all.

B. COMPONENTS OF ESSENTIALISM

Although I argued above that essentialist phenomena can reasonably be construed as related, this argument does not mean that the concept is indivisible. Indeed, psychological essentialism of the sort with which we are concerned (see
S. A. Gelman & Hirschfeld, 1999, for discussion of other sorts of psychological
essentialism) appears to have two related though separable assumptions: (a) a *kind*
assumption, that people treat certain categories as richly structured "kinds," and
(b) an *essence* assumption, that people believe a category has an underlying property (essence) that cannot be observed directly but that causes the observable qualities that category members share.

1. The "Kinds" Assumption

By "kinds" (i.e., "natural kinds"), I mean categories that have many similarities
in common, including nonobvious similarities, and are assumed to capture deep
regularities beyond those that are already known. We have already seen that kinds
are directly expressed in language, via generic noun phrases (or "kind-referring
expressions"; Carlson & Pelletier, 1995). The notion of "kind" is itself universally
expressed lexically (Wierzbicka, 1994). Children and adults also use knowledge
about kinds to form "over-hypotheses" such as "kinds of animals each have a characteristic sound," thus leading to novel inferences even in the absence of specific
information about a novel kind (e.g., that armadillos have a characteristic sound)
(Shipley, 1989, 1993).

Kinds can be distinguished from other forms of conceptual organization (S. A.
Gelman, 1997; Wierzbicka, 1994). On the one hand, they are distinct from individuals (e.g., Lassie is an individual; the set of dogs is a kind). On the other hand,
they are distinct from a variety of other categories or groupings in which instances
share only a small number of superficial features with one another. A category is
any grouping together of two or more discriminably different things; in contrast,
a kind is a category that the cognizer believes to be based in nature, to be discovered rather than invented, and to capture many deep regularities. "Tigers" is a kind;
the set of "striped things" (including tigers, striped shirts, and barber-shop poles)
is not. Members of the category "striped things" have only a single property in
common (stripedness); they do not share nonobvious similarities, nor does the category serve as a basis of induction (Markman, 1989; Mill, 1843). Similarly, the ad
hoc category of "things to take on a camping trip" constitutes a category but not a
kind (Barsalou, 1991).

2. The "Essence" Assumption

Related to but distinct from the notion of "kind" is that of "essence." As an intuitive folk construal, the essence is an underlying property, substance, power,
process, relationship, or entity shared by members of a kind, that one cannot observe directly but that causes the observable qualities that hold a category together.

The essence is believed to confer identity and to be causally responsible for observable similarities among category members (S. A. Gelman et al., 1994; D. Medin, 1989). For example, one plausible essence for the category of tigers might be shared DNA structure, which (according to folk belief) is what ultimately gives tigers their identity. Or to give another example, the causal essence of water may be something like H_2O, which is responsible for various observable properties that water has. Note that the cluster of properties "odorless, tasteless, and colorless" is not an essence of water, despite being true of all members of the category *water,* because the properties "odorless, tasteless, and colorless" lack causal force (see Braisby et al., 1996, and Malt, 1994, for a critique of this view, and S. A. Gelman & Hirschfeld, 1999, for a rejoinder). There are two caveats to this view, however: (a) often the causal essence is not known and instead children and adults have an "essence placeholder" (D. Medin, 1989), and (b) an essence is rarely consulted to determine category membership, for the simple reason that people often do not know (or cannot readily access) the relevant information. In such instances, people use other features instead.

The major difference between kind and essence is that the latter incorporates the former and adds to it the idea that some part, substance, or quality (i.e., the essence) *causes* the properties shared by the kind. In the literature, the two notions have often been treated as interchangeable. However, categories can be bound together in crucial ways, without cognizers considering the causal basis of the kind.

Two pieces of evidence tentatively suggest that, developmentally, a notion of kind may precede a notion of essence. Evidence for use of *kinds* is present by age 2 (in children's use of generic noun phrases), but evidence for appeal to an *essence* (e.g., with the switched-at-birth method) has so far not appeared below age 4 years. Second, the Gottfried, Gelman, & Schultz (in press) study of brain transplants implies that the youngest children (preschool and kindergarten age) have a notion of kind that is *not* tied to a particular known or localized part (i.e., the brain), even though they have sufficient knowledge about the function of the part to enable localizing it. To put this point another way, children do not yet have the adult conception that an animal's psychological essence is housed in the brain, but rather believe that there is an enduring sense of kind that is distinct from the brain. An instructive line for future research should be to use converging methods to try to distinguish "kind" from "essence."

3. Essences and Theories

In distinguishing components of essentialism, the link between essences and theories needs to be clarified. Essences and theories are related in that both posit that categories incorporate nonobvious information that cannot be reduced to observable features. For adults, concepts are influenced by theoretical belief systems and cannot be characterized by statistical information alone (Heit & Rubinstein, 1994; Keil, 1989; Murphy & Medin, 1985; Rips, 1989; see Murphy, 1993, for review). How subjects incorporate different features varies, depending on their theories about the domain (Wisniewski & Medin, 1994). The probability of incorporating novel instances is also dependent on theoretical beliefs rather than statistical correlations (D. L. Medin & Shoben, 1988). The extent to which features are weighted in classification judgments is influenced by causal understandings: properties that are causes are viewed as more central to a concept than properties that are effects (Ahn & Lassaline, 1996), again demonstrating that correlations alone cannot account for the centrality and significance of features in a concept (see also Ahn et al., 1995; Keil, 1989; White, 1995, for further evidence).

Initial evidence suggests a similar pattern for children (Barrett, Abdi, Murphy, & Gallagher, 1993). For example, in a task that required children to categorize novel birds into one of two novel categories, first- and fourth-grade children (ages 6–7 years and 9–10 years, respectively) noticed the association between brain size and memory capacity and used that correlation to categorize new members. Specifically, exemplars that preserved the correlation were more often judged to be category members and to be more typical of the category. The children did not make use of features that correlated equally well but were unsupported by a theory (e.g., the correlation between structure of heart and shape of beak).

However, essentialist concepts and theory-laden concepts are not equivalent. First, essentialized categories need not imply full-fledged explanatory theories (Atran, 1990). Instead, they are "theory-like" in their adherence to nonobvious, theorized entities to account for observable structure. Second, some theory-laden concepts are not essentialized. For example, Murphy and Medin (1985) convincingly made the case that we use theories to classify items such as trash cans, but we do not need to appeal to essentialism in such cases.

C. ESSENTIALISM AND LANGUAGE

A notable aspect of essentialism is its close link to language. In part we have seen this link with generic noun phrases, which signal that categories are kinds (Carlson & Pelletier, 1995). However, a more general assumption implicit in much of the research reviewed earlier is that common nouns map onto kinds (Macnamara, 1986; Markman, 1989; Wierzbicka, 1994) or even onto essentialized categories (Carey, 1995). Conversely, changing what we call a thing can have consequences even when the thing itself does not change. For example, according to the *New York Times* (June 3, 1997), a biologist who conducted cloning research suggested that when and if humans are ever intentionally cloned, doctors will use a different word to refer to the process in order to avoid controversy. In summary, essentializing may be more likely to occur when a concept is encoded in language than when it is not. Certainly, hearing a familiar name can foster essentializing (S. A. Gelman & Markman, 1986), though not every word carries essentialist assumptions (Davidson & Gelman, 1990).

In addition to lexicalization and generic noun phrases as means of conveying essences, the distinction between essential and nonessential properties may be expressed in other ways across languages of the world. For example, in an investigation of Spanish verbs, Sera (1992; Sera, Reittinger, & del Castillo Pintado, 1991) found that the distinction between *ser* and *estar* maps roughly onto a distinction between inherent and accidental properties. Although English does not make the same distinction in its verb system, the propensity to use various kinds of quantifiers or generics may distinguish categories that promote inferences from those that do not.

From a developmental perspective, the precise role of lexicalization and other linguistic markers of essentialism is not entirely clear. Perhaps concepts that are so important as to be essentialized are prime candidates for lexicalization because of their salience, frequency, and stability. Or perhaps having a name helps fix the concept in people's minds, transmit it to new generations, and so reify its existence. Linguistic form class also appears to be important, though to date this line has been underexplored. Markman (1989) suggested that nouns are more likely than adjectives to capture essentialized kinds (see also Hall & Moore, 1997, and Waxman & Markow, 1995, for evidence that nouns imply greater stability than adjectives). These are all promising directions to pursue in future research.

V. Conclusions

A varied set of essentialist-like beliefs emerge early in development (by 3 to 5 years of age): certain categories promote rich inferences, are stable over transformations, have innate structure, and incorporate causal features. These beliefs have both positive and negative implications. On the positive side, they are productive in that they lead children to search for new knowledge and to revise categories on the basis of that knowledge. On the negative side, they appear to promote stereotyping. Thus, essentializing can be viewed as a powerful and persistent myth—persistent over history and perhaps over cultures (Atran, 1990), yet erroneous in its application and details.

The fact that essentialist-like beliefs emerge so early in development, yet receive so little explicit instruction from parents, suggests that essentialism may be a developmental constant. Nonetheless, alongside this constant, developmental changes also occur. Essentialism may start out as an assumption about "kinds," only later incorporating the idea of a causal essence. This tentative conclusion receives support from the fact that evidence for "kinds" has been found in children about 2 to 3 years younger than those showing evidence for essences. Moreover, with age children are increasingly able to incorporate nonessentialized models of concepts (Heyman & Gelman, 1997; Hirschfeld, 1996; M. Taylor, 1996), detailed biological knowledge (Gottfried et al., in press), and statistical information about category structure (Gutheil & Gelman, 1997; Lopez et al., 1992).

Early esentialism might appear to pose a challenge to more traditional theories of children's concepts (e.g., Inhelder & Piaget, 1964), which emphasized the instability of children's concepts and their focus on superficial, accidental, or perceptual features. However, an important point is that essentialism does not posit that perceptual features are unimportant to early concepts. Rather, essentialism carries with it the assumption that a category has two distinct though interrelated levels: the level of observable reality and the level of explanation and cause. This two-tier structure may in fact serve to motivate further development, leading children to develop deeper, more thoughtful understandings (Waxman & Braig, 1996; Wellman & Gelman, 1997). In fact, most developmental accounts of cognitive change include something like this structure, such as equilibration (Inhelder & Piaget, 1958), competition (MacWhinney, 1987), theory change (Carey, 1985), analogy (Goswami, 1996), and cognitive variability (Siegler, 1994). In all these cases—as with essentialism—children consider contrasting representations. Perhaps not surprisingly, then, children look beyond observable features when trying to understand the categories of their world.

ACKNOWLEDGMENTS

This research was supported by National Science Foundation grant BNS-9100348, NICHD grant HD36043, and a J. S. Guggenheim fellowship to the author.

REFERENCES

Adams, A. K., & Bullock, D. (1986). Apprenticeship in word use: Social convergence processes in learning categorically related nouns. In S. A. Kuczaj & M. D. Barrett (Eds.), *The development of word meaning* (pp. 155–197). New York: Springer-Verlag.

Ahn, W.-K., Kalish, C. W., Medin, D. L., & Gelman, S. A. (1995). The role of covariation versus mechanism information in causal attribution. *Cognition, 54,* 299–352.

Ahn, W.-K., & Lassaline, M. E. (1996). *Causal structure in categorization.* Unpublished manuscript, Yale University, New Haven, CT.

Atran, S. (1990). *Cognitive foundations of natural history.* New York: Cambridge University Press.

Au, T. K., Sidle, A. L., & Rollins, K. B. (1993). Developing an intuitive understanding of conservation and contamination: Invisible particles as a plausible mechanism. *Developmental Psychology, 29,* 286–299.

Barrett, S. E., Abdi, H., Murphy, G. L., & Gallagher, J. M. (1993). Theory-based correlations and their role in children's concepts. *Child Development, 64,* 1595–1616.

Barsalou, L. W. (1991). Deriving categories to achieve goals. In G. H. Bower (Ed.), *The psychology of learning and motivation* (pp. 1–64). San Diego, CA: Academic Press.

Barsalou, L. W. (1993). Challenging assumptions about concepts. *Cognitive Development, 8,* 169–180.

Bartsch, K., & Wellman, H. M. (1995). *Children talk about the mind.* New York: Oxford University Press.

Bem, S. (1989). Genital knowledge and gender constancy in preschool children. *Child Development, 60,* 649–662.

Benveniste, E. (1971). *Problems in general linguistics.* Coral Gables, FL: University of Miami Press.

Bloom, A. H. (1981). *The linguistic shaping of thought.* Hillsdale, NJ: Erlbaum.

Bloom, L. (1970). *Language development; form and function in emerging grammars.* Cambridge, MA: MIT Press.

Brace, C. L. (1964). A nonracial approach towards the understanding of human diversity. In A. Montagu (Ed.), *The concept of race.* New York: Free Press.

Braisby, N., Franks, B., & Hampton, J. (1996). Essentialism, word use, and concepts. *Cognition, 59,* 247–274.

Brown, A. L. (1990). Domain-specific principles affect learning and transfer in children. *Cognitive Science, 14,* 107–133.

Brown, R. (1973). *A first language; The early stages.* Cambridge, MA: Harvard University Press.

Bullock, M., Gelman, R., & Baillargeon, R. (1982). The development of causal reasoning. In W. J. Friedman (Ed.), *The developmental psychology of time* (pp. 209–254). New York: Academic Press.

Callanan, M. A. (1990). Parents' descriptions of objects: Potential data for children's inferences about category principles. *Cognitive Development, 5,* 101–122.

Callanan, M. A., & Oakes, L. M. (1992). Preschoolers' questions and parents' explanations: Causal thinking in everyday activity. *Cognitive Development, 7,* 213–233.

Carey, S. (1985). *Conceptual development in childhood.* Cambridge, MA: MIT Press.

Carey, S. (1995). On the origins of causal understanding. In D. Sperber, D. Premack, & A. J. Premack (Eds.), *Causal cognition: A multi-disciplinary approach* (pp. 268–308). Oxford, England: Clarendon Press.

Carey, S., & Spelke, E. (1994). Domain-specific knowledge and conceptual change. In L. A. Hirschfeld & S. A. Gelman (Eds.), *Mapping the mind: Domain specificity in cognition and culture* (pp. 169–200). New York: Cambridge University Press.

Carlson, G. N., & Pelletier, F. J. (Eds.). (1995). *The generic book.* Chicago: University of Chicago Press.

Croft, W. (1990). *Typology and universals.* New York: Cambridge University Press.

Daniel, E. V. (1984). *Fluid signs: Being a person the Tamil way.* Berkeley: University of California Press.

Davidson, N. S., & Gelman, S. A. (1990). Inductions from novel categories: The role of language and conceptual structure. *Cognitive Development, 5,* 151–176.

DeLoache, J. S., & DeMendoza, O. A. P. (1987). Joint picturebook interactions of mothers and 1-year-old children. *British Journal of Developmental Psychology, 5,* 111–123.

Diesendruck, G. (1996). *Essentialism and word learning: A cross-cultural investigation.* Unpublished manuscript, Bar-Ilan University.

Diesendruck, G., Gelman, S. A., & Lebowitz, K. (1998). Conceptual and linguistic biases in children's word learning. *Developmental Psychology, 34,* 823–839.

Dupré, J. (1993). *The disorder of things: Metaphysical foundations of the disunity of science.* Cambridge, MA: Harvard University Press.

Ebeling, K. (1997, April). *The role of shape and intentionality in children's early naming.* Paper presented at the meeting of the Society for Research in Child Development, Washington, DC.

Eder, R. A. (1989). The emergent personologist: The structure and content of $3\frac{1}{2}$, $5\frac{1}{2}$, and $7\frac{1}{2}$-year-olds' concepts of themselves and other persons. *Child Development, 60,* 1218–1228.

Flavell, J. H., Flavell, E. R., & Green, F. L. (1983). Development of the appearance-reality distinction. *Cognitive Psychology, 15,* 95–120.

Fuss, D. (1989). *Essentially speaking: Feminism, nature, and difference.* New York: Routledge.

Gelman, R. (1990). First principles organize attention to and learning about relevant data: Number and the animate-inanimate distinction as examples. *Cognitive Science, 14,* 79–106.

Gelman, R., Durgin, F., & Kaufman, L. (1995). Distinguishing between animates and inanimates: Not by motion alone. In D. Sperber, D. Premack, & A. J. Premack (Eds.), *Causal cognition: A multi-disciplinary debate* (pp. 150–184). Oxford, England: Clarendon Press.

Gelman, S. A. (1988). The development of induction within natural kind and artifact categories. *Cognitive Psychology, 20,* 65–96.

Gelman, S. A. (1997). Developing a doctrine of natural kinds. *Psychology of Language and Communication, 1*(2).

Gelman, S. A., & Coley, J. D. (1990). The importance of knowing a dodo is a bird: Categories and inferences in 2-year-old children. *Developmental Psychology, 26,* 796–804.

Gelman, S. A., & Coley, J. D. (1991). Language and categorization: The acquisition of natural kind terms. In S. A. Gelman & J. P. Byrnes (Eds.), *Perspectives on language and thought: Interrelations in development* (pp. 146–196). Cambridge, England: Cambridge University Press.

Gelman, S. A., Coley, J. D., & Gottfried, G. M. (1994). Essentialist beliefs in children: the acquisition of concepts and theories. In L. A. Hirschfeld & S. A. Gelman, *Mapping the mind: Domain specificity in cognition and culture* (pp. 341–366). New York: Cambridge University Press.

Gelman, S. A., Coley,, J. D., Rosengren, K., Hartman, E., & Pappas, T. (1998). Beyond labeling: The role of maternal input in the acquisition of highly-structured categories. *Monographs of the Society for Research in Child Development.* Series No. 253, vol. 63, No. 1.

Gelman, S. A., Collman, P., & Maccoby, E. E. (1986). Inferring properties from categories versus inferring categories from properties: The case of gender. *Child Development, 57,* 396–404.

Gelman, S. A., Croft, W., Fu, P., Clausner, T., & Gottfried, G. (1998). Why is a pomegranate an "apple"? The role of shape, taxonomic relatedness, and prior lexical knowledge in children's overextensions of "apple" and "dog." *Journal of Child Language, 25,* 267–291.

Gelman, S. A., & Diesendruck, G. (1999). Representation of concepts. In I. E. Sigel (Ed.), *Theoretical perspectives in the development of representational thought* (pp. 87–111). Hillsdale, NJ: Erlbaum.

Gelman, S. A., & Gottfried, G. M. (1996). Children's causal explanations of animate and inanimate motion. *Child Development, 67,* 1970–1987.

Gelman, S. A., & Heyman, G. D. (1997, April). *Thinking about the origins of human dispositions.* Paper presented at the meeting of the Society for Research in Child Development, Washington, DC.

Gelman, S. A., & Hirschfeld, L. A. (1999). How biological is essentialism? In S. Atran & D. Medin (Eds.), *Folk biology* (pp. 403–446). Cambridge, MA: MIT Press.

Gelman, S. A., & Kalish, C. W. (1993). Categories and causality. In R. Pasnak & M. L. Howe (Eds.), *Emerging themes in cognitive development: Vol. 2. Competencies* (pp. 3–32). New York: Springer-Verlag.

Gelman, S. A., & Markman, E. M. (1986). Categories and induction in young children. *Cognition, 23,* 183–209.

Gelman, S. A., & Markman, E. M. (1987). Young children's inductions from natural kinds: The role of categories and appearances. *Child Development, 58,* 1532–1541.

Gelman, S. A., & Medin, D. L. (1993). What's so essential about essentialism? A different perspective on the interaction of perception, language, and conceptual knowledge. *Cognitive Development, 8,* 157–167.

Gelman, S. A., & O'Reilly, A. W. (1988). Children's inductive inferences within superordinate categories: The role of language and category structure. *Child Development, 59,* 876–887.

Gelman, S. A., Rodriguez, T., Nguyen, S., & Koenig, M. (1997, April). *Children's spontaneous talk about kinds: Domain-specificity in use of generics.* Paper presented at the meeting of the Society for Research in Child Development, Washington, DC.

Gelman, S. A., & Tardif, T. Z. (1998). Generic noun phrases in English and Mandarin: An examination of child-directed speech. *Cognition, 66,* 215–248.

Gelman, S. A., & Wellman, H. M. (1991). Insides and essences: Early understandings of the nonobvious. *Cognition, 38,* 213–244.

Gelman, S. A., Wilcox, S. A., & Clark, E. V. (1989). Conceptual and lexical hierarchies in young children. *Cognitive Development, 4,* 309–326.

Golinkoff, R. M., Mervis, C. B., & Hirsh-Pasek, K. (1994). Early object labels: The case for a developmental lexical principles framework. *Journal of Child Language, 21,* 125–155.

Gopnik, A., & Wellman, H. (1994). The theory theory. In L. A. Hirschfeld & S. A. Gelman (Eds.), *Mapping the mind: Domain specificity in cognition and culture* (pp. 257–293). New York: Cambridge University Press.

Goswami, U. (1996). Analogical reasoning and cognitive development. In H. W. Reese (Ed.), *Advances in child development and behavior* (Vol. 26, pp. 91–138). San Diego, CA: Academic Press.

Gottfried, G. (1997, April). *Children's understanding of the brain-as-container metaphor.* Paper presented at the meetings of the Society for Research in Child Development, Washington, DC.

Gottfried, G., Gelman, S. A., & Schultz, J. (in press). Children's understanding of the brain: From early essentialism to biological theory. *Cognitive Development.*

Guillaumin, C. (1980). The idea of race and its elevation to autonomous scientific and legal status. In *Sociological theories: Race and colonialism* (pp. 37–68). Paris: UNESCO.

Gutheil, G., & Gelman, S. A. (1997). Children's use of sample size and diversity information within basic-level categories. *Journal of Experimental Child Psychology, 64,* 159–174.

Hall, D. G., & Moore, C. E. (1997). Red bluebirds and black greenflies: Preschoolers' understanding of the semantics of adjectives and count nouns. *Journal of Experimental Child Psychology, 67,* 236–267.

Heit, E., & Rubinstein, J. (1994). Similarity and property effects in inductive reasoning. *Journal of Experimental Psychology: Learning, Memory, and Cognition, 20,* 411–422.

Heyman, G. D., & Gelman, S. A. (1997). *Children's beliefs about trait origins.* Unpublished manuscript, University of Michigan, Ann Arbor.

Heyman, G. D., & Gelman, S. A. (1998). Young children use motive information to make trait inferences. *Developmental Psychology, 34,* 310–321.

Hickling, A. K., & Wellman, H. M. (1998). *The emergence of everyday causal explanation in foundational knowledge domains.* Unpublished manuscript, University of North Carolina, Greensboro.

Hirschfeld, L. (1995). Do children have a theory of race? *Cognition, 54,* 209–252.

Hirschfeld, L. (1996). *Race in the making: Cognition, culture, and the child's construction of human kinds.* Cambridge, MA: MIT Press.

Hirschfeld, L. A., & Gelman, S. A. (1997). What young children think about the relation between language variation and social difference. *Cognitive Development, 12,* 213–238.

Inhelder, B., & Piaget, J. (1958). *The growth of logical thinking from childhood to adolescence.* New York: Basic Books.

Inhelder, B., & Piaget, J. (1964). *The early growth of logic in the child.* New York: Norton.

James, W. (1983). *The principles of psychology.* Cambridge, MA: Harvard University Press. (Original work published 1890).

Johnson, C. N. (1990). If you had my brain, where would I be? Children's understanding of the brain and identity. *Child Development, 61,* 962–972.

Jones, S., & Smith, L. (1993). The place of perception in children's concepts. *Cognitive Development, 8,* 113–139.

Kaiser, M. K., McCloskey, M., & Proffitt, D. R. (1986). Development of intuitive theories of motion: Curvilinear motion in the absence of external forces. *Developmental Psychology, 22,* 67–71.

Kalish, C. W. (1996). Preschoolers' understanding of germs as invisible mechanisms. *Cognitive Development, 11,* 83–106.

Kalish, C. W., & Gelman, S. A. (1992). On wooden pillows: Young children's understanding of category implications. *Child Development, 63,* 1536–1557.

Keil, F. (1989). *Concepts, kinds, and cognitive development.* Cambridge, MA: Bradford Books/MIT Press.

Keil, F. (1994). The birth and nurturance of concepts by domains: The origins of concepts of living things. In L. A. Hirschfeld & S. A. Gelman (Eds.), *Mapping the mind: Domain specificity in cognition and culture* (pp. 234–254). New York: Cambridge University Press.

Kohlberg, L. (1966). A cognitive-developmental analysis of children's sex-role concepts and attitudes.

In E. Maccoby (Ed.), *The development of sex differences* (pp. 82–173). Palo Alto, CA: Stanford University Press.

Kornblith, H. (1993). *Inductive inference and its natural ground: An essay in naturalistic epistemology.* Cambridge, MA: MIT Press.

Krifka, M. (1995). Common nouns: A contrastive analysis of Chinese and English. In G. N. Carlson & F. J. Pelletier (Eds.), *The generic book* (pp. 398–411). Chicago: University of Chicago Press.

Krifka, M., Pelletier, F. J., Carlson, G. N., ter Meulen, A., Link, G., & Chierchia, G. (1995). Genericity: An introduction. In G. N. Carlson & F. J. Pelletier (Eds.), *The generic book* (pp. 1–124). Chicago: Chicago University Press.

Kuczaj, S. (1976). *-ing, -s and -ed: A study of the acquisition of certain verb inflections.* Unpublished doctoral dissertation, University of Minnesota, Minneapolis.

Liben, L. S., & Signorella, M. L. (Eds.). (1987). *Children's gender schemata* (*New Directions for Child Development,* No. 38). San Francisco: Jossey-Bass.

Locke, J. (1959). *An essay concerning human understanding, Vol. 2.* New York: Dover. (Original work published 1894).

Lopez, A., Gelman, S. A., Gutheil, G., & Smith, E. E. (1992). The development of category-based induction. *Child Development, 63,* 1070–1090.

Lyons, J. (1977). *Semantics* (Vol. 1). New York: Cambridge University Press.

Macnamara, J. (1986). *A border dispute.* Cambridge, MA: MIT Press.

MacWhinney, B. (1987). The competition model. In B. MacWhinney (Ed.), *Mechanisms of language acquisition* (pp. 249–308). Hillsdale, NJ: Erlbaum.

MacWhinney, B. (1991). *The CHILDES project: Tools for analyzing talk.* Hillsdale, NJ: Erlbaum.

Malt, B. C. (1994). Water is not H_2O. *Cognitive Psychology, 27,* 41–70.

Markman, E. M. (1989). *Categorization and naming in children: Problems in induction.* Cambridge: Bradford Books/MIT Press.

Markman, E. M. (1992). Constraints on word learning: Speculations about their nature, origins, and domain specificity. In M. A. Gunnar & M. Maratsos (Eds.), *Modularity and constraints in language and cognition* (pp. 59–101). Hillsdale, NJ: Erlbaum.

Marler, P. (1991). The instinct to learn. In S. Carey & R. Gelman (Eds.), *The epigenesis of mind: Essays on biology and cognition* (pp. 37–66). Hillsdale, NJ: Erlbaum.

Mayr, E. (1982). *The growth of biological thought.* Cambridge, MA: Harvard University Press.

Mayr, R. (1991). *One long argument: Charles Darwin and the genesis of modern evolutionary thought.* Cambridge, MA: Harvard University Press.

McDonald, K. A. (1998, October 30). Genetically speaking, race doesn't exist. *The Chronicle of Higher Education,* p. A19.

Medin, D. (1989). Concepts and conceptual structure. *American Psychologist, 44,* 1469–1481.

Medin, D. L., & Ortony, A. (1989). Psychological essentialism. In S. Vosniadou & A. Ortony (Eds.), *Similarity and analogical reasoning* (pp. 179–195). Cambridge, England: Cambridge University Press.

Medin, D. L., & Shoben, E. J. (1988). Context and structure in conceptual combination. *Cognitive Psychology, 20,* 158–190.

Merriman, W. E., & Bowman, L. L. (1989). The mutual exclusivity bias in children's word learning. *Monographs of the Society for Research in Child Development, 54* (3–4, Serial No. 220).

Mervis, C. B., & Mervis, C. A. (1988). Role of adult input in young children's category evolution. I. An observational study. *Journal of Child Language, 15,* 257–272.

Mill, J. S. (1843). *A system of logic, ratiocinative and inductive.* London: Longmans.

Moser, D. J. (1996). *Abstract thinking and thought in ancient Chinese and early Greek.* Unpublished doctoral dissertation, University of Michigan, Ann Arbor.

Murphy, G. L. (1993). Theories and concept formation. In I. Van Mechelen, J. Hampton, R. Michalski, & P. Theuns (Eds.), *Categories and concepts: Theoretical views and inductive data analysis* (pp. 173–200). San Diego, CA: Academic Press.

Murphy, G. L., & Medin, D. L. (1985). The role of theories in conceptual coherence. *Psychological Review, 92*, 289–316.

Pappas, A., & Gelman, S. A. (1998). Generic noun phrases in mother-child conversations. *Journal of Child Language, 25*, 19–33.

Piaget, J. (1929). *The child's conception of the world.* London: Routledge & Kegan Paul.

Pinker, S. (1994). *The language instinct.* New York: Wm. Morrow.

Rips, L. J. (1989). Similarity, typicality, and categorization. In S. Vosniadou & A. Ortony (Eds.), *Similarity and analogical reasoning* (pp. 21–59). New York: Cambridge University Press.

Rorty, R. (1979). *Philosophy and the mirror of nature.* Princeton, NJ: Princeton University Press.

Rosengren, K., Gelman, S., Kalish, C., & McCormick, M. (1991). As time goes by: Children's early understanding of growth in animals. *Child Development, 62*, 1302–1320.

Rothbart, M., & Taylor, M. (1990). Category labels and social reality: Do we view social categories as natural kinds? In G. Semin & K. Fiedler (Eds.), *Language and social cognition* (pp. 11–36). London: Sage.

Sachs, J. (1983). Talking about the there and then: The emergence of displaced reference in parent-child discourse. In K. E. Nelson (Ed.), *Children's language* (Vol. 4), Hillsdale, NJ: Erlbaum.

Sera, M. D. (1992). To be or to be: Use and acquisition of the Spanish copulas. *Journal of Memory and Language, 31*, 408–427.

Sera, M. D., Rettinger, E., & del Castillo-Pintado, J. (1991). Developing definitions of objects and events in English and Spanish speakers. *Cognitive Development, 6*, 119–143.

Shipley, E. F. (1989). Two kinds of hierarchies: Class inclusion hierarchies and kind hierarchies. *Genetic Epistemologist, 17*, 31–39.

Shipley, E. F. (1993). Categories, hierarchies, and induction. In D. Medin (Ed.), *The psychology of learning and motivation* (Vol. 30, pp. 265–301). San Diego, CA: Academic Press.

Shultz, T. R. (1982). Rules of causal attribution. *Monographs of the Society for Research in Child Development, 47* (1, Serial No. 194).

Siegal, M., & Robinson, J. (1987). Order effects in children's gender-constancy responses. *Developmental Psychology, 23*, 283–286.

Siegler, R. S. (1994). Cognitive variability: A key to understanding cognitive development. *Current Directions in Psychological Science, 3*, 1–5.

Simons, D. J., & Keil, F. C. (1995). An abstract to concrete shift in the development of biological thought: The insides story. *Cognition, 56*, 129–163.

Smith, L. B. (1995). Self-organizing processes in learning to learn words: Development is not induction. *The Minnesota Symposia on Child Psychology, 28*, 1–32.

Smith, L. B., & Heise, D. (1992). Perceptual similarity and conceptual structure. In B. Burns (Ed.), *Percepts, concepts and categories* (pp. 233–272). Amsterdam: North-Holland.

Smith, L. B., Jones, S. S., & Landau, B. (1996). Naming in young children: A dumb attentional mechanism? *Cognition, 60*, 143–171.

Sober, E. (1994). *From a biological point of view.* New York: Cambridge University Press.

Soja, N. N., Carey, S., & Spelke, E. S. (1992). Perception, ontology, and word meaning. *Cognition, 45*, 101–107.

Solomon, G. E. A., Johnson, S. C., Zaitchik, D., & Carey, S. (1996). Like father, like son: Young children's understanding of how and why offspring resemble their parents. *Child Development, 67*, 151–171.

Springer, K. (1992). Children's awareness of the biological implications of kinship. *Child Development, 63*, 950–959.

Springer, K. (1995, April). *The role of factual knowledge in a naive theory of biology.* Paper presented at the meeting of the Society for Research in Child Development, Indianapolis, IN.

Sylvia, C., & Novak, W. (1997). *A change of heart.* Boston: Little, Brown.

Taylor, M. (1996). The development of children's beliefs about social and biological aspects of gender differences. *Child Development, 67*, 1555–1571.

Taylor, M. G., & Gelman, S. A. (1993). Children's gender- and age-based categorization in similarity judgments and induction tasks. *Social Development, 2,* 104–121.

Templeton, A. R. (1998). *American Anthropologist.*

Waxman, S. R., & Braig, B. (1996, April). *Stars and starfish: How far can shape take us?* Paper presented at the International Conference on Infant Studies, Providence, RI.

Waxman, S. R., & Markow, D. B. (1995, April). *Object properties and object kind: 21-month-old infants' extension of novel adjectives.* Poster presented at the meeting of the Society for Research in Child Development, Indianapolis, IN.

Wellman, H. M., & Gelman, S. A. (1997). Knowledge acquisition. In D. Kuhn & R. Siegler (Eds.), *Handbook of child psychology* (5th ed., pp. 523–573). New York: Wiley.

White, P. A. (1995). *The understanding of causation and the production of action: From infancy to adulthood.* Hove, England: Erlbaum.

Wierzbicka, A. (1994). The universality of taxonomic categorization and the indispensability of the concept 'kind.' *Rivista di Linguistica, 6,* 347–364.

Wisniewski, E. J., & Medin, D. L. (1994). On the interaction of theory and data in concept learning. *Cognitive Science, 18,* 221–281.

INFANTS' USE OF PRIOR EXPERIENCES WITH OBJECTS IN OBJECT SEGREGATION: IMPLICATIONS FOR OBJECT RECOGNITION IN INFANCY

Amy Needham
Avani Modi

DEPARTMENT OF PSYCHOLOGY: EXPERIMENTAL
DUKE UNIVERSITY
DURHAM, NORTH CAROLINA 27708

ADVANCES IN CHILD DEVELOPMENT
AND BEHAVIOR, VOL. 27

On one of their first trips to the library, a mother holds her baby boy and points out some of the interesting sights around them. As the baby looks at the rows and rows of bookcases, one can only speculate about what impressions he has of the books on the shelves. Most likely, a young infant (at three months or younger) studying a row of spines belonging to tightly packed books on a shelf would not interpret this display as a collection of individual objects. However, how would his impression of the display change after seeing someone walk up to the shelf he was studying and remove a book? Would he now (or soon, after several such experiences) have the impression of the books as a collection of items on the shelf? And would this experience transfer to other shelves of books in the library? In this chapter, we explore this question of how prior experiences with objects influence infants' perception of displays containing these previously seen objects and objects similar to them.

I. Object Segregation

One of the most important problems in vision is how we determine which surfaces belong together as a single object and which belong to separate objects. Accurate segmentation of a scene is likely to be related to our identification of objects. Perhaps we typically segment a display into its units prior to identifying the object(s) present, but one of the main themes of this chapter is that this process can take place in reverse as well—that sometimes we segment displays into their appropriate objects *because* we recognize or identify the objects in the display. A similar point has been made in the adult literature by Mary Peterson (1994), who has shown that even though we might typically think of figure–ground segregation as something that takes place prior to object recognition, adults sometimes recognize a figure in a display prior to (or while) establishing the figure–ground organization of the display.

Evidence for infants' use of this kind of process would lead to new kinds of research questions being asked. We would want to known when and how infants begin to learn about the types of objects that exist in the world, perhaps first on the basis of features such as shape (round objects, cylindrical objects) or even animacy (animate objects, inanimate objects). The first year of life would be seen as a time for infants to build this catalog of object types, which may over time develop a hierarchical structure [cylindrical objects: those that hold substances (e.g., beverage cans, cups), and those that do not (e.g., hot dogs, candles)]. This framework of knowledge about the objects in the world may be perceptual in origin, but may serve as a foundation to which more conceptual information is added (Eimas, 1994). These ideas for the future of research in this area serve to highlight the potential importance of this process.

A. PHYSICAL AND FEATURAL INFORMATION IN OBJECT SEGREGATION

Most of the research on infants' segregation of displays into objects has been focused on their ability to use certain kinds of visually available information either (a) to group together the visible portions of a partly occluded object or (b) to find a boundary between two spatially contiguous objects. To accomplish either of these tasks, infants must (as Slater et al., 1990, have claimed) engage in "perceptual inference," going beyond what is directly given in the display. Infants must do more than simply perceive the information present in the display, they must also be able to determine what the information suggests about the composition of the display. They must apply rules they have abstracted about the properties of objects to the information present in a display.

Two kinds of information have been somewhat extensively studied: physical information and featural information. Physical information typically refers to facets of objects' interactions with each other, such as their relative or common motions, spatial relations, and support relations. If one has the requisite physical knowledge (e.g., that inanimate objects cannot act on each other at a distance, that the surfaces of a single object cannot be separated by spatial gaps, that all objects require support), then physical information in a display can be used to segment it. Featural information refers to the shapes, colors, patterns, and textures of objects. If one has the knowledge that objects tend to be regular in their featural properties, then abrupt changes in one or more of these features may be perceived as an indication of a boundary between two objects.

The existing literature suggests that to find object boundaries, infants use at least certain kinds of physical information by 2 months of age, and at least certain kinds of featural information by about 4 months of age, and by 8 months of age (if not earlier) infants resolve conflicts in interpretations suggested by these two sources of information by favoring the interpretation suggested by physical information (e.g., S. P. Johnson & Aslin, 1995; Needham, 1997; Needham & Baillargeon, 197; Needham & Kaufman, 1997; see S. P. Johnson, 1997; Needham, Baillargeon, & Kaufman, 1997; and Spelke, 1990, for reviews).

B. PRIOR EXPERIENCE IN OBJECT SEGREGATION

In this chapter, we explore yet another source of information infants may use when segregating displays: prior experiences with objects. As Needham et al. (1987) first suggested, infants may use their prior experiences to form a clear interpretation of a display even when they cannot form a clear interpretation based on other sources of information in the display. Infants could use their prior experiences with objects in at least two ways in interpreting a display. First, they may recognize a specific instance of an object they have seen before, and on this basis alone be able to find its boundaries. For example, the first time an infant daughter sees her mother's key ring, she may encode extensive information about its shape, colors, and materials. The second time she sees the key ring, when it is on the living room table next to the remote control for the television, she may know that it is separate from the remote control, even if she has never seen the remote control before.

The second way infants may use their prior experience is by categorizing a previously unseen object as a member of a category about which they possess some knowledge. For example, after an infant has had experience with her mother's key ring, a key ring rattle, and perhaps even several other instances of key rings observed in the grocery store parking lot, she may not have difficulty determining that a key ring she sees on a neighboring table at a restaurant is separate from an adjacent fork (and predicting exactly where the boundary between the two objects is). By this time, the infant may even have certain expectations about what key rings seem to do (i.e., that they are associated with entry into houses and cars), and what their presence often signals (i.e., an imminent departure).

II. Feature Integration Theory

Adults' recognition and identification of objects has been extensively studied, using a variety of stimuli such as letters, words, and line drawings. Overall, many researchers would agree that the process of object or pattern recognition is at least a three-stage process (Kanwisher, Woods, Iacoboni, & Mazziotta, 1997). First, the basic features of the display are extracted. Next, a representation of the display is created that includes featural information (e.g., shape, color, pattern) from the display. Finally, this representation is compared to representations stored in memory and the object(s) in the display is (are) identified.

The general sequence of processes sketched out above could be further explained in many ways, but one highly influential theory of how we recognize objects is Feature Integration Theory (Kahneman & Treisman, 1984; Kahneman, Treisman, & Gibbs, 1992; Kanwisher, 1991; Lavie, 1997). This name comes from a basic assumption of the theory: that the individual features of an object are first registered as independent entities and are later integrated into a unified representation of an object. According to this theory, an *object file* is formed very early in the process of perceiving an object, and this file is used to collect information about the object, such as its color or shape. Once attention is focused on the information in the object file, an *object token,* or representation of this specific object, is formed. When an object token is formed, the features of the object are bound together (in a process called "binding") as part of this token.

Object tokens are thought to be formed for each newly perceived entity, and each object token is compared with the available object types stored in memory. A successful match between token and type completes the identification process. Of course, we sometimes recognize a previously seen object as something we have seen before without being able to identify it, and this theory allows for recognition of particular tokens even if they have not been matched to a known object type. This aspect of the theory lends itself well to perceptual learning, as it would allow infants to recognize an object they know very little about. One important aspect of this theory for the purposes of the present discussion is that our catalog of known "types" could begin as common and/or simple items such as faces, circles, and squares, and could grow into the rich and complex array of objects known to an adult.

III. Feature Integration Theory in Infancy

Can Feature Integration Theory be used to explain how infants recognize objects? Some research suggests that infants may have difficulty in binding the features of an object to whatever mental representation is formed of the object (Leslie, Xu, Tremoulet, & Scholl, 1998; Xu & Carey, 1996). For example, the results of a number of studies suggest that, like adults, infants rely more on spatiotemporal information than on featural information when keeping track of the identity of objects (Simons, 1996). These studies demonstrate that under certain circumstances, infants respond as though they are unsure whether a change in features between the disappearance and reappearance of an object necessarily means that two distinct entities are involved in the event.

In these studies, infants do not seem to believe that every new set of features should correspond to a new entity. However, other studies show that when the events are simplified considerably, infants respond with surprise when the number of different entities does not equal the number of different sets of features (Wilcox, in press; Wilcox & Baillargeon, 1998).

In Feature Integration Theory terminology, infants apparently (a) do not always open a new object file for each novel set of features they see, (b) do not always return to an old object file when they should, or (c) have difficulty in binding the features of a new object together to form a particular object token. Although little of the existing research in this area would allow us to discriminate between the first two possibilities, some researchers have investigated the binding issue.

In one study, Slater and his colleagues (Slater, Mattock, Brown, Burnham, & Young, 1991) familiarized newborn infants with two stimuli that differed in both color and orientation (e.g., one was a vertical red line and the other was a diagonal green line). The infants were then tested to determine whether they remembered the particular color-orientation compounds they had seen. During test, infants saw one of the stimuli they had seen during familiarization paired with a stimulus representing a novel relation between color and orientation. If the infants were unable to bind together the particular color-orientation combinations they experienced, they should have looked about equally at the familiar and novel combination of color and orientation. However, the results showed that the infants looked reliably longer at the novel combination, indicating that the infants were capable of encoding and remembering the combination of features they experienced in the familiarization phase of the study.

Building on this finding, Bhatt and Rovee-Collier (1994, 1996) have shown (using a different procedure that included lengthy exposure to the familiarization stimulus) that 3-month-old infants can remember feature combinations even after a 24-hour delay. The findings suggest that when given enough time, infants encode extensive and detailed information about objects and remember this information for 24 hours or more. Such findings suggest that infants are usually able to bind a collection of features together to define a particular object (or object token).

Thus, the Leslie et al. (1998) and Xu and Carey (1996) studies may indicate that when spatiotemperal information identifies just one object in a display, and featural information identifies two distinct sets of features, infants tend to favor the interpretation based on spatiotemporal information over that based on featural information. Other studies also suggest that infants pay less attention to featural information when information about, for example, the motion of objects, the spatial layout of objects, the solidity of objects, or the support relations between objects conflicts with the featural information (Kellman & Spelke, 1983; Needham & Baillargeon, 1997; Needham & Kaufman, 1997). In all these cases, research has shown that infants tend to favor the interpretation based on the physical information present in the display rather than the features of the objects. This pattern of findings may reflect the relative ecological validities of the different kinds of information, as physical laws are more inviolable than rules based on featural information (e.g., all objects require support, but not all objects are uniform in shape, color, and pattern). One explanation for this pattern of findings is that infants are sensitive to the ecological validities of the various kinds of information they learn about, and they favor interpretations based on sources of information with higher ecological validity over those based on information with lower ecological validity (Needham, 1997).

Clearly, more evidence is needed before we can determine whether Feature Integration Theory is an appropriate explanation for how infants recognize and identify objects and if so which aspects of infants' abilities differ from those of adults. In this chapter, we review work from our laboratory addressing the issue of how infants encode and represent a collection of features that defines an object.

IV. Infants' Recognition and Categorization of Objects

Many controversies remain about the best way to explain how adults recognize and identify objects, for example, whether the representation used during recognition is viewer centered or object centered (Biederman, 1987; Tarr, Bulthoff, Zabinski, & Blanz, 1997). However, much is known about how adults accomplish these tasks and researchers agree on many basic points. In comparison, much less is known about the development of these processes. In many (if not all) areas of psychology, understanding the origins and development of a process or behavior often leads to fundamental changes in our understanding of the phenomenon in its mature form (Baer, 1982; Baron & Galizio, 1983; Berlyne, 1965; Bijou, 1984; Bugelski, 1956; Reese, 1989; Spelke & Van de Walle, 1993; Toulmin, 1971; Watson, 1926). Object recognition in infancy is an important, but relatively neglected area of study.

A. OBJECT RECOGNITION

Beginning with the groundbreaking work of Fantz (1963), a long history of research findings has supported the conclusion that from birth and even before (see DeCasper, Lecanuet, Busnel, Granier-Deferre, & Maugeais, 1994; DeCasper & Spence, 1986; Hepper, 1991), infants encode and remember stimuli from their environment. Many visual recognition memory studies have provided evidence that infants (even newborns, see Slater et al., 1990, 1991) spend less time looking at a stimulus they have seen before than at a novel stimulus. These studies have dealt with variables that influence infants' recognition, such as the amount of initial study time given and the delay interval between familiarization and test. These studies have indicated that by 5 months of age, infants recognize previously seen stimuli after only modest amounts of familiarization (e.g., Cornell, 1979; Fagan, 1970, 1971, 1974; Lasky, 1980; Martin, 1975; Rose, 1980, 1981). For example, Fagan (1974) examined the length of familiarization 5-month-old infants required to recognize various stimuli on immediate memory tests. He found that although 20 to 30 s of familiarization time was needed for faces, and 17 s for abstract patterns composed of identical elements, as little as 4 s was sufficient for patterns that looked (to adults) very different from each other.

When infants are given extensive amounts of familiarization time with a particular stimulus, as in Rovee-Collier's mobile conjugate reinforcement paradigm, research indicates that infants acquire detailed and lasting representations of the stimulus. For example, infants as young as 2 months of age remember details of the stimulus 24 h after training, and as infants get older, their representations of the stimulus remain detailed for longer periods of time. As the interval between training and testing increases for any particular age, infants notice fewer discrepancies between the training and testing stimuli, suggesting that their representations lose detail over time (Rovee-Collier, 1993; Rovee-Collier & Sullivan, 1980).

Beyond the basic questions of the conditions under which infants remember a previously seen stimulus, researchers have asked whether a prior experience with a specific object affects infants' subsequent perception of the object. This question was investigated in a study by Granrud, Haake, and Yonas (1985) on infants' use of familiar size as a cue for depth. Typically, the use of familiar size as a depth cue has been studied using objects that are likely to have sizes that are quite familiar (e.g., a human face). However, Granrud and his colleagues explored whether familiar size would be used when the familiarity was acquired during a brief period of time at the beginning of the study. Specifically, they tested whether prior experience with two objects that differed in size would facilitate 7-month-old infants' use of familiar size to determine which of the two objects was closer (and potentially reachable) during testing. In their study, infants first participated in a 10-min play session in which two novel experimental objects were featured, one large and one small. In test, equally large versions of both objects were placed in front of the infants, who viewed the display monocularly to eliminate binocular cues.

Granrud et al. reasoned that if the infants' prior experience with the objects influenced perception of the objects' relative distances, then the small object in the play session should be perceived as closer than the large object. If so, they should reach more for the previously small object because the infants tend to reach more for objects they perceive as closer. Exactly this result was obtained.

In summary, the evidence from the object recognition literature leads to three main conclusions. First, infants recognize objects they have seen before if the familiarization time is sufficiently long. Second, when familiarization time is long, infants recognize extensive detailed information about object features. Finally, infants' prior experiences with objects affect their subsequent perception of those objects. These conclusions are important premises for the issues investigated in our own research, described later in the chapter.

From the perspective of Feature Integration Theory, the literature on infant object recognition indicates that infants are able to set up object tokens and that they recognize a previously seen token on subsequent encounters. In the next section we explore evidence about the identification process, in which a particular object token is compared to representations of types that are stored in memory.

B. OBJECT CATEGORIZATION

Some of the earliest work on categorization in infancy was designed to address the question of whether infants form perceptual categories: Do infants form groupings of objects based on perceptual categories such as shape or color? One of the earliest studies on this question was conducted by Ruff (1978). She showed 6- and

9-month-old infants a series of objects that were the same in three-dimensional shape, but different in size, color, and orientation. After the infants were presented several instances of this shape category, they were given test trials featuring two objects, one a novel instance of the same shape category and the other a novel object of a different shape. The results showed that the 9-month-old infants looked reliably longer at the novel-category object than the familiar-category object, but the 6-month-old infants did not show a reliable looking preference. Thus, under the conditions of these experiments, 6-month-old infants either did not form an internal representation of the shape of the familiarization objects or formed it and did not use it to interpret the shapes of the test objects.

Whether infants younger than 9 months of age can form and use categorical representations was a question of considerable interest. A new method was devised by Bomba and Siqueland (1983) to investigate 3- and 4-month-old infants' categorization of abstract, two-dimensional patterns created by a collection of black dots on a white background. The researchers first familiarized infants with several different instances of a shape category; each instance was created by perturbing a prototype shape to a different extent. Then in test, the infants were shown a pair of stimuli they had never seen within the context of the experiment: one was the prototype of the familiarized shape category and the other was the prototype of a different shape category. The results showed that the infants looked reliably longer at the novel-category prototype than at the familiar-category prototype, indicating that they had formed and used a shape category during familiarization.

In further experiments, Bomba and Siqueland (1983), Quinn (1987), and Younger and Gotlieb (1988) used the same general design to explore additional aspects of the categorization context that influenced infants' categorization performance, including memory load, the number of categories represented in the exemplars (exemplars from one or two categories), and the complexity of the patterns used as stimuli. The results of both Bomba and Siqueland (1983) and Quinn (1987) suggest that under conditions of low memory load, infants form a central representation for the category and maintain some memory for the characteristics of individual exemplars. In contrast, under conditions of high memory load, infants tend to form a central representation for the category and do not maintain memory of the individual characteristics.

Studies of young infants' categorization of other kind of stimuli, such as animals, vehicles, colors, spatial relations, faces, and containers, suggest that infants notice what is changing and what is unchanging across a set of exemplar displays and that they use this information to form categories quite readily.

The evidence described above makes clear that even young infants have the ability to categorize objects. Our next question is whether infants' assignment of an object to a particular category (essentially, their identification of the object as a kind of thing they know something about) influences their perception of these objects. Does knowing what kind of object something is help infants perceive it differently? One relevant set of experiments was conducted by Bertenthal and his colleagues, and involved displays known as "point light walkers" (Bertenthal, 1993). These displays are collections of moving lights that would be seen in the side view of a person who had lights on his or her head and major joints and walked across the room in the dark. This collection of moving lights against a black background is readily perceived by adults as a human form when the display is in an upright orientation, but not when it is inverted. Bertenthal and his colleagues reasoned that they could use this orientation specificity of adults' perception of these displays to assess whether infants also recognized the displays as representing a human form.

The 3-, 5-, and 7-month-old infants were shown a canonical and a scrambled walker in the upright and inverted orientations. Scrambled walkers were formed by randomly repositioning points of light and their motion profiles across the computer screen. The results showed that the 3-month-old infants discriminated between the canonical and scrambled walkers in both the upright display and the inverted display, indicating that they were probably discriminating between the displays on the basis of local differences between elements in the two displays rather than perceiving the familiar global structure. At 5 and 7 months of age, however, the infants discriminated between the canonical and scrambled walkers in the upright display but not in the inverted display. These results suggest that, as infants acquire categorical knowledge about the human form, they may use this information to help them make sense even of displays such as point light walkers, which resemble actual humans in only an abstract way.

Another line of research has dealt with infants' perception of displays containing representations of human faces. This research indicates that from birth, the human face may hold special interest for infants (M. H. Johnson, Dziurawiec, Ellis, & Morton, 1991). Thus, one may expect that infants are collecting considerable information about human faces and may use this information to help them interpret face-like displays. Schwartz (1982) compared 5-month-old infants' perception of partly occluded checkerboard displays and partly occluded face displays. She found that the infants did not perceive the visible portions of the checkerboard display as connected behind the occluder, but they did perceive the visible portions of the face display as connected behind the occluder. Vishton, Stulac, and Calhoun (198) obtained similar results: 6-month-old infants reached for partly occluded faces as though they perceived the displays as connected behind the occluder, but did not reach for partly occluded geometric figures.

C. SUMMARY

The studies reviewed in this section suggest two main conclusions. First, extensive evidence indicates that infants as young as 3 months of age can learn categories based on object form, noticing similarities in the shapes of a group of discriminably different objects and regarding a previously unseen member of the category as familiar. Second, the studies by Bertenthal, Schwartz, and Vishton suggest that infants acquire information about categories they experience on a day-to-day basis. Infants use this information to interpret displays.

In the next section we describe our research on infants' ability to segregate objects using their prior experiences in the ways outlined above. Before describing these experiments, we briefly describe our research methods.

V. General Method of Current Studies

The method used in most of our experiments was adapted from that devised by Spelke (e.g., Spelke, Breinlinger, Jacobson, & Phillips, 1993). The infants participated in a familiarization phase and then a test phase. During the *familiarization* phase, the infants saw the stationary test display, a display similar to the test display, and/or a portion of the test display. Many of the experiments reported here involved assessing the effects of slightly different experiences during the familiarization phase. During the *test* phase, the infants saw test events in which a gloved hand took hold of one part of the display and moved it a short distance. For half of the infants, the other part of the display remained stationary (move-apart event); for the other infants, the two parts moved as a whole (move-together event). The rationale was that if the infants perceived the stationary display as a single unit, they would expect it to move as a whole and would be surprised when it did not. Conversely, if the infants viewed the stationary display as composed of more than one unit, they would expect the units to move independently and would be surprised when they did not. If the infants perceived the display's composition to be neither one unit or two units, they were expected to show equal looking at the two test events (such results were found by Kellman & Spelke, 1983). Because infants' surprise at an event is typically manifested by prolonged attention to the event (e.g., Bornstein, 1985; Spelke, 1985), the infants were expected to look reliably longer at the test event that depicted motion inconsistent with their interpretation of the stationary display.

In each experiment, the infant sat on a parent's lap in front of an apparatus consisting of a large display box. The parent was asked to remain calm and neutral, and to close his or her eyes during the test trials.

The infants' looking behavior was monitored by two observers who watched the infant through peepholes in large cloth-covered frames on either side of the apparatus. The observers could not see the familiarization and test events from their viewpoints, and they were not told which condition and/or experiment was being conducted. Each observer held a joystick linked to a computer and depressed the trigger on the joystick when the infant attended to the events. Each trial was divided into 100-ms intervals, and the computer determined in each interval whether the two observers agreed on the direction of the infant's gaze. Interobserver agreement was calculated for each trial on the basis of the number of intervals in which the computer registered agreement, out of the total number of intervals in the trial. Agreement per trial per infant averaged 92% across experiments. The primary (i.e., more experienced) observer's looking times were used to determine the end of the trials.

An experimenter stationed beside the apparatus controlled the familiarization and test events using precise, second-by-second scripts that were practiced until they were performed smoothly and accurately. A metronome beating softly once per second helped the experimenter adhere to the scripts.

The infants received one to three familiarization trials at the start of the experiment. In some cases, familiarization trials were quite brief and ended when the infant had accumulated a preset amount of looking time at the display. In other cases, familiarization trials ended when the infant either (a) looked away from the display for 2 consecutive seconds after having looked for 10 cumulative seconds or (b) looked at the display for a maximum of 30 consecutive seconds. Following the familiarization trial(s), the infants received two to six test trials (experiments with older subjects typically had two trials, and experiments with younger subjects typically had six trials). In each test trial, the test event was repeated continuously until the computer signaled the end of the trial. A test trial typically ended when the infant either (a) looked away from the event for 2 consecutive seconds after looking for the minimum amount of time for that experiment (6–8 s, depending upon the length of the event cycle), or (b) looked at the event for a maximum of 60 cumulative seconds. When a trial ended, an experimenter lowered a curtain in front of the apparatus. During the intertrial interval, the test objects were quickly returned to their starting positions and the curtain was then lifted again to begin a new trial.

A between-subjects design was used in all of the experiments reported in this chapter; each infant saw only the move-apart test event or the move-together test event. Although this design prevents a direct assessment of each infant's percept of the display, it allows us to determine the group percept over the age range tested, assuming that this percept is consistent over the infants in the group. We believe that a between-subjects design may be a more sensitive measure of infants' initial interpretation of the display, because it avoids cross-contamination of infants' responses to the two test events. It also provides a more realistic situation to infants, as each infant is shown that a given display is either composed of one unit or two separate units but not both.

Finally, the number of infants tested in each condition ranged from 6 to 18 across experiments. The infants' looking times at the two test events were compared by means of analyses of variance and planned comparisons. Results are reported as statistically reliable of the *p* values associated with them were smaller than .05.

VI. Initial Study

Although our goal was to investigate the effects of a brief prior exposure to one portion of a display on infants' perception of the display, we began this research by first determining infants' perception of the composition of a display consisting of two parts with distinctly different features (see Figure 1): a tall, blue box with white squares and a curved yellow cylinder (Needham & Baillargeon, 1998). After a familiarization trial during which the display was seen stationary, the infants were shown a test display in which a gloved hand took hold of the cylinder and moved it a short distance to the side. Half of the infants saw the cylinder move apart from the box, which remained stationary throughout the event (move-apart event), and half saw the box move with the cylinder as a single unit (move-together event). The infants were 4.5, 6.5, 7.5, and 8 months old.

The results showed that for the 4.5- and 6.5-month-old infants, the mean looking time was about the same whether they saw the move-apart or the move-together test event, indicating that the composition of the display was ambiguous to them (Needham, 1998). Two other groups were given no familiarization trial prior to seeing one of the two test events, and they also had about the same mean looking times. In contrast, following the familiarization trial, the 7.5- and 8-month-old infants perceived the display as clearly composed of two separate units. Further studies revealed that even 4.5-month-old infants can use object features to determine object boundary locations, but that they do so only when the features of objects are very simple (Needham, 1998, 1999d).

Test Events

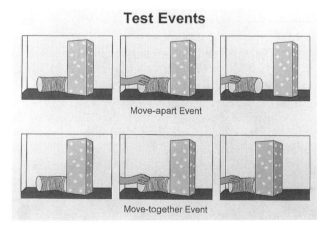

Fig. 1. Schematic drawing of the cylinder and box display and the move-apart and move-together test events shown to the infants in the experiments described in sections VII and VIII. Reprinted from *Infant Behavior and Development,* Vol. 21, A. Needham & R. Baillargeon, "Effects of prior experience in 4.5-month-old infant's object segregation," p. 4, Copyright © 1998, with permission from Elsevier Science.

TABLE I

Mean Looking Times of Infants of Four Ages Who Saw
the Cylinder and Box Displayed in the Original Studies

| | Test event (in seconds) | |
| | Move-apart[a] | Move-together |
Age		
8 months	26.8*	39.2
7.5 months	34.8*	49.0
6.5 months	38.6	30.3
4.5 months	39.7	37.5

[a]*mean is reliably different ($p < .05$) from the other mean in that row.

VII. Recognition-Based Process

In the present section and the next one, a series of experiments is described in which 4.5-month-old infants were given prior experience with an object either identical or similar to an object to be seen in the test display, and the effects of this experience on infants' responses to the test events described above were assessed.

A. EFFECTS OF PRIOR EXPERIENCE WITH A TEST OBJECT

1. Effects of Immediate Prior Experience

Our next step was to give 4.5-month-old infants a brief exposure to either the cylinder or the box immediately prior to testing. If the infants were able to make use of this prior experience to help them perceive the display as clearly composed of two separate pieces, they should look reliably longer at the move-together event (which is counter to this interpretation) than at the move-apart event (which is in line with this interpretation). In our first study, we gave infants a 5-s exposure to the tall blue test box alone immediately prior to the test event, which was move-apart for half of the infants and move-together for the other infants. The mean looking time was significantly longer for the move-together than the move-apart test event, indicating that the infants perceived the display as composed of two separate units. These findings suggest that 4.5-month-old infants can make use of their prior experiences with objects to determine the locations of object boundaries in a display containing these objects. However, we sought further evidence to support this conclusion by assessing the effects of a brief prior exposure to the cylinder.

We used the same procedure, except that we showed the cylinder alone rather than the box alone prior to testing. The mean looking times were about the same for both the test events, indicating that the infants did not use the prior experience when segregating the test display. Although several interpretations of this finding are possible, we decided to determine whether infants' use of prior exposure depends upon having sufficient time to process the object during the initial exposure. Studies have shown that infants need more time to process more complex displays sufficiently for later recognition (e.g., Fagan, 1974), and the cylinder seemed more complex than the box. We therefore decided to increase the length of the initial prior exposure to the cylinder to 15 s. After seeing the cylinder alone for 15 s, the mean looking time was reliably longer for the move-together than the move-apart event, indicating that the infants used the prior experience to segregate the test objects into two separate pieces.

One conclusion that can be drawn from these results is that infants recognize the portion of the test display seen prior to testing. Another conclusion is that recognizing the previously seen object allows infants to segment the test display into two separate units. Infants use their prior experience with a portion of the test display to help them form an interpretation of the display that would be ambiguous to them without the prior experience. These conclusions are important because they indicate that infants interpret the sequence of experiences in much the same way as adults.

2. Effects of Delay and Context Change

Our next step was to determine the effects of delay and context on infants' use of prior experiences for segregating a display. In two studies designed to assess the effects of time, a delay of about 24 h (Mean delay = 24 h, 10 min) was introduced between the initial experience with the test object and the presentation of the test events (Needham & Baillargeon, 1998; Needham & Modi, 1999b). The infants were 4.5 months old. An experimenter visited each infant in his or her home and showed the infant either the test box or the test cylinder for approximately 2 min. Fagan (1970, 1971, 1973) had found this familiarization time sufficient for recognition in 5-month-old infants with delays of 1 to 14 days. About 24 h later, the infant was brought to the laboratory for the test phase. Again, half of the infants saw the move-apart event and half saw the move-together event. In both studies, the mean looking time was reliably longer for the move-together than the move-apart event. The infants who had seen the box prior to testing looked reliably longer at the move-together than at the move-apart event only in the second block of test trials (trials 3–6), but the infants who saw the cylinder prior to testing looked reliably longer at the move-together than at the move-apart event over all six test trials. The reason for this difference is unclear, although we are exploring the possibility that the cylinder's complexity and unfamiliarity may make it more distinctive and more memorable than the box. These findings suggest that even when the initial and subsequent views of the object occur about 24 h apart and in different contexts, infants are still able to use the prior experience to segment the test display into two separate units.

3. Effects of Lengthier Delays

In a follow-up study currently under way (Needham & Modi, 1999b), the delay between familiarization and test is 72 h. So far, the results are not promising, leading us to suspect that some time between 24 and 72 h after their initial exposure to one of the test objects in their home, infants are no longer able to use the prior exposure to segregate the test display they see in the laboratory. If this finding holds up, infants' failure after a 72-h delay will not be consistent with the retention functions that Rovee-Collier and her colleagues have found in infants (see Rovee-Collier, 1993, and Rovee-Collier & Hayne, for a review of this work). Specifically, their research shows that even 3-month-old infants remember their prior experience with a mobile for around 9 days after training. However, Rovee-Collier's procedures differ in many ways from ours. Two important differences are the amount of familiarization the infants receive of the relevant object or situation (about 30 min in Rovee-Collier's studies vs. 2 min in ours), and the similarity in context during the initial and subsequence encounters with the test stimulus (training and testing in the home in Rovee-Collier's studies vs. familiarization in the home and testing in the laboratory in our studies). These two factors (and possibly others) could contribute to the longer retention in her studies than in ours.

B. EFFECTS OF PRIOR EXPERIENCE WITH A SIMILAR OBJECT

The findings of the experiments described above did not indicate the processes infants use in segregating a display. Recognition of the previously seen object might be required for infants to benefit from the prior experience when segregating the test display, but the recognition process can be characterized in different ways. One possibility is that infants encode much about the object during their initial brief exposure to it, and that their recognition of the previously seen object requires a close match between the features of the object on the first and second encounters. Alternatively, infants may not encode specific information about the object during the initial brief exposure, but can "recognize" the object without a close match in features. Perhaps prior experience with any object of the same shape or color as the corresponding test object would be sufficient to facilitate infants' segregation of the test display.

In an attempt to answer questions such as these and produce a more complete explanation of the factors influencing infants' use of their prior experiences in perceiving objects, we conducted a series of experiments on the effects of prior experiences with objects similar but not identical to the test objects on infants' segregation of the test display (Needham, in press; Needham & Lockhead, 1999; Needham & Modi, 1999a).

We can learn what infants encode about a briefly seen object and how this information is represented in memory by studying the kinds of "errors" that infants make in this task. If we gave infants a brief prior exposure to an object very different from the object composing the test display, we would expect that infants' segregation of the test display would be unaffected. However, as the features of the previously seen object become more similar to those of the relevant portion of the test display, we can examine the conditions under which infants respond as though they recognize one of the test objects.

The method used in these studies was the same as in the studies described in the preceding section with one exception. Our pilot testing indicated that infants who were shown a brief familiarization with a different box looked equally at the two test events in every condition we tried—no matter how similar the different boxes were. Equal looking at the two test events is the pattern of results we obtained when the infants had received either (a) no familiarization at all, or (b) familiarization with the entire test display. Thus, we speculated that the infants who received a brief prior experience with a box different from the test box (a) did not notice the connection between the familiarization box and the test display, and (b) could benefit from seeing the entire test display after seeing the familiarization box and before seeing the test event. To test this speculation, we used a three-phrase procedure, with a brief familiarization trial first (typically featuring a single object), then a longer familiarization trial featuring the entire test display, and finally the test trials featuring either the move-apart or the move-together test event. We reasoned that infants may apply their prior experience to the segregation of the test display more readily if they were given the opportunity to study the test display prior to seeing the test events.

1. Change in Orientation of Box

In the first experiment, we investigated how changes in the box seen during familiarization and test would affect infants' segregation of the test display (Needham, in press). The first change we explored was a change in the orientation of the box they would see as part of the test display. During the first familiarization trial, the infants saw the test box lying on the floor of the apparatus in a horizontal orientation rather than in the vertical orientation in which it would be seen as part of the test display. After this familiarization trial and that featuring the entire display, each infant was shown one of the test events. The results showed that the mean looking time was reliably longer for the move-together than the move-apart event, indicating that infants made use of the prior experience with the test box in a different orientation to segregate the test objects into two separate units.

These results showed that a change in orientation of the object did not prevent infants' recognition of the object as part of the test display. In many ways, these results make contact with the adult literature. One possibility is that the representations infants use in object recognition are object-centered rather than viewer-centered (Biederman, 1987; Tarr et al., 1997). Another possibility is that infants can engage in a mental manipulation of their representation of an object akin to mental rotation studied in adults (Shepard & Metzler, 1971). Both of these possibilities are still quite speculative and await further experimental exploration.

2. *Changes in Features of Box*

The results of the first experiment indicated that a rather pronounced change in the spatial orientation of the test box did not prevent infants' recognition of the box in the test display. Our next question was whether infants would be similarly "liberal" in their transfer of information from one object to another object with features that differed from those of the first object. The changes introduced here were not extensive: only the background color and texture element color and shape were altered between familiarization and test. The size, viewing orientation, and placement of texture elements in the familiarization and test boxes were identical. Instead of the blue box with white squares (which they would see as part of the test display), the infants were shown a purple box with yellow circles.

The results of the first experiment showed that, after a 5-s familiarization with the purple box, the mean looking times were about the same for the two test events, indicating that the infants did not make use of this prior experience to interpret the test display. We hypothesized that the familiarization box was not similar enough to the test box for infants to apply their experience to the segregation of the test display. Therefore, in our next experiment we chose to increase the similarity between the familiarization and test boxes to see whether this change might facilitate infants' use of their prior experience.

In the second experiment, the familiarization box was the same as the test box with one exception: the texture elements on the familiarization box were red squares, and those on the test box were white squares. The procedure was identical to the study just reported. The results showed that the mean looking times in this experiment were also equal for the two test events, again indicating that the infants did not bring to bear their prior experience with the familiarization box to segment the test display. Once again, we sought to increase the similarity between the familiarization and test boxes, so we changed the color of the familiarization box's texture elements from red to yellow. The procedure was identical to the study just reported, and the results showed that the infants still showed no preference for either test event.

In our final study, we changed the texture elements on the familiarization box once again, hoping to make this box similar enough to the test box that infants would make use of their experience with the familiarization box to segment the test display into two separate pieces. We changed the texture elements on the familiarization box to white circles, and put the infants through the same procedure as in the other studies. The results showed that the mean looking times for the move-together event were reliably longer than for the move-apart event, indicating that the infants perceived the test display as composed of two separate units.

Therefore, they must have applied their prior experience with the familiarization box to their segregation of the test display. Thus, when the familiarization box was only minimally different from the test box, the infants applied their experience with one to the segregation of a display containing the other. One important aspect of this finding is that it shows at least some limited ability to transfer knowledge (e.g., that this is a separate object) straight from one object to another object that they perceive to be different. One possibility is that this ability to transfer knowledge from one object to another becomes more robust with development, so that by later in the first year of life it could occur even without the support of extremely high perceptual similarity between the objects. We will return to this topic later.

3. Summary

Together, the findings of this set of experiments suggest that infants treat orientational discrepancies between familiarization and test differently from featural differences. A difference in spatial orientation that is quite noticeable (horizontal vs. vertical orientation) did not prevent infants from applying their prior experience from one object to the other. In contrast, even what seems to adults to be a very small difference in the features of the box seen during familiarization and test prevented infants from applying their prior experience with one box to segment a display containing the other box. The infants' ability therefore seems strikingly adult-like, because for adults the features of an object—and not its spatial orientation or some other irrelevant factor—determine the object's identity. These findings are much like those of others (e.g., Bhatt & Rovee-Collier, 1994, 1996; Quinn & Eimas, 1996; Slater et al., 1991; Wilcox, in press; Wilcox & Baillargeon, 1998), and they support the idea that infants attend to and analyze object features when determining the identities of objects.

4. Changes in Features of Cylinder

Our next set of studies began an investigation of the situations within our paradigm that may reveal errors in feature integration. We were interested in determining whether recognition errors are more likely when the familiarization cylinder was the same color as the test box than when this cylinder was a different color from both test objects. This kind of error could result from a process akin to illusory conjunctions that have been found in adults (Kanwisher, 1991; Lavie, 1997; Treisman & Gelade, 1980).

As discussed in section II, illusory conjunctions are thought to occur during preattentive processing of stimuli, when the features of objects have been processed in at least a superficial way, but the features have yet to be bound to the particular object files they are associated with. After attention has been focused on the objects, though, these features are bound to the relevant object tokens. Considerable evidence suggests that infants are capable of focused attention (M. H. Johnson, 1996; Richards, 1989), but when stimulus-encoding time is limited, infants may make analogous kinds of errors that influence their recognition judgments in the same way was illusory conjunction errors do in adults.

We have discussed the evidence indicating that infants can remember stimulus compounds (Bhatt & Rovee-Collier, 1994, 1996; Slater et al., 1991). However, whether infants use object features to form a unique representation of an object that they refer back to when seeing the same object again is a topic of some debate (Wilcox & Baillargeon, 1998; Xu and Carey, 1996). Thus, although infants may remember which features determine the unique identity of an object in some situations, in other situations they may not. They can use object features to determine object identity, for example, looking at features as a basis for recognition, but they may not succeed in noticing changes in features in all the situations in which the older child or adult would be successful.

The first situation we considered was one in which the infants received prior experience with a cylinder that was the same as the test cylinder except that it was blue—the same blue as the test box—and the test cylinder was yellow. If, after seeing the blue cylinder, the infants mistakenly believe they have had experience with either the yellow cylinder or the blue box of the test display, they may expect the display to consist of two separate pieces, just like infants who have prior experience with one of the test objects. As before, we expected that if the infants segregate the test objects, they would look reliably longer at the move-together than the move-apart test event. In contrast, if the infants regarded the blue cylinder as being too different from the yellow cylinder to help them segment the test display, they should look about equally at the move-apart and move-together test events.

In this first study, we gave the infants a 15-s exposure to the blue cylinder alone prior to testing, as prior research indicated that 15 s was (and 5 s was not) sufficient time to encode enough of the cylinder to recognize it on a subsequent encounter (Needham & Baillargeon, 1998). The results showed that the mean looking time was about equal for the move-apart and move-together events, indicating that the infants did not use the prior experience to segregate the test objects. These results suggest that after 15 s of exposure to the blue cylinder, the infants were not confused about whether they had seen a blue or a yellow cylinder—they responded as though they were sure that they had not seen part of the test display before.

In a subsequent study, we explored the consequences of reducing this familiarization time to a level that our previous research indicated was insufficient for infants to encode enough of the cylinder's features to recognize it on a subsequent encounter. We thought this situation might be analogous to the brief stimulus presentations that have led to illusory conjunctions in adult studies. Infants were given a 5-s exposure to the blue cylinder prior to seeing the move-apart or move-together test events (Needham & Modi, 1999a). The results showed the male infants, but not female infants, looked reliably longer at the move-together than at the move-apart event, indicating that they may have thought that they had seen part of the test display before when they had not actually done so.

One possible explanation for these findings is that the brief exposure time allowed the male infants to encode the shape but not the color of the cylinder. According to this argument, a prior exposure to a cylinder of any color, as long as it was the same shape as the test cylinder, would be used by the male infants to segregate the test objects. To test this possibility, we conducted another study in which a cylinder of a different color from that seen in the test display was shown in the 5-s familiarization at the beginning of the session (Needham & Modi, 1999a). The infants saw an orange cylinder (a bright orange that was actually somewhat similar to the yellow of the test cylinder) during the brief familiarization trial.

The results indicated that neither the male nor the female infants looked reliably longer at the move-together than at the move-apart event, showing that the male infants would not use a prior experience with a cylinder of just any color to segment the test display. These results suggest that infants may experience illusory conjunctions under conditions of brief stimulus exposure, just as adults do.

These results also suggest that the male infants may have processed color information from the objects during the first 5 s of the familiarization trial, but did not link together the color and the shape of the object. By 15 s of processing time, this linkage had apparently taken place. The female infants (who did not seem to experience the illusory conjunction) may process information much more quickly or much more slowly than the male infants in this situation, as their responses are consistent with both of these possibilities. More research is needed to investigate the possibilities.

Our next step in investigating illusory conjunctions in infancy will be to test the effects of prior experience with two boxes that have different components of the test box's features—for example, a blue box with yellow squares and a purple box with white squares during familiarization and a blue box with white squares in the test display. The issue is whether infants will combine features from the two boxes, as adults do in analogous situations (Lavie, 1997). We hope to explore other situations that could shed light on the question of whether infants keep track of the features of objects seen simultaneously or sequentially in the paradigm we have developed.

5. Summary

The results of the experiments summarized in this section suggest that for infants to bring to bear a prior exposure with a similar object when segregating a display, the familiarization and test objects must be *highly* similar. Infants seem to encode considerable information about an object when they first see it, even for as short a time as 5 s, and to require a close match between their initial and subsequent encounters with an object to believe that they have seen the object before. However, in certain situations, infants may misremember having seen a certain object before when the features of the initially seen object consist of a mixture of the features of the two objects in the test display.

One may wonder how often the conditions we created in the lab would actually occur in the real world: Would infants often see either the identical object or an extremely similar object prior to seeing the object next to a novel object? If not, is the use of prior experiences to segregate objects a very common or theoretically interesting phenomenon? We wondered whether infants might overcome some of their featural specificity demonstrated in these studies if they had exposure to a *collection* of objects similar to those seen as part of the test display.

VIII. Categorization-Based Process

As described in the introduction, we thought it was possible that infants could make use of category knowledge to help them segment displays into individual units. The literature shows that even young infants can make categories of objects they encounter. We wondered whether infants would make use of this generalized knowledge about a group of objects to segment a display containing an object that could be considered a member of that category.

A. CATEGORIES EXPERIENCED WITHIN THE LAB

1. 4.5-Month-Old Infants
Our first step in addressing the above question was to see whether infants would make use of a prior experience with a group of objects, none of which would be an effective cue on its own, and none of which was identical to what would be seen in the test display (Needham & Lockhead, 1999). To accomplish these goals, we again used our cylinder-and-box test display and the same method described in the preceding section. In the initial 5-s familiarization trial, we presented infants a display consisting of the three boxes that were ineffective in helping the infants segregate the test objects into two separate units: the purple box with yellow circles, the blue box with red squares, and the blue box with yellow squares. We knew from the studies reported in the preceding section that infants did not use any of these boxes, presented alone, to help them segment the test display. However, presenting all three of these boxes at once might lead infants to form a category of "tall, thin boxes with texture elements" that would include the test box and allow infants to see the cylinder and box as separate units.

The results were positive—the mean looking time was reliably longer for the move-together than the move-apart event, suggesting that the infants were able to form a category that (a) was general enough to include the test box as one of its members and (b) facilitated the infants' segregation of the test display into two separate units. However, another possibility is that simply seeing any three boxes together in the familiarization trial would facilitate infants' segregation of the test display. To test this possibility, we conducted another experiment identical to that just described except that the infants saw three *identical* boxes (all blue with yellow squares, the one we considered to be most similar to the test box) during the 5-s familiarization. The results showed that the mean looking times were about equal for the two test events. Together, the results of the two experiments indicate that infants can form a category of boxes that is broad enough to include the test box after being exposed to three different boxes but not three instances of one box alone.

We wanted further tests of the above conclusions, specifically the idea that infants form a general representation of a kind of box that encompasses the box seen in the test display. One way to manipulate the kind of representation infants form as a result of the familiarization trial is to make the features of all three boxes identical, as described above. Another way may be to show infants only two of the three boxes. This seemingly minor manipulation could produce an important difference in the nature of the representation infants create if the following characterization of infants' formation of a representation is correct.

When infants are presented two different objects from the same category, they may notice the differences between the objects. However, when presented with three different objects, they may notice not only the differences among the three objects but also the similarities, and on the basis of the similarities create a categorical representation that encompass all three objects. If so, infants should not form a representation general enough to include the text box after seeing any two of the three different boxes described above.

To investigate this issue, infants were shown two of the three different boxes used in the first study in this section (Needham & Lockhead, 1999). The method was the same except that during the 5-s familiarization trial, the infants were shown either (a) the purple box with yellow circles and the blue box with yellow squares or (b) the blue box with red squares and the blue box with yellow squares. Results showed that the mean looking time was about equal for the move-apart and the move-together test events, indicating that they did not receive information in the familiarization trial that facilitated their segregation of the cylinder-and-box test display.

These results provide additional evidence in favor of the interpretation offered for the results of the first study in the section: Infants form a categorical representation that is general enough to include the test box when they are shown three different boxes that are all similar to the test box, but not when they are shown three identical boxes or two different boxes. Infants evidently need experience with different exemplars of a category, and they need more than one set of differences, to generalize across these differences to form a representation of the category to which these objects could belong. Infants use this category knowledge to determine that the test box and cylinder are separate objects even though they have seen neither of these objects before.

2. 9.5-Month-Old Infants

Another demonstration of infants' use of category information to segment a display came in a series of studies involving older infants, who were 9.5 months old (Needham & Kaufman, 1997; Needham, Kaufman, & Modi, 1999). This line of studies began as an investigation of infants' use of featural and spatial information to form an interpretation of a display composed of two pieces that could or could not be connected. The displays are shown in Figure 2. They were composed of two rectangular boxes arranged in depth so that the back box was visible to the right of the front box. In the parallel display, the boxes' front surfaces were parallel to each other and the two boxes were separated in depth by a noticeable gap. In the angled displays, the edge of the back box hidden by the front box was moved toward the front box, so that the left edge of the back box could have been touching (and possibly attached to) the front box. In the Similar-angled display, the two boxes were decorated with the same color and pattern; in the Dissimilar-angled display, the two boxes were decorated with different colors and patterns.

The infants received one familiarization trial in which the stationary display was visible. In the test events, rather than moving the objects in the display, the experimenters moved a large, thin screen (38 cm square) either between the two portions of the display (screen-between event) or behind the entire display (screen-behind event). Six experimental conditions were formed by crossing the three displays with the two events. Infants were assigned randomly to these conditions in a completely between-subjects design. Our rationale was that if the infants interpreted the display as a single unit, the screen-between event would be seen as a violation of solidity, and therefore the mean looking time would be reliably longer for the screen-between than the screen-behind event. In contrast, if they saw the display as composed of two separate units, the mean looking time for the two events would be about equal.

These displays were created to explore infants' use of two kinds of information—about the spatial relations between objects and about the features of the objects. We expected that using the spatial layout to segment the displays would lead the infants to see the parallel display as composed of two separate pieces and the angled displays as ambiguous. We also expected that using the available featural information would lead the infants to see the similar displays as composed of a single unit and the dissimilar display as composed of two separate units.

The results showed that for the infants who saw the Parallel display, the mean looking times were about the same for the screen-between and the screen-behind events, indicating that the infants used the spatial layout of the display rather than the features of the display to interpret the display as composed of two separate units. For the infants who saw the angled displays, responses to the test events depended upon whether they saw the similar or dissimilar display. For the infants who saw the Similar-angled display, the mean looking time was reliably longer for the screen-between than for the screen-behind event, but for the infants who saw

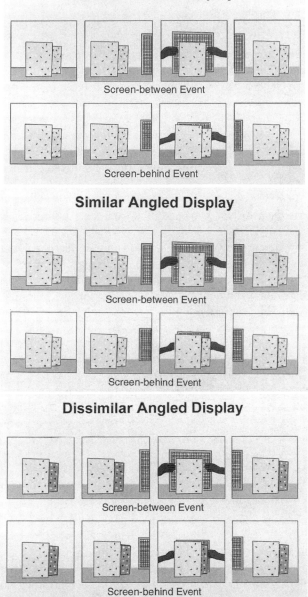

Fig. 2. Schematic drawing of the Similar parallel, Similar angled, and Dissimilar angled test displays and the screen-between and screen-behind test events used in the Needham and Kaufman (1997) studies. The effects of prior exposure to a group of displays like the Similar angled test display (that were shown to be composed of a single piece or two separate pieces) on the infants' responses to the screen-between test event was studied by Needham, Kaufman, and Modi (1999). These studies are described in section VII.

the Dissimilar-angled display, the mean looking time was about equal for the two test events.

These results suggest that the infants regarded the spatial layout of the Parallel display as unambiguous information about the display's composition as two separate pieces. In contrast, the infants seemed to regard the angled spatial layout as ambiguous information about the display's composition, because they made use of the color and pattern of the two portions of the display to interpret the two angled displays differently. As has been shown in previous research, infants seem to favor interpretations based on physical information—the spatial layout of the display—over interpretations based on featural information (Needham, 1997; Needham & Baillargeon, 1997).

The goal of the next study was to explore whether prior exposure to a set of displays similar to the test display would influence infants' interpretation of test display. In this study (Needham, Kaufman, & Modi, 1999), the infants were given three familiarization trials, each featuring a display similar in color and pattern to the Similar-angled test display and the same as this test display in size and shape. The familiarization boxes could be attached to each other to make a single object (one-object experience condition) or could be separate objects (two-objects experience condition). In each of the familiarization trials, one of the familiarization displays was deposited on the stage in such a way that its composition (as a single unit or two separate units) was clear, but once the display was in place on the stage, its spatial orientation looked just like the test display. Specifically, the experimenter deposited the connected boxes on the stage with one hand grasping one of the two-part object and deposited the separated boxes using one hand on each box and placing them on the stage one after the other. Half of the infants were in the one-object experience condition and half were in the two-object experience condition. The infants in both conditions saw the same test event—the Similar-angled display and the screen-between event.

Because the test event depicts a movement of the screen that would be possible if one thought the test display was composed of two separate pieces, but impossible if one thought the test display was composed of a single piece, we expected that if the infants perceived the test display as composed of a single unit, they would look reliably longer at the test event than if they perceived the test display as composed of two separate units. Evidence in favor of infants' use of their prior experience with the familiarization displays to help them segment the test display would be found if the infants who were in the one-object experience condition looked reliably longer at the test event than the infants in the two-objects experience condition. Exactly this result was obtained, even though the infants in the two-objects experience condition probably had to override a tendency to see the test display as a single unit (as found by Needham & Kaufman, 1997).

An additional study was conducted to determine whether the prior exposure to three different displays similar to the test display was necessary (as it was for the younger infants in the studies described in the previous section) for infants to apply their prior experience to the segmentation of the test display. This study was identical to the one just described, except that the infants saw just one of the three familiarization displays used in the prior experiment on each of the three familiarization trials. Based on our previous findings with younger infants described in the previous section, we expected that infants may not apply their prior experience with a single display to their interpretation of the test display. We were surprised to find that our results were no different from the original experiment: the mean looking time was reliably longer for the infants in the one-object experience than the two-objects experience condition.

The final study of this series was designed to determine whether infants discriminated between the familiarization display and the test display in this context. The familiarization display was light purple with bright yellow and white squares, and the test display was light blue with dark blue and white squares. Because there is evidence that infants' color vision system functions quite well by 4 months of age (see Kellman & Banks, 1998, for a review), it seemed clear that by 9.5 months of age, infants should be capable of discriminating between displays on the basis of color alone. However, we have found no evidence that infants do discriminate between these displays in the context of this experiment. These findings suggest that infants may apply their experience with the purple box to their segmentation of the blue test display because they do not notice that the display has changed. These findings are intriguing because they suggest a counterintuitive developmental progression in which young infants notice very small changes in an object on successive views, but older infants do not notice bigger changes. Further research is needed to explore this possible progression.

B. CATEGORIES EXPERIENCED OUTSIDE THE LAB

One way that category membership could facilitate infants' accurate object perception is to help them identify the kinds of objects that are exceptions to the general rules they are learning to find object boundaries. For example, as a rule, objects tend to be internally uniform in shape, color, and pattern, but for some categories of objects, this heuristic would be the exception rather than the rule. For example, brushes typically have a bristle portion and a handle portion that look very different from each other but are physically connected. If one were to segment a paintbrush based on featural information alone, one would expect that the bristle portion would not be connected to the handle portion. Thus, acquiring information about the category of brushes and how they look and function would be helpful when trying to determine object boundary locations in displays containing brushes.

We wanted to investigate the development of category knowledge and infants' use of it in segregating a display consisting of a paintbrush such as one might use

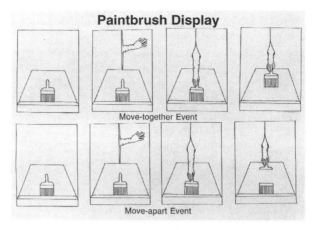

Fig. 3. Schematic drawing of the paintbrush test display and the move-together and move-apart test events used in the studies described in section VIII.

to paint the outside of a house (Needham, 1999b). The brush was composed of several distinct-looking parts: a yellow wooden handle, a bright chrome band binding the bristles to the handle, and a medium sized (6 cm × 8 cm) segment of black bristles. The brush lay against a slanting surface with the bristles down; in this orientation, the infants could see the entire brush. In the test event, a gloved hand took hold of the handle of the brush and pulled it up along the slanted surface. Half of the infants saw the brush (handle and bristles) move as a whole unit (move-together event); half saw the handle break away from the rest of the brush (move-apart event) (see Figure 3). If the infants segregated the objects on the basis of featural information alone, they should perceive the brush as consisting of more than one unit and look reliably longer at the move-together than at the move-apart event. In contrast, if the infants made use of category knowledge about brushes to segregate the objects, they should perceive the brush as a single unit and look longer at the move-apart than at the move-together test event.

Our results showed that for 12-month-old infants, the mean looking time was longer for the move-apart than the move-together test event, but for 8-month-old infants, the mean looking times were the same. These results suggest that between 8 and 12 months of age, infants acquire knowledge about brushes needed to override the interpretation of the display based solely on featural information. This knowledge allows infants to determine that the different-looking portions of the brush are actually connected to each other.

Although Carey and her colleagues have proposed that learning the words for objects facilitates infants' ability to individuate objects (e.g., Xu & Carey, 1996), we know of no evidence indicating (and we think it is unlikely) that 1-year-old children know the words *brush* or *paintbrush*.

To support our position that this process is not language-mediated, we are currently looking at younger infants' use of category knowledge about another kind of object that is more commonly experienced in the world by younger infants: key rings. If 6- or 7-month-old infants make use of category knowledge about key rings to see their distinct-looking parts as connected, this evidence would support our knowledge- or visual experience-based (rather than language-based) account of how infants' segregation rules are altered over time.

IX. Summary and Conclusions

We have described three ways in which infants use their prior experiences with objects when segregating displays. First, infants use their prior experiences with specific objects when segregating displays containing those objects. This effect occurs even over delays of 24 h and even when the context of the familiarization and test events are different.

Second, infants sometimes use a prior experience with an object similar to one present in the test display. Our work has shown that changes in the spatial orientation of the object between familiarization and test may be less disruptive than changes in the features of the object. This difference may signal a basic similarity in the ways in which infants and adults process object identity. At least some portions of Feature Integration Theory may be used to explain infants' object recognition, as our findings suggest that infants use an object's features to determine whether they have seen it before. Further evidence in this regard came from data indicating that infants may experience illusory conjunctions between features such as the shape and color of an object.

Finally, infants use a prior experience with a group of similar objects, perhaps by forming a general categorical representation that encompasses the characteristics of these objects. These categories may be formed after very brief exposures with three exemplars in the laboratory or with more lengthy exposures with any number of exemplars they encounter in their everyday experiences.

A. USE OF PRIOR EXPERIENCES VERSUS LEARNING IN GENERAL

One question about this work is how the use of prior experiences with particular objects or types of objects may be related to infants' more general learning about the physical relations between objects and the features of objects. Extensive research has shown that infants make use of general rules to determine where object boundaries should be. For example, their physical knowledge tells them that, in general, surfaces that move together are typically part of the same object. Their featural (or configural) knowledge tells them that because objects are generally regular in shape, color, and pattern, abrupt changes in these features typically signal an object boundary. The research summarized here implies that infants use their prior experiences with specific objects and types of objects to form exceptions to these general rules. In the following section, we describe a proposed developmental process linking infants' general knowledge and the recognition- and categorization-based processes we have discussed in this chapter.

B. PROPOSED DEVELOPMENTAL SEQUENCE

We think that infants probably first develop some general-purpose heuristics such as those just described, or perhaps even more primitive rules. Presumably, the initial forms of these general rules would not be entirely accurate and could be revised as infants notice failures of the rules and gain more information about the physical or featural domain (e.g., see Baillargeon, 1995).

Failures of and exceptions to the rules may attract infants' attention and may lead infants to collect information about frequently seen objects that do not conform to general rules. For example, an infant who has not had much exposure to paintbrushes may develop knowledge about paintbrushes used during a renovation of his or her home, and may come to learn that these objects held by his or her parents do not look like they should be single objects (based on a general featural analysis), but nevertheless are single objects. At this point in the process, this knowledge could be applied to these paintbrushes in different locations within the house for as long as the infant's memory allowed, but would be limited to these particular paintbrushes (these object tokens, according to Feature Integration Theory).

The next development that occurs could be a broadening or generalization of this representation, into an object type. As infants experience more exemplars that could be grouped together as the same type, and as their compositions consistently violated what would be expected according to the more general rules, infants may develop categorical representations for types of objects such as paintbrushes or more generally brushes or even more generally things with handles. These categorical representations could help infants to be accurate in segregating previously unseen objects that fit within the perceptual representation of what an object of that type tends to look like.

These categorical representations could be a beginning part of emerging knowledge about particular types of objects. Once infants form a representation for a particular type of object, they would be able to elaborate on this basic representation, adding information about typical locations of or uses for this type of object. Eimas's (1994) ideas about perceptual and conceptual representations differing mostly in amount (rather than in kind) of information are consistent with our ideas about the development of this kind of knowledge.

By the time persons reach adulthood, they have established an extensive network of perceptual and conceptual representations, and they may almost automatically identify many of the objects they see. Adults' segregation of many scenes may be primarily recognition- or identification-based, and they may fall back on their more general rules only when encountering an unknown object, such as a bizarre new toy received as a baby gift or a fancy new breadmaker that needed to be disassembled for cleaning. According to this perspective, the development of a network of representations would be a key task during infancy and early childhood that could contribute in important ways to efficient and veridical interpretation of the world. One of the goals of our future research is to explore the development of this representational network.

C. VISUAL-ORAL AND VISUAL-MANUAL CONNECTIONS

We have restricted our discussion in this chapter to situations in which infants make use of visually obtained experiences when segregating displays, but infants probably could make use of, for example, orally obtained experiences and apply these cross-modally to the visual segregation of a display. Ongoing research in our laboratory indicates that infants' learning of the general featural rules they use to segment displays may be facilitated by the development of more active visual and oral exploration of objects (Needham, 1999c; Rochat, 1989).

Current research also suggests that infants make use of a visual prior experience with an object to prepare actions on the object that are appropriate (Needham, 1999a). In one study, 12-month-old infants were shown to reach differently for a display depending upon whether it had been shown to consist of a single piece or two separate pieces. This visual prior experience seemed to facilitate 12-month-old (but not 9-month-old) infants' manual actions on the display.

D. CONCLUSION

In this chapter, we have shown that beginning early in the first year of life, infants use knowledge gained about specific objects and types of objects when determining object boundary locations. That infants are not limited to interpreting displays based on featural or physical information is important, because many studies have indicated that early in life, infants' use of this knowledge leaves them with ambiguous interpretations of displays (S. P. Johnson & Aslin, 1995; Kellman & Spelke, 1983; Needham, 1998; Spelke et al., 1993). Although recent findings lead one to conclude that infants do begin to develop their general knowledge early in the first year, the use of this knowledge early in infancy may be constrained by limitations in infants' basic information-processing abilities. Thus, the ability to recognize a specific object or type of object would play an especially important role in allowing young infants to make clear and accurate interpretations of the objects in the world. However, this ability is useful throughout the life span because segregating displays based on recognition or categorization (when possible)

Needham, A. (1997). Factors affecting infants' use of featural information in object segregation. *Current Directions in Psychological Science, 6,* 26–33.

Needham, A. (1998). Infants' use of featural information in the segregation of stationary objects. *Infant Behavior and Development, 21,* 47–76.

Needham, A. (1999a). How infants grasp two adjacent objects: Effects of perceived display composition on infants' actions. *Developmental Science, 2,* 219–233.

Needham, A. (1999b). *Infants' perception of a paintbrush: Use of functional versus configural knowledge to segregate a display.* Manuscript in preparation.

Needham, A. (1999c). *The development of infants' use of featural information to find a boundary between two adjacent objects: Relations to object exploration skills.* Manuscript under review.

Needham, A. (1999d). *The role of shape in 4-month-old infants' segregation of adjacent objects.* Manuscript under review.

Needham, A. (in press). *Object recognition and object segregation in 4.5-month-old infants. Journal of Experimental Child Psychology.*

Needham, A., & Baillargeon, R. (1997). Object segregation in 8-month-old infants. *Cognition, 62,* 121–149.

Needham, A., & Baillargeon, R. (1998). Effects of prior experience in 4.5-month-old infants' object segregation. *Infant Behavior and Development, 21,* 1–24.

Needham, A. Baillargeon, R., & Kaufman, L. (1997). Object segregation in infancy. In C. K. Rovee-Collier & L. P. Lipsitt (Eds.), *Advances in infancy research* (Vol. 11, pp. 1–44). Norwood, NJ: Ablex.

Needham, A., & Kaufman, J. (1997). Infants' integration of information from different sources in object segregation [Special issue]. *Early Development and Parenting, 6,* 137–147.

Needham, A., Kaufman, J., & Modi, A. (1999). *Effects of prior experience with similar objects on infants' object segregation.* Manuscript in preparation.

Needham, A., & Lockhead, G. (1999). *Infants' use of a categorical representation in object segregation.* Manuscript in preparation.

Needham, A., & Modi, A. (1999a). *Illusory recognition in 4.5-month-old infants' object segregation.* Manuscript in preparation.

Needham, A., & Modi, A. (1999b). *The role of memory in infants' object segregation.* Manuscript in preparation.

Peterson, M. A. (1994). Object recognition processes can and do operate before figure-ground organization. *Current Directions in Psychological Science, 3,* 105–111.

Quinn, P. C. (1987). The categorical representation of visual pattern information by young infants. *Cognition, 27,* 145–179.

Quinn, P. C., & Eimas, P. D. (1996). Perceptual organization and categorization in young infants. In C. K. Rovee-Collier & L. P. Lipsitt (Eds.), *Advances in infancy research* (Vol. 10, pp. 1–36). Norwood, NJ: Ablex.

Reese, H. W. (1989). Rules and rule-governance: Cognitive and behavioristic views. In S. C. Hayes (Ed.), *Rule-governed behavior: Cognition, contingencies, and instructional control* (pp. 3–84). New York: Plenum.

Richards, J. E. (1989). Sustained visual attention in 8-week-old infants. *Infant Behavior and Development, 12,* 425–436.

Rochat, P. (1989). Object manipulation and exploration in 2- to 5-month-old infants. *Developmental Psychology, 25,* 871–884.

Rose, S. A. (1980). Enhancing visual recognition memory in preterm infants. *Developmental Psychology, 16,* 85–92.

Rose, S. A. (1981). Developmental changes in infants' retention of visual stimuli. *Child Development, 52,* 227–233.

Rovee-Collier, C. K. (1993). The capacity for long-term memory in infancy. *Current Directions in Psychological Science, 2,* 130–135.

Rovee-Collier, C. K., & Hayne, H. (1987). Reactivation of infant memory: Implications for cognitive development. In H. W. Reese (Ed.), *Advances in child development and behavior* (Vol. 20, pp. 185–238). Orlando, FL: Academic Press.

Rovee-Collier, C. K., & Sullivan, M. W. (1980). Organization of infant memory. *Journal of Experimental Psychology, 6,* 798–807.

Ruff, H. A. (1978). Infant recognition of the invariant form of objects. *Child Development, 49,* 293–306.

Schwartz, K. (1982). *Perceptual knowledge of the human face in infancy.* Unpublished doctoral dissertation, University of Pennsylvania, Philadelphia.

Shepard, R. N., & Metzler, J. (1971). *Mental rotation of three-dimensional objects. Science, 171,* 701–703.

Simons, D. J. (1996). In sight, out of mind: When object representations fail. *Psychological Science, 7,* 301–305.

Slater, A., Mattock, A., Brown, E., Burham, D., & Young, A. (1991). Visual processing of stimulus compounds in newborn infants. *Perception, 20,* 29–33.

Slater, A., Morison, V., Somers, M., Mattock, A., Brown, E., & Taylor, D. (1990). Newborn and older infants' perception of partly occluded objects. *Infant Behavior and Development, 13,* 33–49.

Spelke, E. S. (1985). Preferential looking methods as tools for the study of cognition in infancy. In G. Gottlieb & N. Krasnegor (Eds.), *Measurement of audition and vision in the first year of postnatal life* (pp. 323–363). Norwood, NJ: Ablex.

Spelke, E. S. (1990). Principles of object perception. *Cognitive Science, 14,* 29–56.

Spelke, E. S., Breinlinger, K., Jacobson, K., & Phillips, A. (1993). Gestalt relations and object perception: A developmental study. *Perception, 22,* 1483–1501.

Spelke, E. S., & Van de Walle, G. A. (1993). Perceiving and reasoning about objects: Insights from infants. In N. Eilan, R. McCarthy, & B. Brewer (Eds.), *Spatial representation* (pp. 132–161). Oxford: Basil Blackwell.

Tarr, M. J., Bulthoff, H. H., Zabinski, M., & Blanz, V. (1997). To what extent do unique parts influence recognition across changes in viewpoint. *Psychological Science, 8,* 282–289.

Toulmin, S. (1971). The concept of "stages" in psychological development. In T. Mischel (Ed.), *Cognitive development and epistemology* (pp. 25–60). New York: Academic Press.

Treisman, A., & Gelade, G. (1980). A feature integration theory of attention. *Cognitive Psychology, 12,* 97–136.

Vishton, P. M., Stulac, S. N., & Calhoun, E. K. (1998). Using young infants' tendency to reach for object boundaries to explore perception of connectedness: Rectangles, ovals, and faces. *Infant Behavior and Development, 21,* 99.

Watson, J. B. (1926). What the nursery has to say about instincts. In M. Bentley, K. Dunlap, W. S. Hunter, K. Koffka, W. Kohler, W. McDougall, M. Prince, J. B. Watson, & R. S. Woodworth (Eds.), *Psychologies of 1925: Powell Lectures in Psychological Theory* (pp. 1–35). Worcester, MA: Clark University Press.

Wilcox, T. (in press). Object individuation: Infants' use of shape, size, pattern, and color. *Cognition.*

Wilcox, T., & Baillargeon, R. (1998). Object individuation in infancy: The use of featural information in reasoning about occlusion events. *Cognitive Psychology 37,* 97–155.

Xu, F., & Carey, S. (1996). Infants' metaphysics: The case of numerical identity. *Cognitive Psychology, 30,* 111–153.

Younger, B. A., & Gotlieb, S. (1988). Development of categorization skills: Changes in the nature or structure of infant form categories? *Developmental Psychology, 24,* 611–619.

PERSEVERATION AND PROBLEM SOLVING
IN INFANCY

Andréa Aguiar
Renée Baillargeon

DEPARTMENT OF PSYCHOLOGY
UNIVERSITY OF ILLINOIS AT URBANA-CHAMPAIGN
CHAMPAIGN, ILLINOIS 61820

ADVANCES IN CHILD DEVELOPMENT
AND BEHAVIOR, VOL. 27

I. Introduction

One of the hallmarks of human problem solving is its *efficiency*. When solutions to problems are known and easily retrieved from memory, we prefer retrieving them over computing them anew. As an illustration, consider the following situation. A college student participating in an experiment is asked the answer to the problem "122 × 11." After a few seconds, the subject answers "1342." On the next trial, the subject is again given the problem "122 × 11" and immediately answers "1342." Rather than laboriously recomputing the problem's solution, the subject swiftly and efficiently retrieves it from memory.

Despite its many obvious advantages, our tendency to retrieve past solutions from memory has at least one potential drawback. Past solutions can be helpful only if they are indeed appropriate for the problems at hand. To return to our example, consider what would happen if the subject was given the problem "122 × 13" in a later trial and mistakenly assumed that this was the same problem as before. The subject would once again retrieve the solution "1342," yielding a perseverative error. In this chapter, *perseveration* is defined as the retrieval of a familiar solution in a context in which a significant change has been introduced so that the familiar solution is no longer appropriate; for the subject to succeed, a novel solution must be computed.

Infants, like adults, produce perseverative errors, and developmental researchers have long been interested in understanding infants' perseverative tendencies. In this chapter, we summarize the research we have been conducting over the past 5 years on the perseverative responses of infants aged 6.5 to 11 months in a variety of tasks. The central perspective of our work, as illustrated by the preceding comments, is that perseveration is best understood as efficient problem solving gone awry. Familiar solutions are retrieved where novel solutions should have been computed.

Before describing our research, we briefly discuss prior work on infant perseveration. For the most part, this work has involved very different tasks from our own and has yielded very different answers to the riddle of infants' perseverative errors. After outlining these differences, we introduce our research and outline the plan of this chapter.

II. Perseveration in Memory-and-Motor Tasks

A. TRADITIONAL MEMORY-AND-MOTOR TASKS

Most of the research on infants' perseverative errors has focused on tasks that require infants (a) to update and remember information about objects and (b) to use this information to select appropriate motor responses. For ease of reference, we will refer to tasks with this dual requirement as "memory-and-motor" tasks.

The first infant memory-and-motor task was developed by Piaget (1954, pp. 44– 46) to examine infants' ability to search manually for an object hidden in one of two locations. This task has been used extensively by developmental researchers (for reviews, see Bremner, 1985; Diamond, 1985; Harris, 1987; Sophian, 1984; Wellman, Cross, & Bartsch, 1986). For example, in a classic longitudinal study, Diamond (1985) tested infants every 2 weeks from 6 to 12 months of age. On each trial, a toy was hidden in one of two identical wells, which were then covered with cloths. Next, a delay was introduced; the length of the delay was slowly increased across testing sessions. During the delay, the experimenter used a verbal distractor (e.g., counting aloud) to attract the infants' attention and thus prevent them from simply staring at the correct well throughout the delay. Following the delay, the infants were allowed to search for the toy. Side of hiding was reversed three to five times in each session. Of particular interest were reversal trials (termed B trials) that followed correct trials (termed A trials): would the infants search at the correct well on the B trials, or would they perseverate, returning to the (now empty) well they had searched successfully on the A trials? Two main results were obtained. First, all of the infants produced perseverative errors on the B trials. Second, longer delays were necessary with age to elicit perseverative errors: thus, whereas delays of less than 1 s produced errors at 7.5 months, 3-s delays were needed at 8 months, 6-s delays at 9 months, 8-s delays at 10 months, and over 10-s delays at 12 months.

B. NOVEL MEMORY-AND-MOTOR TASKS

A number of experiments with novel memory-and-motor tasks have added significantly to our understanding of the conditions under which perseverative errors occur in these tasks (e.g., Diedrich, Thelen, Corbetta, & Smith, 1998; Hofstadter & Reznick, 1996; Munakata, 1998; Smith, McLin, Titzer, & Thelen, 1995). To illustrate this point, two such experiments are described next, one by Hofstadter and Reznick (1996) and one by Smith et al. (1995).

Hofstadter and Reznick (1996) examined 5-month-old infants' *visual search* for an object hidden in one of two locations. As in Diamond's (1985) experiment, a toy was lowered in one of two identical wells, which were then covered with cloths. Next, a transparent and an opaque screen were raised, hiding the wells. After a 3-s delay, the opaque screen was lowered, leaving the transparent screen in place (to prevent manual search responses). Visual search on the A and B trials was measured by the direction of the infant's first gaze toward a well. The results indicated that, on the B trials, the infants had a significant tendency to gaze first at the well that was correct on the preceding A trial, thus producing a perseverative error.

Smith et al. (1995) examined whether 8-month-old infants would still make perseverative errors if *no toy* was hidden. The infants sat in front of two identical wells covered with lids; one lid was labeled the A lid and the other the B lid. In each test trial, an experimenter grasped and waved one of the lids before returning it to its initial position. After a 3-s delay, the infants were allowed to reach. The A lid was used for two test trials (A trials) and the B lid for two additional trials (B trials). The results indicated that the infants had a significant tendency to reach for the A lid on the B trials. Perseverative errors were thus observed despite the fact that no toy was hidden and the infants simply watched the experimenter wave one of the lids covering the wells.

Although the tasks devised by Hofstadter and Reznick (1996) and Smith et al. (1959) differ from the Piagetian two-location search task in several key respects, both are still memory-and-motor tasks according to the two criteria listed earlier: in each task, success on the B trials depended on the infants being able (a) to update and remember information (e.g., to remember in which of the two wells the object had been hidden or which of the two lids had been cued) and (b) to use this information to select one or two alternative motor responses (e.g., to direct their gaze to the left or right well or to reach for the left or right lid).

Not surprisingly, current accounts of perseveration in memory-and-motor tasks (e.g., Ahmed & Ruffman, 1998; Diamond, 1991; Diedrich et al., 1998; Hofstadter & Reznick, 1996; Marcovitch & Zelazo, in press; Munakata, 1998; Smith et al., 1995; Zelazo & Zelazo, 1998) typically refer to limitations in (a) infants' ability to update and maintain information in working memory across trials, and/or (b) infants' ability to use this information to select a novel motor response over a previously successful but no longer appropriate response. Decreases with age in perseveration are generally attributed to improvements in these two abilities with neurological maturation and (primarily motor) experience.

III. Perseveration in Tasks Other Than Memory-and-Motor Tasks

A. NONMEMORY-AND-MOTOR TASKS

1. Previous Tasks

In the mid 1990s, we began exploring the nature and causes of infants' perseverative errors in tasks *other* than memory-and-motor tasks. We were aware that perseverative errors had been reported in a number of detour tasks (e.g., Lockman & Pick, 1984; Mackenzie & Bigelow, 1986; Rieser, Doxsey, McCarrell, & Brooks, 1982). These tasks were similar to memory-and-motor tasks in that infants had to select one of two alternative motor responses on each trial; the tasks differed from memory-and-motor tasks, however, in that infants did not need to update and re- member information to determine which of the two motor responses was appro- priate, because the necessary information was perceptually available.

To illustrate, Lockman and Pick (1984) examined 12- and 18-month-old infants' ability to use the shortest route to reach their mothers. The infants and their moth- ers were positioned on opposite sides of an 8-foot-long barrier, near the left or right end; the two ends were used on alternate trials. The barrier was short enough for the infants to see their mothers clearly, but too tall for the infants to climb over it. The results indicated that on the initial trial, the infants in both age groups almost always went to their mothers by the shortest route (e.g., around the right end of the barrier if they stood near that end). On subsequent trials, however, only the 18- month-olds changed their response and used the shortest route to reach their moth- ers; the 12-month-olds tended to repeat their first response, going to their mothers via the same route across trials. The younger infants thus perseverated even though their mothers were clearly visible above the barrier so that the infants had no need to update and remember their mothers' position across trials.

2. Our Own Tasks

In our research, we used two novel series of tasks. The tasks in the *first* series (Aguiar, 1998; Aguiar & Baillargeon, 1999b; Aguiar, Rives, & Baillargeon, 1997) were similar to those of Lockman and Pick (1984), Mackenzie and Bigelow (1986), and Rieser et al. (1982) in that infants had to select one of two motor re- sponses based on information that was perceptually available rather than stored in memory. Our tasks were adapted from Piaget's (1954, pp. 180–183) support task. In this task, a toy is placed on the far end of a support such as a cloth, and infants must pull the near end of the cloth to bring the toy within reach. In our tasks, in- fants aged 7, 9, and 11 months were shown two clothes placed side by side; one had a toy on its far end and one had a toy beyond it (the oldest infants were tested with a somewhat more complex arrangement of the cloths and toys). After infants succeeded at retrieving the toy, the location of the two cloths was reversed; the question of interest was whether, in the reversal trial, the infants would (a) pull the correct cloth and retrieve the toy or (b) perseverate, pulling the cloth on the same side as the cloth they had pulled on the preceding trial.

Our *second* series of tasks (Aguiar, 1998; Aguiar & Baillargeon, 1996, 1998, 1999a, 1999c) differed maximally from memory-and-motor tasks in that infants not only did not have to update and remember information about objects but also did not have to select one of two alternative motor responses. Tasks in this second series involved the violation-of-expectation paradigm (e.g., Baillargeon, 1995,

1998). In this paradigm, infants typically see an expected event, which is consistent with the belief or expectation under examination, and an unexpected event, which violates it. With appropriate controls, longer looking at the unexpected than at the expected event provides evidence that infants detect the violation in the unexpected event. In our tasks, infants aged 6.5, 7.5, and 8.5 months were shown containment events. During the familiarization trials, infants saw an object being lowered into a much wider container. During the test trials, the same object was lowered into two novel containers, one slightly larger (large-container event) and one smaller (small-container event) than the object. Past research (Sitskoom & Smitsman, 1995) has shown that by 6.5 months of age, infants realize that a rigid object can be lowered into a container that is wider but not narrower than the object. Our containment tasks examined whether infants would (a) detect the violation shown in the small-container test event or (b) perseverate, carrying forth the same expectation ("the object will fit into the container") they had formed during the familiarization trials.

Infants in both our support and containment tasks produced perseverative errors. To account for these results, together with those of Lockman and Pick (1984), Mackenzie and Bigelow (1986), and Rieser et al. (1982), we have been developing a model of perseveration in nonmemory-and-motor tasks. As might be expected, this model differs radically from current accounts of perseveration in memory-and-motor tasks (e.g., Ahmed & Rufman, 1998; Diamond, 1991; Diedrich et al., 1998; Hofstadter & Reznick, 1996; Marcovitch & Zelazo, in press; Munakata, 1998; Smith et al., 1995; Zelazo & Zelazo, 1998). As mentioned earlier, these accounts typically refer to limitations in (a) infants' ability to update and remember information about objects and (b) infants' ability to select a new motor response over a previously successful but no longer appropriate alternative response. Because neither of these limitations could be used to explain the perseverative errors observed in our containment tasks, we opted for a very different approach focused on limitation in infants' problem-solving abilities.

B. ORGANIZATION OF THE CHAPTER

The rest of this chapter is divided into four sections. In the first, we describe our problem-solving model of perseveration in nonmemory-and-motor tasks. In the second and third sections, we describe the results of our support and containment experiments and discuss how these results provide evidence for our model. Finally, in the fourth section, we return to the perseverative errors that have been observed in memory-and-motor tasks and explore ways in which our problem-solving model can be elaborated to account for these errors. Our hope is that a single model can eventually be developed that accounts for errors in *both* memory-and-motor and nonmemory-and-motor tasks and thus offers a unified account of perseveration in infancy.

IV. A Problem-Solving Model of Infant Perseveration in Nonmemory-and-Motor Tasks

Before describing our model of infant perseveration in nonmemory-and-motor tasks, we make two comments about its domain of application. First, our model focuses primarily on tasks of the following format: to start, infants receive one or more trials (termed the A trials) in which they are given the same problem; next, infants receive one or more trials (termed the B trials) in which they are given a problem that is largely similar to the initial problem except that a crucial feature has been changed so that the original solution is no longer valid; for infants to succeed, a new response must be produced. Second, our model applies only to tasks that infants are capable of solving: perseveration on the B trials is never due to infants lacking the knowledge and cognitive skills necessary to detect the change introduced or to respond to it appropriately.

A. THREE ASSUMPTIONS

Our model rests on three main assumptions which are described in turn.

1. First Assumption

The first assumption is that at the start of each A and B trial in a testing session, infants conduct an *initial analysis* of the problem before them to categorize it as novel or familiar; that is, they judge whether the problem is one they are encountering for the first time in the session or one they have encountered earlier in the session. If infants conclude that the problem is novel, they perform a *further analysis* of the problem and compute its solution. In contrast, if infants conclude that the problem is familiar, they do not conduct a further analysis of the problem but instead simply retrieve their previous solution (for related ideas, see Baillargeon, 1993; Logan, 1988; Suchman, 1987).

2. Second Assumption

The second assumption is that infants perseverate on the B trials when their initial analysis of the problem is too incomplete to allow them to detect the crucial change that has been introduced. As a result, infants mistakenly categorize the problem as similar to that on the preceding A trials. Instead of computing a novel solution, infants retrieve their prior solution, resulting in a perseverative error.

3. Third Assumption

The third assumption, which is depicted in Figure 1, is that whether infants perseverate or respond correctly on the B trials depends to a large extent on their level of expertise at the task. We believe that *novice* infants (i.e., infants with little experience at the task) are more likely to perseverate on the B trials than are *expert* infants (i.e., infants with more experience at the task).

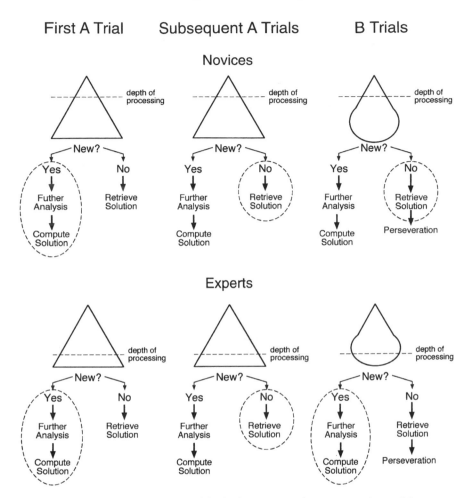

Fig. 1. *Schematic description of the third assumption of our perseveration model.*

a. Novice Infants.   When categorizing a problem, novice infants tend to engage in a shallow analysis of the problem that bypasses many of its crucial features. On the first A trial, this shallow analysis is sufficient to yield a correct categorization of the problem as novel; because infants are encountering the problem for the first time in the test session, a correct categorization would be expected on almost any analysis, however superficial. Having categorized the problem as novel, novices then conduct a further analysis of the problem and compute its solution. On the subsequent A trials, novice's shallow initial analysis is again sufficient to yield a correct categorization of the problem as familiar; because the problem is in fact the same as that on the preceding A trials, a correct categorization would again be expected on almost any analysis. Having categorized the problem as familiar, infants do not conduct any further analysis but instead simply retrieve and execute their prior solution.

Novices' shallow initial analysis is thus sufficient to lead them to perform correctly on all of the A trials. Difficulties arise only on the B trials, when the change in the problem involves a feature that typically falls outside the set of features that novices spontaneously attend to when performing their (shallow) initial analysis of the problem. Because they fail to detect the change introduced, novices mistakenly categorize the problem as familiar and hence retrieve their previous solution, resulting in a perseverative error. Novices' difficulties on the B trials constitute the primary focus of this chapter.

b. Expert Infants. In contrast to novices, expert infants tend to engage on both A and B trials in a deeper initial analysis of the problem that takes into account a greater number of its crucial features. As a result, experts are more likely to detect the change introduced in the B trials and hence to categorize and respond to the problem correctly.

4. Summary of Assumptions

In summary, we believe that the key to perseveration in nonmemory-and-motor tasks lies in problem categorization: infants perseverate when they mistakenly categorize a novel problem as familiar and thus go on to retrieve their previous solution rather than compute a new one. In turn, the key to problem categorization lies in problem analysis: infants mistakenly categorize a novel problem as familiar when their initial analysis of the problem is too shallow to allow them to notice that a crucial feature has been changed. When discussing the findings of our support and containment experiments, we will attempt to flesh out our claims about problem categorization and analysis. We believe that these claims are important not only for the insights that they may yield about infant perseveration, but also, more generally, for the light that they may shed on infant problem solving. As mentioned at the start of this chapter, our view is that perseveration is best understood as efficient problem solving gone awry; from this perspective, perseveration provides a fascinating window through which to explore the strengths and limitations of human problem solving from its origins onward.

B. SUPPORTING EVIDENCE FROM RELATED LITERATURES

Findings from several research areas outside infancy provide evidence for our problem-solving model of perseveration in nonmemory-and-motor tasks. Below we briefly describe three sets of such findings.

1. Distinction between Computation-Based and Retrieval-Based Problem Solving

A number of neuropsychological findings support the distinction between computation-based and retrieval-based problem solving (e.g., Murthy & Fetz, 1992; Posner & Raichle, 1994). In one experiment, Posner and Raichle (1994, pp. 105–129) used positron emission tomography (PET) to examine adults' brain activity during a verb-generation task. The participants were asked to read a list of 40 nouns and after each noun to produce a verb that represented an appropriate use of the noun (e.g., hammer–pound). The PET images revealed that the pathway activated when the subjects were computing their responses included the left frontal cortex, the anterior cingulate cortex, the left posterior temporal cortex, and the right cerebellum. However, when the subjects were tested with the same list of nouns following 15 min of practice, so that they were now simply retrieving their previous responses, no activation was observed in these areas; instead, a different pathway was activated that included the buried insular cortex in both hemispheres. The computation of new responses and retrieval of old responses thus produced activation in two different brain pathways.

2. Perseveration Produced by the Miscategorization of a Problem

Results from the traditional problem-solving literature provide evidence for the notion that perseveration occurs when subjects mistakenly categorize a problem as similar to one encountered earlier in a testing session. In the classical experiments of A. S. and E. H. Luchins (e.g., Luchins, 1942, 1946; Luchins & Luchins, 1950), adults and elementary school children solved two sets of five pencil-and-paper problems in which they were asked how to obtain a specific volume of liquid from a large tank using any or all of three empty jars (A, B, and C). The volume of liquid to be obtained and the capacity (measured in quarts) of the three jars changed from problem to problem. The first set of problems was solved most efficiently by the formula $B - A - 2C$. All but one of the problems in the second set could be solved by this formula or more efficiently by simpler formulas such as $A - C$ or $A + C$; the remaining problem could be solved only by the $A - C$ formula. Most adults and children continued to use the formula they had generated for the first set of problems when solving the second set. Indeed, the participants' perseverative tendency was so robust that most failed to notice that the original formula actually led to an incorrect answer in the $A - C$ problem. Consistent with our hypotheses about categorization and perseveration, the authors observed in additional experiments that only participants "who treated each problem as possessing individual requirements" (Luchins & Luchins, 1950, p. 295) tended to show little or no perseverative tendency.

3. Distinction between Novices' and Experts' Problem Categorization

Many results from the adult literature on expertise are consistent with our hypothesis that infants who are novices or experts at a task consider different information when categorizing problems (e.g., Anderson, 1987; Cheng, 1985; Chi, Feltovich, & Glaser, 1981; Ericsson & Charness, 1994; Johnson & Mervis, 1994; Reimann & Chi, 1989). For example, Chi et al. (1981) asked physics experts (Ph.D. students in physics) and novices (undergraduate students who had just completed a mechanics course) to categorize 24 problems from a standard physics textbook. Analysis of the participants' sorts indicated that the experts categorized the problems based on principles of mechanics, whereas the novices categorized the problems based on the concrete objects (e.g., springs and pulleys) mentioned in the problems.

V. Perseveration in Support Tasks

In this section, we review experiments conducted with three support tasks of increasing difficulty. As mentioned earlier (in section III), these tasks resembled memory-and-motor tasks in that infants were required on each trial to perform one of two alternative motor responses (i.e., pull on a left or a right cloth). These tasks differed from memory-and-motor tasks, however, in that infants did not need to update and remember information on each trial to decide which motor response was appropriate: all of the information necessary to make this decision was perceptually available. Our three tasks and their results are described in turn.

A. TOY-ATTACHED TASK

Several researchers have reported that infants less than 8 months of age typically do not pull on the near end of a cloth to bring within reach a toy placed on the far end of the cloth (e.g., Aguiar, 1997; Kolstad & Aguiar, 1995; Matthews, Ellis, & Nelson, 1996; Piaget, 1952; Willatts, 1984). However, Kolstad and Aguiar (1995) found that infants as young as 6.5 months of age will pull on a cloth to bring a toy within reach if they are first shown that the toy is *attached* to the cloth. Kolstad and Aguiar concluded that when the toy and cloth are separate, young infants are unable to think of an appropriate solution for retrieving the toy; the solution of pulling on the cloth to bring the toy within reach is not yet in their repertoire and does not occur to them. When the toy and cloth are attached, however, infants view them as a single, composite object; because they already know how to act on one portion of a composite object to make possible an action on a different portion of the object (e.g., grasping a nursing bottle and bringing its nipple to the mouth), in-

A Trial

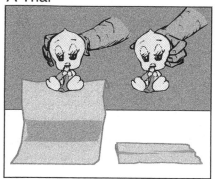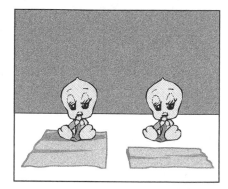

B Trial

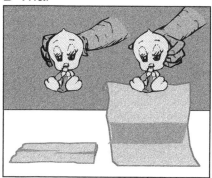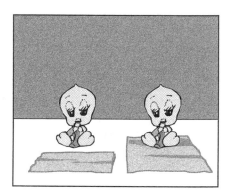

Fig. 2. Schematic drawing of the test trials in the toy-attached task.

fants have no difficulty determining what action to perform to retrieve the toy attached to the cloth.

Our first support task was based on this result (Aguiar, 1998; Aguiar & Baillargeon, 1999b; Aguiar et al., 1997). In the task, 7- and 9-month-old infants were shown two cloths lying side by side. As depicted in Figure 2, one cloth had a toy attached to its far end and the other cloth was folded in half and had an identical toy placed beyond it. After the infants succeeded in retrieving the attached toy on two trials, the location of the two toy-cloth pairs was reversed. The question of interest was whether the infants would pull the cloth with the attached toy or would perseverate, pulling the cloth on the same side as the cloth they had pulled in the preceding trials.

1. Procedure

Participants were tested using a two-phase procedure that consisted of a pretest and a test phase. Infants' actions during both phases were videotaped and later coded through frame-by-frame analyses.

During the *pretest* phase, each infant sat on a parent's lap at a table across from an experimenter. To start, the infants received pretest trials with a single toy and cloth. These trials were designed to introduce the task to the infants, and also to ensure that the infants could solve single toy–cloth problems. The toy was a bright attractive toy such as a Tweety Bird doll (throughout the experiment, new toys were introduced as needed to maintain the infants' interest). The bottom of the toy was velcroed to the far end of a cream-colored felt cloth. At the start of the first trial, the experimenter held up the toy and cloth, calling the infant's attention to each of them. Next, the experimenter placed the cloth and toy on the table in front of the infant; the near end of the cloth was within the infant's reach, but the toy was not. Next, the infant was encouraged to retrieve the toy (e.g., "Can you get it?"). The parent was instructed to restrain the infant while the cloth and toy were being placed on the table and to release him or her when the experimenter asked the infant to retrieve the toy. If the infant failed to pull on the cloth and retrieve the toy, the trial was repeated up to two times, usually with a different toy; if the infant still failed to retrieve the toy after three trials, the session was terminated. If the infant succeeded in retrieving the toy, then he or she received two additional pretest trials that were identical to the initial one, with one exception: after depositing the cloth and toy on the table, the experimenter placed a large opaque screen on the table between the infant and the cloth and toy; the screen was then immediately removed. The reason for this procedure is explained below.

Following the pretest phase, the *test* phase began. At the start of the first test trial, the experimenter placed one cream-colored cloth on the table to one side of the infant's midline and then folded the cloth in half, toward the infant. Next, the experimenter introduced two identical attractive toys, such as Tweety Bird dolls (see Figure 2). One toy was held above and beyond the folded cloth; the other toy, which was held on the opposite side of the infant's midline, had a cloth attached to its bottom. The experimenter squeaked the two toys, placed them down on the table, and then tapped them simultaneously until the infant had looked at each of them. For half of the infants, the attached toy–cloth pair was on the right and the unattached toy–cloth pair was on the left; for the other infants, the positions of the two pairs were reversed. Next, as in the last two pretest trials, the screen was placed between the infant and the toy–cloth pairs for a brief interval; this procedure was adapted from that of Hofstadter and Reznick (1996) and was intended to prevent the infants from simply reaching for whichever toy–cloth pair they happened to look at last when the experimenter tapped them. After the screen was removed, the infants were encouraged to reach, as in the pretest trials. The first trial was repeated until the infants succeeded in retrieving the attached toy on two consecutive trials, termed the A trials. The infants typically took two to six trials to complete these trials. Infants who did not complete two successful A trials (with the same toy) within six trials were eliminated from the sample. The infants who succeeded on two consecutive A trials were given one additional trial, termed the B trial, that was identical to the A trials except that the position of the two toy–cloth pairs was reversed.

The infants' responses on the B trial were assigned to one of two main categories. Infants were said to have produced a *correct* response if they pulled the cloth in the attached toy–cloth pair while focusing primarily on the toy (as opposed to, say, the cloth itself, the experimenter, and so on). Infants were said to have produced a *perseverative* response if they pulled the cloth in the unattached toy–cloth pair while again attending to the toy. In rare instances where the infant pulled both cloths simultaneously, the toy the infant looked at was used to determine which cloth was being pulled intentionally.

2. Results and Interpretations

As shown in Table I, the results of the B trial revealed a reliable difference between the responses of the 7- and 9-month-old infants: whereas most of the younger infants produced perseverative responses by continuing to pull the cloth on the same side as they had pulled on the A trials, most of the older infants produced correct responses, pulling the cloth with the attached toy.

Consistent with our model, we assume that the 7-month-old infants perseverated because their initial analysis of the B-trial problem was too shallow to allow them to register the change in the location of the two toy–cloth pairs. As a result, the infants categorized the B-trial problem as similar to that on the preceding A trials. This miscategorization in turn led the infants to retrieve their previous solu-

TABLE I

7-, 9-, and 11-Month-Old Infants' Performance in the Support Tasks

	Response on the B trial	
Task	Pull cloth at previous location (perseverate)	Pull cloth at new location (succeed)
Toy-attached		
7 months	×	
9 months		×
Toy unattached		
9 months	×	
11 months		×
Gap		
11 months	×	

tion, leading to a perseverative error. In contrast, the 9-month-old infants engaged in a more complete initial analysis of the B-trial problem. This analysis enabled the infants to notice the change in the location of the two toy–cloth pairs. Accordingly, the infants categorized the B-trial problem as distinct from that on the preceding A trials and proceeded to analyze the problem further and compute a new appropriate solution.

Why did the 7-month-old infants engage in a shallow and the 9-month-old infants in a deeper initial analysis of the B-trial problem? We believe that the answer to this question has to do with infants' level of expertise at solving problems involving the retrieval of composite objects—objects that are made up of different parts such as a nursing bottle, a rattle, and the attached toy–cloth pair in our task. As mentioned earlier, 6.5-month-old infants readily pull on the near end of a cloth to bring within reach a distant toy when they are shown that the toy is actually attached to the far end of the cloth, thus forming a single composite object (Aguiar, 1997; Kolstad & Aguiar, 1995). However, pilot data collected with infants aged less than 6 months indicated that these younger infants were less likely to succeed at retrieving the attached toy. One implication of these results is that, although the 7-month-old infants in the present experiment were able to solve problems involving the retrieval of composite objects, this ability was still a relatively new acquisition. By contrast, the 9-month-old infants had about 2 months additional practice at retrieving composite objects. It is plausible that as a result of such practice infants come to automatically encode more detailed information about composite objects in their initial analysis. After all, one can gain access to a distant portion of a composite object by acting on a nearer portion that is *attached* but not *disjoint* (e.g., one can gain access to the nipple of a nursing bottle by acting on the bottle only if the bottle and nipple are actually attached at the time). It would make sense that with experience infants would come to closely and routinely attend to the arrangement of the portions of a composite object prior to acting on it. Such an encoding would have helped the 9-month-old infants in our experiment track the location of the attached toy–cloth pair on each trial, thereby facilitating their successful performance.

We are not suggesting that 7-month-old infants never attend to the arrangement of the distinct portions of composite objects. If this were the case, it would be difficult to explain the 7-month-old infants' performance on their first successful A trial. Our suggestion is that the infants attended to the arrangement of each toy–cloth pair only in their *further* analysis of the problem when they were computing its solution. In the B trial, the infants never carried out this further analysis because they miscategorized the problem as familiar, and thus simply retrieved their previous, A-trial solution.

What information did the 7-month-old infants include in their shallow initial analysis of the B-trial problem? The present data do not allow us to offer a precise answer to this question. One possibility is that the infants focused on the global context of the problems and were swayed by the overall similarities across trials in the testing room, experimenter, procedure, stimuli, and so on. Another possibility is that the infants' initial analysis was more limited in scope and that, like the physics novices in the experiment of Chi et al. (1981), the infants attended primarily to the concrete entities involved in the problems ("yep, toys and cloths, same old thing").

B. TOY-UNATTACHED TASK

Our second support task (Aguiar, 1998; Aguiar & Baillargeon, 1999b; Aguiar et al., 1997) was similar to our first with one important exception: in the attached toy-cloth pair, the toy was no longer velcroed to the cloth but simply rested on it (see Figure 3). This difference was perceptible only when the experimenter held up the

A Trial

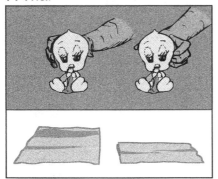 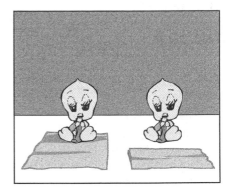

B Trial

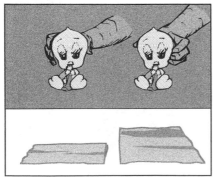 

Fig. 3. Schematic drawing of the test trials in the toy-unattached task.

toy; when the toy and cloth were on the table, they were indistinguishable from the attached toy–cloth pair in our first task.

1. Procedure

Participants were 9- and 11-month-old infants. The infants were tested using the same procedure as in the toy-attached task, with a few exceptions. First, the single toy and cloth used in the three pretest trials were no longer attached. Second, at the start of each test trial, the experimenter placed the two cloths simultaneously on the table, on either side of the infant's midline, and then folded one of the cloths in half. Next, the experimenter introduced the two toys, and the procedure then continued as in the toy-attached task.

2. Results and Interpretations

The results revealed a reliable different between the responses of the younger and older infants on the B trial: whereas most of the 9-month-old infants perseverated and pulled the cloth on the same side as the cloth they had pulled on the A trials, most of the 11-month-old infants responded correctly and pulled the cloth on which the toy rested (see Table I).

Consistent with our model, we believe that the 9-month-old infants perseverated in the toy-unattached task because (a) their initial analysis of the B-trial problem was too shallow to enable them to register the change in the location of the two toy–cloth pairs; (b) they consequently miscategorized the problem as similar to that on the preceding A trials; (c) this miscategorization in turn led them to retrieve their previous solution, resulting in a perseverative error. In contrast, the 11-month-old infants succeeded at the task because (a) they engaged in a deeper and more complete analysis of the two toy–cloth pairs that allowed them to detect the change in the location of the toy–cloth pairs; (b) they accordingly categorized the B-trial problem as novel; and therefore (c) they went on to compute its solution.

Why did the 9-month-old infants engage in a shallow and the 11-month-old infants in a deeper initial analysis of the B-trial problem? We believe that the answer to this question has to do with infants' level of expertise at solving problems involving the retrieval of objects resting on supports. As mentioned earlier, it is not until infants are about 8 months of age that they spontaneously pull on the near end of a support to bring within reach a toy placed on the far end of the support (e.g., Aguiar, 1997; Kolstad & Aguiar, 1995; Matthews et al., 1996; Piaget, 1952; Willatts, 1984). These findings suggest that although the 9-month-old infants in the present experiment were able to solve problems involving the retrieval of supported objects, this ability was still a relatively new acquisition. By contrast, the 11-month-old infants had about 2 months additional practice at retrieving supported objects. It seems reasonable to suppose that as a result of such practice infants come to automatically encode more detailed information about object-support pairs; after all, one can retrieve an object by pulling on a support when the object rests *on* but not *beyond* the support, and it makes sense that with experience infants come to closely and routinely attend to whether an object is on or beyond a support before acting on it. This more detailed encoding would have helped the 11-month-old infants in our experiment track the location of the supported toy on the initial analysis of each of the trials, thereby contributing to their successful performance.

Why did the 9-month-old infants perseverate in the toy-unattached but not the toy-attached task? In accordance with our model, we believe that the answer to this question has to do with infants' initial analysis of the B-trial problem in each task. We suggested earlier that, by 9 months of age, infants automatically encode detailed information about composite objects. In the toy-unattached task, however, there were *no* composite objects. If the infants simply noted in their initial analysis of the B-trial problem in the unattached-toy task that there were two distinct objects, a toy and a cloth, on either side of the midline, without attending particularly to whether the toy in each pair was on or beyond the cloth, then they would have lacked the necessary information to judge that the B trial was indeed different from the preceding A trials and called for a novel solution.

Once again, we are not suggesting that 9-month-old infants never attend to the arrangement of objects and their supports. Clearly, the 9-month-old infants in the toy-unattached task had to do so on their first successful A trial. However, we believe that these infants attended to the arrangement of the toy and cloth in each pair only in their *further* analysis of the problem when they were computing its solution. In the B trial, the infants never carried out this further analysis because they miscategorized the problem as familiar and therefore simply retrieved their previous, A-trial solution.

C. GAP TASK

Our third support task (Aguiar, 1998; Aguiar & Baillargeon, 1999b; Aguiar et al., 1997) was similar to our toy-unattached task, with one important exception: the toy–cloth pair involving a toy standing behind a folded cloth was replaced with a new toy-two-cloths pair (see Figure 4). In this pair, two smaller cloths, separated by a gap, were laid on the table; the toy rested on the farther of the two cloths. The total length of the two cloths and gap equalled that of the single cloth in the toy–cloth pair.

1. Procedure

Participants were 11-month-old infants. The infants were tested using the same procedure as in the toy-unattached task, with the following exception. At the start of each test trial, the experimenter placed the single cloth and two small cloths on the table, on either side of the midline. Next, the experimenter introduced the two toys, and the procedure continued as in the toy-unattached task.

A Trial

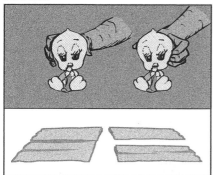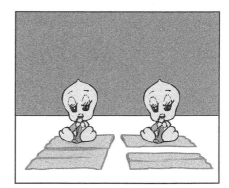

B Trial

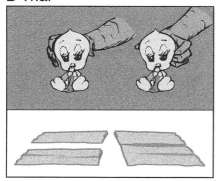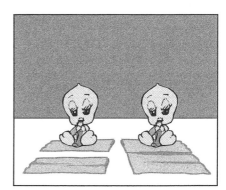

Fig. 4. Schematic drawing of the test trials in the gap task.

2. Results and Interpretations

Comparison of the B-trial responses of the 11-month-old infants in the toy-unattached and gap tasks revealed a reliable difference: whereas most of the infants in the toy-unattached task had responded correctly, most of the infants in the gap task perseverated, pulling the cloth on the same side as the cloth they had pulled on the preceding A trials (see Table I). In accordance with our model, we assume that the infants in the gap task perseverated because their initial analysis of the B-trial problem was too shallow to enable them to register the change that had been introduced. As a result, the infants miscategorized the problem as similar to that on the preceding A trials. This miscategorization in turn led the infants to retrieve their previous solution, resulting in a perseverative error.

Why did the 11-month-old infants perseverate in the gap but not the toy-unattached task? We suggested earlier that the 11-month-old infants in the toy-unattached task, who were experienced at retrieving supported objects, might have included in their initial analysis of the B-trial problem information as to whether each toy was on or beyond its support. Such information was sufficient, in the toy-unattached task, to help the infants track the location of the two toy–cloth pairs and hence correctly categorize the B-trial problem and avoid perseveration. In the gap task, however, each toy rested *on* a cloth; therefore, an initial analysis that simply checked whether a toy was on or off a support would not have provided sufficient information to correctly track the location of the toy–cloth and toy–two-cloths pairs. A more detailed analysis was required that also included information about whether the portion of cloth on which the toy rested was effectively connected to the portion of cloth within reach. Presumably, with practice at solving gap problems such as the one used here, infants would come to include more detailed support information in their initial analyses of the problems, thereby avoiding perseveration.

D. PRIOR EVIDENCE OBTAINED WITH A DIFFERENT SUPPORT TASK

It might be objected that our results are inconsistent with those of experiments conducted with a different support task (Matthews et al., 1996; Willatts, 1985), which yielded no evidence of perseveration. Matthews et al. (1996) tested infants every 4 weeks between 7 and 15 months of age in the following support task: two identical cloths lay side by side on a table, and a toy was placed on the far end of one of the cloths. After the infants successfully retrieved the toy on two or three trials (A trials), the toy was moved to the other cloth (B trials). The results indicated that the infants produced few perseverative errors across all testing sessions. Willatts (1985) found no evidence of perseveration in a similar task with 9-month-old infants.

How can we reconcile these results with our own? Our experiments indicated that more complex support tasks were needed with age to elicit perseverative errors: the 7-month-old infants perseverated in the toy-attached task, the 9-month-old infants perseverated in the toy-unattached but not the toy-attached task, and the 11-month-old infants perseverated in the gap but not the toy-unattached task. Our interpretation of these results was that with experience, infants routinely encode information about more and more crucial features in their initial analysis of support problems, and as a result are more likely to detect changes in these features on B trials. In the task used by Matthews et al. (1996) and Willatts (1985), the infants were given problems involving a *single* toy. Therefore, as long as the infants' initial analysis of the problem on each trial included the toy's location, they could categorize the problem correctly and know whether to retrieve their previous solution or compute a new one. In all our tasks, in contrast, the infants were given problems involving *two* toys. Hence, more information had to be included in the infants' initial analyses of the problems to differentiate between the two toy–cloth pairs and achieve correct categorizations.

The results of Matthews et al. (1996) and Willatts (1985), rather than being inconsistent with our own, thus provide further evidence that the more complex the support task, the more information must be included in infants' initial analyses of the problems for perseveration to be avoided, and hence the older the age at which infants are likely to succeed at the task.

E. TOY-UNATTACHED TASK REVISITED

One way of construing the results reported so far is that infants who have little experience at solving support problems can be prevented from perseverating on B trials by being given simpler problems for which they routinely include change-relevant information in their initial analyses of the trials. Thus, we could say that 9-month-old infants who perseverate in the toy-unattached task can be helped either by attaching the toy that rests on the cloth *to* the cloth (as in our toy-attached task), or by using a single toy (as in the task of Matthews et al., 1996, and Willatts, 1985). Could infants be prevented from perseverating in other ways? We conducted additional experiments to address this question.

The point of departure for these experiments was the intuition that, although infants might focus primarily on the arrangement and location of the toys and cloths in their initial analyses of support problems, they might also encode some information about the global context of the problems. This intuition suggested that the introduction of a *salient contextual change* in the B trials might be detected by infants, leading to correct categorization and responding.

In one experiment (Aguiar, 1998; Aguiar & Baillargeon, 1999b), 9-month-old infants were tested with a procedure similar to that of our original toy-unattached task, with one important exception: one experimenter tested the infant in the A trials and a different experimenter tested the infant in the B trial. At the end of the A trials, the A experimenter stepped behind a large curtain, and the B experimenter then emerged from behind this curtain to continue the infant's testing.

Comparison of the responses on the B trial of the 9-month-old infants in our original toy-unattached task and in the two-experimenters version of the task yielded a significant difference: unlike the infants in our original task, most of the infants in the two-experimenters task responded correctly on the B trial. Further experiments are planned to establish exactly how having a second experimenter test the infants in the B trial prevented their perseverating. For example, did the infants succeed because they knew that different people often behave differently and hence realized that the B experimenter might well give them a different problem than the A experimenter? Did the infants become distracted by the change in experimenter and essentially forget the A trials? Or was it simply that the change in experimenter was perceptually highly salient for the infants and had the same effect that might be expected from any other salient contextual change, such as a drastic change in the appearance of the test rooms?

Whatever the final outcome of these future experiments, two conclusions can already be drawn from the results of our two-experimenters task. First, having two different experimenters administer the A and B trials helps prevent 9-month-old infants from perseverating in the toy-unattached task. Second, infants' initial analyses of support problems include information about not only objects and their supports but also about more global contextual features of the problems, since changes in some of these features can lead infants to categorize problems as novel.

F. SUMMARY OF FINDINGS IN SUPPORT TASKS

The results of our support tasks are easily summarized. First, infants at each age produced perseverative errors. Second, the older the infants, the more complex the task needed to be in order to elicit errors. Thus, the 7-month-old infants perseverated in the toy-attached task, the 9-month-old infants in the toy-unattached but not the toy-attached task, and the 11-month-old infants in the gap but not the toy-unattached task. Finally, infants were less likely to produce perseverative errors if different experimenters administered the A and B trials.

These results are consistent with our model of infant perseveration and suggest that as infants gain experience with support problems, they routinely encode more and more crucial features in their initial analyses of the problems. Thus, the 9- but not the 7-month-old infants in the toy-attached task encoded in their initial analysis of the problem on each trial the location of the attached toy–cloth pair. Similarly, the 11- but not the 9-month-old infants in the toy-unattached task encoded the location of the toy–cloth pair in which the toy rested on as opposed to beyond the cloth. These more detailed encodings enabled the infants to detect the location change introduced in the B trial; as a result, they correctly categorized the problem as novel and computed a new solution, thereby avoiding perseveration.

VI. Perseveration in Containment Tasks

In this section, we review experiments conducted with two containment tasks of increasing difficulty. Both tasks involved a violation-of-expectation paradigm rather than an object-manipulation paradigm. As mentioned earlier, the tasks differed maximally from memory-and-motor tasks in that infants (a) had no need to update and remember information about objects and (b) were not required to select and perform one of two alternative motor responses across trials: infants simply looked at the event they were presented on each trial. The two tasks and their results are described in turn.

A. BALL TASK: CONTAINER AND NO-CONTAINER CONDITIONS

Our first task was based on the results of an experiment by Sitskoorn and Smitsman (1995). These results, which are described in more detail later, suggested that

6- but not 4-month-old infants realize that the width of an object relative to that of a container determines whether the object can be lowered into the container. In our task, 6.5-month-old infants first received familiarization trials (A trials) followed by test trials (B trials). During the familiarization trials, the infants saw a large ball being lowered into a much wider container. During the test trials, the infants saw the same ball being lowered into two novel containers, one slightly larger (large-container event) and one considerably smaller (small-container event) than the ball (Aguiar, 1998; Aguiar & Baillargeon, 1996, 1999a). The question of interest was whether the infants would (a) detect the violation shown in the small-container event, and hence look reliably longer at this event than at the large-container event, or (b) perseverate by carrying forth the same expectation ("the ball will fit into the container") they had formed during the familiarization trials, and hence look about equally at the two test events.

A second group of 6.5-month-old infants was tested in a control condition (no-container condition) identical to the container condition, with one exception: during the familiarization trials, the wide container was absent and the ball was simply lowered to the apparatus floor. We reasoned that because these infants (a) could not form an expectation during the familiarization trials that the ball would fit into the container and hence (b) could have no such expectation to apply to the test trials, they should detect the violation in the small-container test event and hence should look reliably longer at this event than at the large-container test event.

1. Procedure

The infants in the container and no-container conditions were tested using a two-phase procedure that included a familiarization and a test phase (for brevity's sake a prefamiliarization phase involving a single trial is not described here; see Aguiar & Baillargeon, 1998, for details). During the *familiarization* phase, the infants in the container condition received three trials (see Figure 5). At the start of each trial, a large ball attached to the lower end of a rod was held directly above a very wide and shallow container, so that their widths could be visually compared. After a few seconds, a screen hid the ball and container. The ball was briefly raised above the screen and then lowered back behind the screen into the container. Finally, the screen was removed to reveal the ball resting on the bottom of the container. The infants in the no-container condition saw identical familiarization trials, except that the wide container was absent and the ball was simply lowered to the apparatus floor (see Figure 5).

During the *test* phase, the infants in the two conditions received four test trials. On alternate trials, the infants saw two test events identical to the familiarization event except that a different container was used (see Figure 6). In one event (large-container event), the container was taller and slightly wider than the ball; in the other event (small-container event), the container was taller but only half as wide as the ball. When the screen was removed, at the end of each test event, the infants saw the ball's rod protruding above the container's rim, suggesting that the ball

Container Condition

  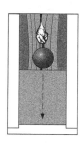 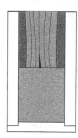 

No-container Condition

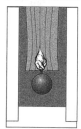  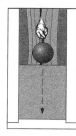 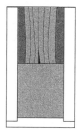 

Fig. 5. Schematic drawing of the familiarization events in the container and no-container conditions of the ball task.

was inside the container. The order of presentation of the two test events was counterbalanced across infants.

Within each familiarization and test trial, the event was repeated continuously until the trial ended. This occurred when the infant either (a) looked away from the event for 2 consecutive seconds after having looked for at least 11 cumulative seconds (the duration of one event cycle) or (b) looked at the event for 60 cumulative seconds without looking away for 2 consecutive seconds.

2. Results and Interpretations

As shown in Table II, the results of the no-container condition indicated that the infants looked reliably longer at the small- than at the large-container test event. These results suggested that the infants (a) understood that the width of the ball relative to that of each container determined whether the ball could be lowered into the container; (b) determined that the ball could fit into the large but not the small container; and hence (c) were surprised in the small-container event when the screen was removed to reveal the rod protruding from the container's rim. These results confirmed those of Sitskoorn and Smitsman (1995) and provided further evidence that, by 6.5 months of age, infants realize that an object cannot be lowered into a narrower container.

Large-container Test Event

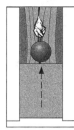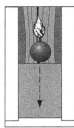

Small-container Test Event

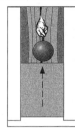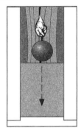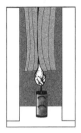

Fig. 6. Schematic drawing of the test events in the container and no-container conditions of the ball task.

In contrast to the infants in the no-container condition, those in the container condition tended to look equally at the small- and large-container test events. Consistent with our model, we believe that the infants responded as they did because (a) their initial analysis of each test event was too shallow to enable them to register the crucial change in the container's width; (b) they miscategorized each test event as similar to the event shown during the familiarization trials; and hence (c) they retrieved the expectation they had formed about the familiarization event ("the ball will fit into the container") and applied it to each test event. Because this expectation was correct for the large- but not the small-container test event, the infants failed to respond appropriately to the latter event.

Why did the infants in the container condition engage in a shallow initial analysis of each test event? In accordance with our model, we believe that the answer to this question has to do with infants' level of expertise at reasoning about the width of objects and containers in containment events. As mentioned earlier, Sitskoorn and Smitsman (1995) found that 6- but not 4-month-old infants succeeded at their task. These findings suggest that, although the 6.5-month-old infants in our task were able to reason about the width of objects and containers (recall that the infants in the no-container condition readily detected the violation in the small-

TABLE II

6.5-Month-Old Infants' Performance in the Ball Task

Condition	Equal looking times at small- and large-container events (perseverate)	Longer looking time at small- than large-container event (succeed)
	Response on test trials	
Container	×	
No-container		×
Occluder		×
Basket	×	
Reduced-opening		×

container test event), this ability was still a relatively new acquisition. One might predict that with more extensive experience at reasoning about the relative widths of objects and containers, infants come to automatically encode this information in their initial analyses of containment events, thereby avoiding perseveration. Data collected with 8.5-month-old infants using the container condition procedure (Aguiar & Baillargeon, 1999a) support this prediction: these older infants responded with prolonged looking to the small-container test event, even though they saw the ball being lowered into the wide container (rather than to the apparatus floor) during the familiarization trials.

What information did the infants in the container and no-container conditions include in their shallow initial analyses of the test events? We suspect that the no-container infants immediately noticed when watching the test events that the ball, instead of being lowered to the apparatus floor, was now being lowered into a container. This change was sufficient to lead the infants to categorize the test events as novel and consequently to pay careful attention to them as they unfolded. In contrast to the no-container infants, the container infants noted only that the test events, like the familiarization event, involved a ball being lowered into a container. Such limited information was insufficient to enable the infants to categorize and respond to the test events correctly.

B. BALL TASK: OCCLUDER AND BASKET CONDITIONS

Our speculations about the contents of the initial analyses performed by the infants in the container and no-container conditions suggest that the infants focused primarily on the *type* of event occuring in the familiarization and test trials (e.g., Baillargeon, 1995, 1998, 1999). Research on infants' acquisition of physical knowledge indicates that infants form distinct event categories (such as occlusion, containment, collision, and support events), and reason and learn separately about each event category. From this perspective, one could argue that the infants in the no-container condition succeeded (i.e., detected the violation in the small-container test event) because they saw a containment event during the test but not the familiarization trials. The infants detected this change in event category in their initial analyses of the test events, allowing them to categorize and respond to the events correctly. In contrast, the infants in the container condition, who saw a containment event during both the familiarization and test trials, were lulled by this similarity in event category to conclude that they were seeing the same event, resulting in perseverative responding.

These speculations led to two predictions. One was that if the infants were shown an occluder rather than a container during the familiarization trials, they should detect a change in event category—from occlusion to containment—during their initial analyses of the test trials. Like the infants in the no-container condition, the infants should then categorize the test events as novel and respond to them appropriately. The other prediction was that increasing the perceptual distinctiveness of the familiarization and test containers should have little effect on the infants' performance. Like the infants in the container condition, the infants should focus primarily, in their initial analyses of the test events, on the fact that these again involved a containment event, and they should respond perseveratively.

1. Procedure

To evaluate these predictions, 6.5-month-old infants were tested in two conditions (Aguiar, 1998; Aguiar & Baillargeon, 1996, 1999a). In both conditions, the infants saw the same small- and large-container test events as the infants in the container and no-container conditions. Only the familiarization event was different (see Figure 7). In one condition (occluder condition), the bottom and back of the wide familiarization container used in the container condition were removed to form a rounded occluder; the ball was simply lowered to the apparatus floor behind the occluder. This manipulation was derived from work by Hespos and Baillargeon (1999). In the second condition (basket condition), the wide familiarization container used in the container condition was replaced with a wide square wicker basket. In the container condition, the wide familiarization container differed from the test containers in height and diameter, but it resembled these containers in a number of respects: all three containers were cylindrical, were covered with a bright contact paper, were decorated with bright decals, and had their upper and lower edges outlined in black. Compared to the wide familiarization container, the basket was even more different perceptually from the test containers, since it differed from these containers in height and width as well as in shape, texture, color, and pattern.

Occluder Condition

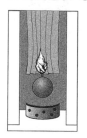 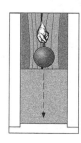 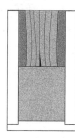  

Basket Condition

 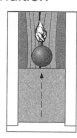 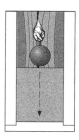  

Fig. 7. Schematic drawing of the familiarization events in the occluder and basket conditions of the ball tasks.

2. Results and Interpretations

The results of the occluder and basket conditions supported our predictions (see Table II). Like the infants in the no-container condition, those in the occluder condition looked reliably longer at the small- than at the large-container test event. Furthermore, like the infants in the container condition, those in the basket condition looked about equally at the two test events. Together, these results provide strong evidence that 6.5-month-old infants in our task focus primarily, in their initial analyses of the test events, on whether these events belong to the same or to a different category than the familiarization event. The infants in the no-container and occluder conditions, who saw events from different categories in the familiarization and test trials, succeeded at the task. In contrast, the infants in the container and basket conditions, who saw containment events in both the familiarization and test trials, did not; even salient differences in the width, height, texture, and appearance of the familiarization and test containers had no detectable effect on the infants' initial analysis and categorization of each test event.

3. Related Findings

The finding that the infants in our task were more likely to err when shown familiarization and test events of the same as opposed to different event categories may be related to adults' performance in tasks where they are asked questions with a distorted term, such as "How many animals of each kind did Moses take on the ark?" Most adult participants answer questions of this type without noticing that Noah was replaced by Moses (e.g., Erickson & Mattson, 1981; Reder & Kusbit, 1991). Reder and Kusbit (1991) argued that participants fail to notice this distortion because they make an incomplete match between the representation of the question and their previously stored proposition that contains the answer. However, adults readily pick up the distortion if, for instance, Nixon replaces Noah (Erickson & Mattson, 1981). According to Reder and Kusbit, this result occurs because the participants' partial match process is sensitive to the level of conceptual similarity between the words in the distorted question and the participants' previously stored representation of the answer. Participants overlook substitutions such as Moses for Noah because the two words invoke similar concepts (i.e., Moses and Noah are both biblical characters of the old Testament), but they detect substitutions such as Nixon for Noah because the two words invoke very different concepts.

C. BALL TASK: REDUCED-OPENING CONDITION

We have argued that the infants in the container and basket conditions responded perseveratively to the small- and large-container test events because their initial analyses of these events (a) indicated that they were again containment events and (b) included no information about the relative widths of the ball and container in each event. Could infants be *induced* to include such crucial information in their initial analyses of the test events? The last condition of our ball task was designed to address this question (Aguiar, 1998; Aguiar & Baillargeon, 1996, 1999a).

This condition was based on the intuition that because the wide container used in the container condition familiarization trials was markedly larger than the ball, even a cursory comparison of the widths of the ball and container was sufficient for the infants to ascertain that the one could easily fit into the other. We hypothesized that a task that required the infants to attend more closely to the widths of the ball and container during the familiarization trials might induce them to do the same in the test trials, resulting in a better performance.

1. Procedure

To test this hypothesis, 6.5-month-old infants were tested in a condition (reduced-opening condition) identical to the container condition, with one exception: during the familiarization trials, a cover with a central opening was placed on the wide container (see Figure 8). The cover reduced the opening of the container, so that the ball now fit snugly into the container. We reasoned that the infants would now need to attend more closely to the widths of the ball and container to determine whether the one could indeed be lowered into the other. This more careful

Reduced-opening Condition

 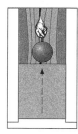  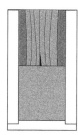 

Fig. 8. Schematic drawing of the familiarization event in the reduced-opening condition of the ball task.

comparison might induce the infants to attend similarly to the relative widths of the ball and container during their initial analyses of the test events, resulting in successful performances.

2. Results and Interpretations

The results confirmed our hypothesis: after receiving familiarization trials in which the opening of the wide container was reduced, the infants looked reliably longer at the small- than at the large-container test event (see Table II).

Together, the results of the container and reduced-opening conditions suggest that although the infants did not spontaneously include information about the relative widths of the ball and container in their initial analyses of the test events (container condition), they could be induced to do so if they were given familiarization trials requiring a careful rather than a cursory comparison of the widths of the ball and container (reduced-opening condition). Such trials apparently had the effect of increasing the salience of this comparison process for the infants, making them more likely to include appropriate information about the relative widths of the ball and container in their initial analyses of the test events.

3. Implications for the Results of the No-Container and Occluder Conditions

The results of the reduced-opening condition may also have implications for the results of the no-container and occluder conditions. One might ask why the infants in these conditions did not begin to respond perseveratively across the test trials. That the infants who saw the small-container test event first did not perseverate is not surprising because this event violated their expectations about containment events; this outcome no doubt motivated the infants to pay careful attention to each subsequent event to determine whether it, too, would violate their expectations. However, what of the infants who saw the large-container test event first? Why did these infants not respond perseveratively on the remaining test trials, looking equally at the large- and small-container events?

At least two possibilities come to mind. The first is that infants are unlikely to perseverate if a change is introduced after a single trial: recall that the infants would have seen the large container in the first test trial and the small container in the second one. In the conditions in which perseveration was observed, the infants saw the same object and container (wide container, basket) on three successive familiarization trials prior to the test trials. Although this explanation may seem plausible, pilot data suggest that it is unlikely. These data were obtained in a condition identical to the container condition except that the wide container was introduced only in the *last* familiarization trial; during the first two familiarization trials the ball was simply lowered to the apparatus floor, as in the no-container condition. Despite the fact that the wide container was present for a single trial, the infants still responded perseveratively in the test trials, looking equally at the small- and large-container test events.

A second explanation is that the infants in the no-container and occluder conditions who saw the large-container test event first were in the same position as the infants in the reduced-opening condition: because the ball and large container were very similar in width, the infants had to compare them carefully to determine whether containment was possible. This process in turn increased the likelihood that the infants would include information about the width of the container in their initial analysis of the small-container event, thereby ensuring a successful performance.

The findings discussed in this section are generally consistent with evidence from the literature on adults' skill acquisition that initial training trials influence the kinds of strategies and computations adults use on later trials when processing novel stimuli (e.g., Doane, Alderton, Sohn, & Pellegrino, 1996; Kerr & Booth, 1978; Medin & Bettiger, 1994; Pellegrino, Doane, Fischer, & Alderton, 1991; Schmidt & Bjork, 1992). For example, in a visual discrimination task (e.g., Doane et al., 1996), adults were found to be significantly better at judging whether two random polygon stimuli were similar or different if they were initially trained on pairs of polygons that were highly similar and thus required a precise comparison strategy, as opposed to pairs that were highly dissimilar and thus could be judged by means of a more global comparison strategy.

D. PRIOR EVIDENCE OBTAINED WITH A DIFFERENT CONTAINMENT TASK

It might be objected that our interpretation of the results of the container and basket conditions is inconsistent with the results of Sitskoorn and Smitsman (1995). The 6-month-old infants in their experiment were habituated to two events presented on alternate trials. In both events, a block was repeatedly lowered into and lifted from a box with an opening at the top; one event involved a small block and a box with a small opening, and the other event involved a large block and a box with a large opening. Following habituation, the block and box pairs were rearranged, and the infants saw two test events. In one (large-opening event), the *small* block was lowered into the box with the *large* opening. In the other event (small-opening event), the *large* block was lowered into the box with the *small* opening (the box's side rims were partly collapsible). The results indicated that the infants looked reliably longer at the small- than at the large-opening event. From the perspective of the interpretation proposed in the previous sections, these results are puzzling. Why did the infants not perseverate during the test trials and look equally at the test events they were shown, like the infants in our container and basket conditions? Why did the infants perform instead like the infants in our no-container, occluder, and reduced-opening conditions?

One possible explanation for the discrepancy between our results and those of Sitskoorn and Smitsman (1995) is that these authors changed *both* the object and the container on alternate habituation and test trials. In our task, in contrast, the object—the ball—remained the same throughout the experimental session; only the container was changed. It seems plausible that, when observing containment events in which an object is lowered into a container, infants have a natural bias to attend more to the (moving) object than to the (stationary) container. Such a bias could lead infants to include some information about the features (e.g., width) of the object in their initial analysis of the event on each trial. A change in the object's features would thus be likely to be noticed, and to lead to a correct categorization of the event as novel.

These speculations suggest that 6.5-month-old infants might be less likely to perseverate if tested in a task in which the object rather than the container was changed across trials. For example, infants might see events involving a medium-size container and a small ball (familiarization event), medium ball (medium-ball test event), or large ball (large-ball test event).

E. BALL TASK: RESULTS WITH 7.5-MONTH-OLD INFANTS

We reported earlier that 6.5-month-old infants perseverated in the container condition of our ball task, but that 8.5-month-old infants did not (Aguiar, 1998; Aguiar & Baillargeon, 1996, 1999a). In an additional experiment, we tested 7.5-month-old infants in the same condition (Aguiar & Baillargeon, 1999c). Like the 6.5-month-old infants, these older infants tended to look equally at the small- and large-container test events (see Table III), suggesting that (a) their initial analysis of each test event was too shallow to enable them to detect the change in the container's width; as a result (b) they miscategorized each test event as similar to the familiarization event; and thus (c) they retrieved the expectation they had formed about this event ("the ball will fit into the container") and applied it to each test event.

In our experiments with 6.5-month-old infants, we found that there were at least two ways of preventing perseverative responding in these infants. One way was to

TABLE III

6.5-, 7.5-, and 8.5-Month-Old Infants' Performance in the Ball and Quantitative-Ball Tasks

	Response on test trials	
Condition	Equal looking times at small- and large-container events (perseverate)	Longer looking time at small- than at large-container event (succeed)
Ball task		
Container		
6.5	×	
7.5	×	
8.5		×
No container		
6.5		×
7.5		×
Reduced-opening		
6.5		×
7.5	×	
Quantitative-ball Task		
Container		
6.5		×
7.5	×	
8.5		×

show the infants events from different event categories in the familiarization and test trials (no-container and occluder conditions); we suggested that this change in event category was noted by the infants in their initial analyses of the test events, leading to correct categorization and responding. The other way was to show the infants a familiarization event that required them to perform a more careful comparison of the widths of the ball and container (reduced-opening condition); we speculated that this experience made the width-comparison process more salient for the infants and as a result induced them to include information about the widths of the ball and container in their initial analysis of each test event.

Would the same manipulations also be effective in preventing perseverative responding in 7.5-month-old infants? To find out, we tested two additional groups of infants, one with the no-container and one with the reduced-opening procedure (see Table III). The results of the no-container condition were similar to those we had obtained with the 6.5-month-old infants: the infants looked reliably longer at the small- than at the large-container test event, suggesting that they detected the violation in the small-container test event. The results of the reduced-opening condition, however, were different from those we had obtained with the 6.5-month-old infants. Like the 7.5-month-old infants in the container condition, those in the reduced-opening condition tended to look equally at the small- and large-container test events.

Why was the reduced-opening manipulation not effective in preventing perseveration in the 7.5-month-old infants? We suspect that because these infants were somewhat more experienced than the 6.5-month-old infants at reasoning about width in containment tasks, they were easily able to determine that the ball would fit into the container, even when its opening was reduced. Hence, the manipulation did not succeed in making the width comparison process more salient for the infants and thus inducing them to include width information in their initial analyses of the test events.

F. QUANTITATIVE-BALL TASK

Our second containment task (Aguiar & Baillargeon, 1999a, 1999c) was similar to the container condition of the ball task with one exception: during the test events, the ball and container were shown successively, rather than simultaneously, so that their widths could not be visually compared (during the familiarization event, the widths of the ball and wide container could be visually compared at the end of each event cycle when the screen was removed to reveal the ball resting inside the wide container; see Figures 9 and 10). Thus, as in the ball task, infants had to compare the width of the ball to that of each test container to detect the violation in the small-container test event. The present task differed from the ball task, however, in that infants had to encode and remember the width of the ball in order to compare it to that of each test container.

Our label for the present task—the quantitative-ball task—is derived from the distinction drawn in computational models of everyday physical reasoning between quantitative and qualitative reasoning strategies (e.g., Forbus, 1984). A strategy is said to be *quantitative* if it requires subjects to encode and use information about absolute quantities (e.g., object A is "this" wide, where "this" stands for some absolute measure of A's width). In contrast, a strategy is said to be *qualitative* if it requires subjects to encode and use information about only relative quantities (e.g., object A is wider than object B). The ball task could be solved by means of a qualitative strategy: infants could visually compare the widths of the ball and container at the start of each test event when the ball was held above the container. The present task, however, could be solved only by means of a quantitative strategy: infants had to encode and remember the width of the ball to determine whether it could fit into each test container.

1. Procedure

Participants were 6.5- and 7.5-month-old infants. The procedure was similar to that of the container condition of the ball task, except that the familiarization and

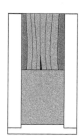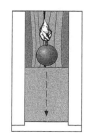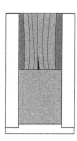

Fig. 9. Schematic drawing of the familiarization event in the quantitative-ball task.

test events were modified so that the ball was no longer held above the container. At the start of each trial, only the container was present, resting on the apparatus floor. After a few seconds, the container was hidden by the screen, and the ball was introduced into the apparatus, above the screen. Next, the ball was lowered behind the screen into the container. As in the ball task, the screen was then removed to reveal either the ball resting inside the wide container (familiarization event), or the ball's rod protruding above the small or large container (test events).

Large-container Event

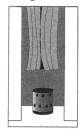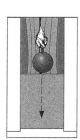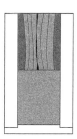

Small-container Event

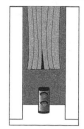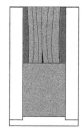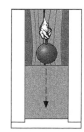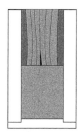

Fig. 10. Schematic drawing of the test events in the quantitative-ball task.

2. Results and Interpretations

As shown in Table III, the 6.5-month-old infants looked reliably longer at the small- than at the large-container test event, whereas the 7.5-month-old infants tended to look equally at the two events. The results of the quantitative-ball task thus mirrored those obtained with the 6.5- and 7.5-month-old infants in the reduced-opening condition of the ball task. We believe that this similarity is not accidental but instead reflects the fact that similar factors were at work in the two tasks.

Let us first consider the 6.5-month-old infants. We argued earlier that reducing the opening of the wide container in the familiarization event forced the infants to attend more closely to the widths of the ball and container; this experience made the width comparison process more salient for the infants and induced them to include information about the widths of the ball and container in their initial analyses of the test events. We suspect that, in the quantitative-ball task, having to remember the ball's width in the familiarization event again had the effect of making more salient for the infants the width comparison process; as a result, the infants were more likely to attend to the widths of the ball and container in their initial analyses of the test events.

Let us now turn to the 7.5-month-old infants. We suspect that these infants perseverated in both the reduced-opening condition of the ball task and the quantitative-ball task for the same reason: they were somewhat more experienced than the 6.5-month-old infants at comparing the widths of objects and containers. For these more experienced infants, reducing the opening of the wide container or showing the ball and wide container successively did not make the process of comparing the widths of the ball and container noticeably more effortful or salient. Consequently, the infants were not induced by these manipulations to attend to the widths of the ball and container in their initial analyses of the test events. In future experiments, we plan to explore whether more challenging manipulations (e.g., combining the manipulations used here in a reduced-opening quantitative-ball task) might prove effective in taxing the limits of 7.5-month-old infants' reasoning and thus in preventing them from responding perseveratively.

In another experiment (Aguiar & Baillargeon, 1998), we tested 8.5-month-old infants in the quantitative-ball task. The infants looked reliably longer at the small- than at the large-container test event, suggesting that they detected the violation in the small-container test event (see Table III). Presumably, these older infants were sufficiently experienced at reasoning about width in (either qualitative or quantitative) containment tasks that they automatically encoded information about the widths of the ball and container in their initial analyses of the test events.

Put together, the results obtained with the 6.5-, 7.5-, and 8.5-month-old infants in the quantitative-ball task form a rather unusual developmental pattern (see Table III): the 6.5- and 8.5-month-old infants succeeded at the task, but the 7.5-month-old infants did not. As should be clear from the preceding discussion, however, we believe that the 6.5- and 8.5-month-old infants were successful for somewhat different reasons. The older infants were at the stage where they routinely encoded information about the widths of objects and containers in their initial analyses of containment events. In contrast, the young infants were merely induced to encode width information in their initial analyses of the small- and large-container test events, because the challenge of having to remember the ball's width made the width-comparison process more salient for them. The 7.5-month-old infants were not so induced, presumably because having to remember the ball's width to compare it to that of the container posed little difficulty for them.

G. SUMMARY OF FINDINGS IN CONTAINMENT TASKS

The results of our containment tasks can be summarized as follows. First, both 6.5- and 7.5-month-old infants responded perseveratively to the ball task test events in some conditions, carrying forth—inappropriately in the context of the small-container test event—the expectation they had formed about the familiarization event. Second, infants responded perseveratively to the ball task test events if they saw containment events during both the familiarization and test trials, but not if they saw events from another event category during the familiarization trials. The 6.5-month-old infants failed to detect the violation in the small-container test event (a) when the ball was lowered into the wide container or basket during familiarization, but not (b) when the ball was lowered to the apparatus floor or behind the occluder. Similarly, the 7.5-month-old infants tended to look equally at the small- and large-container test events (a) when the ball was lowered into the wide container during familiarization, but not (b) when the ball was lowered to the apparatus floor. Third, the 6.5-month-old infants did not perseverate, even when shown containment events in both familiarization and test, if the familiarization event was modified so that comparing the widths of the ball and container required greater attention or effort from the infants. Two modifications proved effective in this respect: one was reducing the opening of the wide container, and the other was showing the container and ball successively. Fourth, the 7.5-month-old infants did not benefit from either of these modifications, presumably because they were not sufficiently taxing to require significantly more attention or effort from these older and somewhat more experienced infants.

The results of our containment tasks are consistent with those of our support tasks (described in section V). Together, these two sets of results point to four main conclusions. First, infants aged 6.5 to 11 months produce perseverative errors in nonmemory-and-motor tasks. Second, with experience, infants include more and more crucial information in their initial analyses of problems, and as a result are less likely to perseverate at tasks that depend on more detailed encodings (e.g., 7-month-old infants perseverated in the toy-attached task, but 9-month-old infants did not, and 7.5-month-old infants perseverated in the quantitative-ball task but

8.5-month-old infants did not). Third, novice infants can be induced to include in their initial analyses of problems crucial features they do not yet routinely encode, by being given in the familiarization or A trials more taxing problems that require greater attention or effort in the processing of these features (e.g., 6.5-month-old infants perseverated in the container but not the reduced-opening condition of the ball task). Finally, novice infants are also less likely to perseverate if some of the changes introduced in the test or B trials involve features infants do spontaneously attend to in their initial analyses of the trials (e.g., 9-month-old infants persever-ated in the toy-unattached but not the two-experimenters-toy-unattached task, and 6.5-month-old infants perseverated in the container and basket but not the no-con-tainer and occluder conditions of the ball task).

These results provide strong support for our model of infant perseveration. In the future, we plan to expand our model in several directions. First, we will seek to confirm our results using new object-manipulation and violation-of-expectation tasks. Second, we will continue our attempts to specify what information infants do and do not include in their initial analyses of problems and events, and how this information is affected by changes in task context and experience. Finally, we plan to explore how our model can be elaborated to account for the perseverative errors that have been observed in memory-and-motor tasks. This last issue is discussed in more detail in the next section.

VII. Revisiting Infant Perseveration in
Memory-and-Motor Tasks

As we discussed in section II, most of the research on infant perseveration has tended to be focused on memory-and-motor tasks—tasks such as Piaget's (1954) two-location search task that require infants (a) to update and remember informa-tion about objects and (b) to use this information to select one of two alternative motor responses. We also mentioned that, in keeping with the particular require-ments of memory-and-motor tasks, accounts of perseveration in these tasks typi-cally refer to limitations in (a) infants' ability to update and maintain information in working memory across trials and/or (b) infants' ability to use this information to select a novel motor response over a previously successful but no longer ap-propriate response.

Such accounts could not easily explain the findings of the support and contain-ment tasks reported in this chapter. In the support tasks, infants perseverated even though they were not required to update and remember information about objects: the toys and cloths all lay visible before them. In the containment tasks, infants again perseverated even though these tasks differed maximally from memory-and-motor tasks. First, infants were not required to produce one of two alternative mo-tor responses—they simply looked at the event before them. Second, infants were not required to update and remember information about objects. What changed in the test trials was the width of the containers, which were always plainly visible; although the ball was not visible after it was lowered into the test containers, it remained the same throughout the experiment. Thus, infants had no need to update and remember information to respond appropriately to the test events.

A. COULD OUR MODEL BE EXTENDED TO MEMORY-AND-MOTOR TASKS?

If current accounts of perseveration in memory-and-motor tasks cannot readily be extended to explain perseveration in nonmemory-and-motor tasks, could the reverse be true? Could our account of perseveration in nonmemory-and-motor tasks be elaborated to explain infants' perseverative errors in memory-and-motor tasks?

The memory-and-motor task literature (reviewed in section II) indicates that *novice* infants who have just begun to search for hidden objects typically perseverate with delays of 0 to 1 s, whereas more *expert* infants who have been able to search for longer periods of time err only with longer delays. For ease of description, we will refer to tasks with delays of 0 to 1 s as immediate-search tasks, and to tasks with longer delays as delayed-search tasks.

1. Immediate-Search Tasks

Our model can readily account for the perseverative errors of novice infants in immediate-search tasks. Specifically, we would argue that (a) infants' initial analysis of the problem on B trials is too shallow to enable them to register the change in the hiding location of the toy; (b) infants consequently miscategorize the problem as similar to that on the preceding A trials; and hence (c) infants retrieve their prior solution, leading to perseverative errors. On this account, novices' perseverative errors in immediate-search tasks are thus analogous to the perseverative errors we found in our support and containment tasks.

2. Delayed-Search Tasks

However, our model cannot as easily explain the perseverative errors of infants who are more expert at searching for hidden objects in delayed-search tasks. The fact that these infants perseverate only with a delay suggests that they do initially encode the change introduced in the B trials, but lose access to this information over time. In addition, the fact that longer delays are necessary with age to elicit errors suggests that older or more expert infants can retain information about the hiding location of an object for longer intervals. How could our model be elaborated to explain these effects?

Findings from the literature on the development of self-produced locomotion and its impact on spatial cognition (e.g., Acredolo, 1985, 1990; Acredolo, Adams, & Goodwyn, 1984; Bai & Bertenthal, 1992; Bertenthal, Campos, & Barrett, 1984;

Bremner, 1985; Horobin & Acredolo, 1986; Kermoian & Campos, 1988) suggest the following hypothesis. As infants learn to move independently about their environment, they develop more effective ways of encoding information about the locations of desired objects. This improved encoding not only helps infants remember the locations that objects occupy, but also helps them remember these locations for longer intervals. Such memory developments would be highly beneficial. For example, a standing infant, who sees a forbidden yet highly attractive remote-control device across a room on one end of a couch, might drop down to the floor (thus losing sight of the device) and crawl around an armchair and coffee table to reach the device. Being able to remember the precise location of the device long enough to reach it would present obvious advantages for the infant.

3. Changes in Infants' Encoding of Location Information

What changes in infants' encoding of location information might result in their improved memory performance in search tasks? Several possibilities exist, all of which might hold true. For example, one possibility is that when infants form the goal of retrieving an object, they learn to link or bind more tightly in memory the description of the goal object to information about its current location (for a discussion of binding processes in memory, see Cohen & Eichenbaum, 1993). Under these conditions, calling the goal object to mind would thus simultaneously remind infants of its location (e.g., as infants, after being momentarily distracted, set course once again for the remote-control device).

Results from the adult problem-solving literature provide some support for this possibility (e.g., Chase & Simon, 1973): when faced with a problem, chess and physics experts typically interconnect crucial features to form a large cohesive cluster in memory, whereas novices tend to keep crucial features in small separate units. One would expect that the links experts establish among the crucial features of a problem make them more accessible in memory and allow experts to recall more of the features, even after a delay, when computing the problem's solution.

Another possible change in infants' encoding of location information is that the encoding becomes more elaborate with increasing locomotor experience. A more detailed encoding of an object's location would result in a stronger memory trace, allowing the information to remain accessible in memory for a longer period of time (see, e.g., Stein, Littlefield, Bransford, & Persampieri, 1984, for a discussion on the effects of elaboration on memory).

The spatial orientation literature provides evidence that is consistent with this possibility. Bertenthal et al. (1984) conducted an experiment in which 8-month-old infants with or without locomotor experience sat at a table in a small room with a window on either side; one of the windows was unremarkable in appearance ("plain window"), but the other was surrounded by bright stripes and flashing lights that served as a salient landmark for the window ("landmark window"). To start, the infants were trained to orient to the landmark window at the sound of a buzzer; after a short delay, an experimenter appeared at the window and talked to the infants. Following training, the infants were wheeled to the opposite side of the table. The question of interest was whether, at the sound of the buzzer, the infants would turn in the same direction as before (to what was now the plain window), or would turn in the opposite direction toward the landmark window. The results indicated that the infants with locomotor experience turned toward the landmark window on the majority of the trials, whereas the prelocomotor infants were about equally likely to turn toward the landmark or the plain window. The authors concluded that the development of self-produced locomotion leads to more consistent use of landmark information. Such a conclusion supports the notion proposed above that with self-produced locomotion comes a more detailed and extensive encoding of location information.

Infants' encoding of location information might improve in yet other ways. Horobin and Acredolo (1986) tested infants aged 8 to 10 months in a delayed-search task and found that the infants with more experience at self-locomotion were more likely to maintain visual fixation on the hiding place of the object during the delay and hence were more likely to succeed at finding the object (see also Acredolo et al., 1984; Bai & Bertenthal, 1992). To be sure, most researchers who use memory-and-motor tasks today do not allow infants to use this simple strategy to keep track of the hiding place of the object (see section II). Nevertheless, the results of Horobin and Acredolo, like those of Bertenthal et al. (1984), support the point that with the development of self-produced locomotion, infants develop new and more effective ways of keeping track of the locations of objects. Maintaining visual fixation and referring to landmarks are two such ways; no doubt others remain to be discovered.

B. ELABORATING OUR MODEL

According to our model of perseveration in nonmemory-and-motor tasks such as our support and containment tasks, infants perseverate on B trials because their initial analysis of the problem is too shallow to enable them to detect the crucial change introduced; as a result, infants miscategorize the problem as being similar to that on the preceding A trials and retrieve their previous solution, leading to a perseverative error. Our discussion of infant's perseverative errors in memory-and-motor tasks such as delayed-search tasks suggests another, slightly different path to perseveration. Specifically, infants in these tasks notice in their initial analysis of the problem on B trials that the object has been hidden in a new location, but this location information decays rapidly during the delay imposed before infants are allowed to search. At the end of the delay, infants return to the contents of their initial analysis. However, because these contents are degraded and no longer include information about the new hiding location of the object, infants conclude—based on the remaining contents of their initial analysis—that they are again faced with the same problem as in the preceding A trials; infants thus retrieve their previous solution, leading to a perseverative response.

Another assumption of our model of perseveration in nonmemory-and-motor tasks is that infants' initial analysis of a problem tends to be shallow when they are novices at the task. As they become expert, infants come to automatically encode more and more of the crucial features of the problem in their initial analysis; as a result, they are more likely to detect changes in these features and to respond to them appropriately. Our discussion of infants' perseveration in delayed-search tasks suggests that, here again, expertise plays a crucial role. We proposed that, as infants become skilled at self-produced locomotion, they learn to encode location information in more and more effective ways. As a result, infants are able to retain information about the hiding location of the object in their initial analysis of the problem on B trials for longer and longer delays.

Our analysis of memory-and-motor tasks does not even begin to deal with the vast literature on these tasks, nor does it make clear how the many variations that have been shown to increase or decrease perseverative responding in these tasks have their effects. Such an extensive analysis is clearly beyond the scope of this chapter. All we meant to accomplish here was to show one way our model of perseveration in nonmemory-and-motor tasks could be extended to account for perseveration in memory-and-motor tasks. Experiments are planned to test this new account and to ascertain how well it compares to existing accounts.

VIII. Concluding Remarks

We have presented a model of infant perseveration in nonmemory-and-motor tasks, reviewed evidence from support and containment tasks that supports this model, and finally examined how our model could be extended to account for infant perseveration in more traditional memory-and-motor tasks, such as delayed-search tasks. Although obviously preliminary and in need of greater elaboration and refinement, we believe that the approach proposed here nevertheless holds great promise. First, it helps place infant perseveration in the broader context of human problem solving, and brings to light striking continuities in infants' and adults' responses to repeated events and problems. Second, it makes clear that a full account of infants' responses to events and problems will require detailed analyses of (a) the contents of infants' representations in specific task situations and (b) the changes that take place in these representations as infants acquire expertise at the tasks.

ACKNOWLEDGMENTS

This research was supported by a grant from CAPES-Brasilia/Brasil (BEX-2688) to the first author and by a grant from the National Institute of Child Health and Human Development (HD-21104) to the second author. We would like to thank Dov Cohen, and Judy DeLoache for helpful comments and Rebecca Bloch, Deepa Block, Laura Brueckner, Beth Cullum, Susan Hespos, Laura Glaser, Lisa Kaufman, Marsha Keeler, Valerie Kolstad, Laura Kotovsky, Melsie Minna, Helen Raschke, April Rives, Teresa Wilcox, and the undergraduate assistants at the Infant Cognition Laboratory at the University of Illinois for their help with the data collection. We would also like to thank the parents who kindly agreed to have their infants participate in the research.

REFERENCES

Acredolo, L. P. (1985). Coordinating perspectives on infants spatial orientation. In R. Cohen (Ed.), *The development of spatial cognition* (pp. 115–140). Hillsdale, NJ: Erlbaum.

Acredolo, L. P. (1990). Individual differences in infant spatial displacement. In J. Colombo & J. Fagen (Eds.), *Individual differences in infancy: Reliability, stability, prediction* (pp. 321–340). Hillsdale, NJ: Erlbaum.

Acredolo, L. P, Adams, A., & Goodwyn, S. W. (1984). The role of self-produced movement and visual tracking in infant spatial orientation. *Journal of Experimental Child Psychology, 38,* 312–327.

Acredolo, L. P., & Evans, D. (1980). Developmental changes in the effects of landmarks on infants spatial behavior. *Developmental Psychology, 16,* 312–318.

Aguiar, A. (1997, May). *Infants' problem solving: 6.5-month-olds' performance in a means-end support task.* Paper presented at the meeting of the Midwestern Psychological Association, Chicago, IL.

Aguiar, A. (1998, April). *Perseverative errors in action and non-action tasks: Implications for a model of problem solving in infancy.* Paper presented at the International Conference on Infant Studies, Atlanta, GA.

Aguiar, A., & Baillargeon, R. (1996, April). *6.5-month-olds' reasoning about containment events.* Paper presented at the International Conference on Infant Studies, Providence, RI.

Aguiar, A., & Baillargeon, R. (1998). 8.5-month-old infants' reasoning about containment events. *Child Development, 69,* 636–653.

Aguiar, A., & Baillargeon, R. (1999a). *Evidence of perseveration in a violation-of-expectation task: 6.5-month-old infants' reasoning about containment events.* Manuscript submitted for publication.

Aguiar, A., & Baillargeon, R. (1999b). *Infants' performance in means-ends support tasks: Is recall memory a key factor in bringing about perseverative errors?* Manuscript in preparation.

Aguiar, A., & Baillargeon, R. (1999c). *New evidence of perseveration in a violation-of-expectation task: 7.5-month-old infants' reasoning about containment events.* Manuscript in preparation.

Aguiar, A., Rives, A., & Baillargeon, R. (1997, April). *Young infants' problem solving in means-end support sequences.* Paper presented at the meeting of the Society for Research in Child Development, Washington, DC.

Ahmed, A., & Ruffman, T. (1998). Why do infants make A-not-B errors in a search task, yet show memory for the location of hidden objects in a non-search task? Developmental Psychology, 34, 441–453.

Anderson, J. R. (1987). Skill acquisition: Compilation of weak-method problem solutions. *Psychological Review, 94,* 192–210.

Bai, D. L, & Bertenthal, B. I. (1992). Locomotor experience and the development of spatial search skills. *Child Development, 63,* 215–226.

Baillargeon, R. (1993). The object concept revisited: New directions in the investigation of infants' physical knowledge. In C. E. Granrud (Ed.), *Visual perception and cognition in infancy* (pp. 265–315). Hillsdale, NJ: Erlbaum.

Baillargeon, R. (1995). A model of physical reasoning in infancy. In C. K. Rovee-Collier & L. P. Lipsitt (Eds.), *Advances in infancy research* (Vol. 9, pp. 305–371). Norwood, NJ: Ablex.

Baillargeon, R. (1998). Infants' understanding of the physical world. In M. Sabourin, F. I. M. Craik, & M. Robert (Eds.), *Advances in psychological science* (Vol. 2, pp. 503–529). London: Psychology Press.

Baillargeon, R. (1999). Young infants' expectations about hidden objects: A reply to three challenges. *Developmental Science*.

Bertenthal, B. I., Campos, J. J., & Barrett, K. C. (1984). Self-produced locomotion: An organizer of emotional, cognitive, and social development in infancy. In R. N. Emde & R. J. Harmon (Eds.), *Continuities and discontinuities in development* (pp. 175–210). New York: Plenum.

Bremner, J. G. (1985). Object tracking and search in infancy: A review of data and a theoretical evaluation. *Developmental Review, 5,* 371–396.

Chase, W. G., & Simon, H. A. (1973). Perception in chess. *Cognitive Psychology, 4,* 55–81.

Cheng, P. W. (1985). Restructuring versus automaticity: Alternative accounts of skill acquisition. *Psychological Review, 92,* 414–423.

Chi, M. T. H., Feltovich, P. J., & Glaser, R. (1981). Categorization and representation of physics problems by experts and novices. *Cognitive Science, 5,* 121–152.

Cohen, N. J., & Eichenbaum, H. (1993). *Memory, amnesia, and the hypocampal system.* Cambridge, MA: MIT Press.

Diamond, A. (1985). Development of the ability to use recall to guide action, as indicated by infants' performance in AB. *Child Development, 56,* 868–883.

Diamond, A. (1991). Neuropsychological insights into the meaning of object concept development. In S. Carey & R. Gelman (Eds.), *The epigenesis of mind* (pp. 67–110). Hillsdale, NJ: Erlbaum.

Diedrich, F. J., Thelen, E., Corbetta, D., & Smith, L. B. (1998). *Perseverative errors in infancy as a window on dynamic perception-action memories.* Manuscript submitted for publication.

Doane, S. M., Alderton, D. L., Sohn, Y. W., & Pellegrino, J. W. (1996). Acquisition and transfer of skilled performance: Are visual discrimination skills stimulus specific? *Journal of Experimental Psychology: Human Perception and Performance, 22,* 1218–1248.

Erickson, T. A., & Mattson, M. E. (1981). From words to meaning: A semantic illusion. *Journal of Verbal Learning and Verbal Behavior, 20,* 540–552.

Ericsson, K. A., & Charness, N. (1994). Expert performance: Its structure and acquisition. *American Psychologist, 49,* 725–747.

Forbus, K. D. (1984). Qualitative Process Theory. *Artificial Intelligence, 24,* 85–168.

Harris, P. L. (1987). The development of search. In P. Salapatek & L. B. Cohen (Eds.), *Handbook of infant perception* (Vol. 2, pp. 155–207). Orlando, FL: Academic Press.

Hespos, S. J., & Baillargeon, R. (1999). *Infants' reasoning about height in occlusion and containment events: A surprising discrepancy.* Manuscript submitted for publication.

Hofstadter, M., & Reznick, J. S. (1996). Response modality affects human infant delayed-response performance. *Child Development, 67,* 646–658.

Horobin, K. M., & Acredolo, L. P. (1986). The role of attentiveness, mobility history, and separation of hiding sites on stage IV search behavior. *Journal of Experimental Child Psychology, 41,* 114–127.

Johnson, K. E., & Mervis, C. B. (1994). Microgenetic analysis of first steps in children's acquisition of expertise in shorebirds. *Developmental Psychology, 30,* 418–435.

Kermoian, R., & Campos, J. J. (1988). Locomotor experience: A facilitator of spatial cognitive development. *Child Development, 59,* 908–917.

Kerr, R., & Booth, B. (1978). Specific and varied practice of a motor skill. *Perceptual and Motor Skills, 46,* 395–401.

Kolstad, V., & Aguiar, A. (1995, March). *Means-end sequences in young infants.* Paper presented at the meeting of the Society of Research in Child Development, Indianapolis, IN.

Lockman, J. J., & Pick, H. L. (1984). Problems of scale in spatial development. In C. Sophian (Ed.), *Origins of cognitive skills* (pp. 3–26). Hillsdale, NJ: Erlbaum.

Logan, G. D. (1988). Toward an instance theory of automatization. *Psychological Review, 95,* 492–527.

Luchins, A. S. (1942). Mechanization in problem solving: The effect of Einstellung. *Psychological Monographs, 54*(6, Serial No. 248).

Luchins, A. S. (1946). Classroom experiments on mental set. *Journal of American Psychology, 59,* 295–298.

Luchins, A. S., & Luchins, E. H. (1950). New experimental attempts at preventing mechanization in problem solving. *Journal of General Psychology, 42,* 279–297.

Mackenzie, B. E., & Bigelow, E. (1986). Detour behavior in young human infants. *British Journal of Developmental Psychology, 4,* 139–148.

Marcovitch, S., & Zelazo, P. D. (in press). The A-not-B errors: Results from a logistic meta-analysis. *Child Development.*

Matthews, A., Ellis, A. E., & Nelson, C. A. (1996). Development of preterm and full-term infant ability on AB, recall memory, transparent barrier detour, and means-end tasks. *Child Development, 67,* 2658–2676.

Medin, D. L., & Bettiger, J. G. (1994). Presentation order and recognition of categorically related examples. *Psychonomic Bulletin and Review, 95,* 492–527.

Munakata, Y. (1998). Infant perseveration and implications for object permanence theories: A PDP model of the AB task. *Developmental Science, 2,* 161–184.

Murthy, V. N., & Fetz, E. E. (1992). Coherent 25- to 35-Hz oscillations in the sensorimotor cortex of awake behaving monkeys. *Proceedings of the National Academy of Sciences U.S.A., 89,* 5670–5674.

Pellegrino, J. W., Doane, S. M., Fisher, S. C., & Alderton, D. (1991). Stimulus complexity effects in visual comparisons: The effects of practice and learning context. *Journal of Experimental Psychology: Human Perception and Performance, 17,* 781–791.

Piaget, J. (1952). *The origins of intelligence in childhood.* New York: International Universities Press.

Piaget, J. (1954). *The construction of reality in the child.* New York: Basic Books.

Posner, M. I., & Raichle, M. E. (1994). *Images of mind.* New York: Scientific American Library.

Reder, L. M., & Kusbit, G. W. (1991). Locus of the Moses illusion: Imperfect encoding, retrieval, or match? *Journal of Memory and Language, 30,* 385–406.

Reimann, P., & Chi, M. T. H. (1989). Human expertise. In K. J. Gilhooly (Ed.), *Human and machine problem solving* (pp. 161–191). New York: Plenum.

Rieser, J. J., Doxsey, P. A., McCarrell, N. J., & Brooks, P. H. (1982). Wayfinding and toddlers' use of information from an aerial view of a maze. *Developmental Psychology, 18,* 714–720.

Schmidt, R. A., & Bjork, R. A. (1992). New conceptualizations of practice: Common principles in three paradigms suggest new concepts for training. *Psychological Science, 3,* 207–217.

Sitskoorn, S. M., & Smitsman, A. W. (1959). Infants' perception of dynamic relations between objects: Passing through or support? *Developmental Psychology, 31,* 437–447.

Smith, L. B., McLin, D., Titzer, B., & Thelen, E. (1995, March). *The task dynamics of the A-not-B error.* Paper presented at the meeting of the Society for Research in Child Development, Indianapolis, IN.

Sophian, C. (1984). Developing skills in infancy and early childhood. In C. Sophian (Ed.), *Origins of cognitive skills* (pp. 27–56). Hillsdale, NJ: Erlbaum.

Stein, B. S., Littlefield, J., Bransford, J. D., & Persampieri, M. (1984). Elaboration and knowledge acquisition. *Memory & Cognition, 12,* 522–529.

Suchman, L. A. (1987). *Plans and situated actions: The problem of human-machine interaction.* Cambridge, UK: Cambridge University Press.

Wellman, H. M., Cross, D., & Bartsch, K. (1986). Infant search and object permanence: A meta-analysis of the A-not-B error. *Monographs of the Society for Research in Child Development, 51*(3, Serial No. 214).

Willatts, P. (1984). The stage IV infant's solution to problems requiring the use of supports. *Infant Behavior and Development, 7,* 125–134.

Willatts, P. (1985). Adjustments of means-ends coordination and the representation of spatial relations in the production of search errors by infants. *British Journal of Developmental Psychology, 3,* 259–272.

Zelazo, P. R., & Zelazo, P. D. (1998). The emergence of consciousness. In H. H. Jasper, L. Descarries, V. F. Castellucci, & S. Rossignol (Eds.), *Consciousness at the frontiers of neuroscience: Advances in neurology* (Vol. 77, pp. 149–165). Philadelphia: Lippincott-Raven.

TEMPERAMENT AND ATTACHMENT: ONE CONSTRUCT OR TWO?

Sarah C. Mangelsdorf

DEPARTMENT OF PSYCHOLOGY
UNIVERSITY OF ILLINOIS AT URBANA-CHAMPAIGN
CHAMPAIGN, ILLINOIS 61820

Cynthia A. Frosch

CENTER FOR DEVELOPMENTAL SCIENCE
UNIVERSITY OF NORTH CAROLINA AT CHAPEL HILL
CHAPEL HILL, NORTH CAROLINA 27599

181

ADVANCES IN CHILD DEVELOPMENT
AND BEHAVIOR, VOL. 27

I. Introduction

Since the 1950s a wealth of research has been conducted on the social-emotional development of young children. The focus of this research has tended to be on either the child or the parent as the major determinant of the child's developmental outcome. For example, in two very different traditions, infant emotional development is described either in terms of the child's innate temperament (e.g., Kagan, 1982, 1984) or in terms of the quality of the attachment relationship between parent and child (e.g., Sroufe, 1985, 1996). A particularly striking point is that for many years these two traditions were conducted in parallel, with few attempts to incorporate both constructs into research investigations, and with little or no interaction between researchers from the two different perspectives. However, despite this apparent independence, the research in these two areas has a number of important areas of convergence.

In this chapter, we explore the question of whether temperament and attachment are the same or two distinctly different constructs. We discuss similarities and differences between the constructs of temperament and attachment, and present an overview of the methodological and conceptual issues related to these lines of inquiry into young children's social and emotional development.

II. How Are Temperament and Attachment Similar and Different?

Both temperament and infant–caregiver attachment relationships are thought to be major organizers of early social-emotional development (Goldsmith, Bradshaw, & Reisser-Danner, 1986). In addition, both individual differences in young children's temperaments and differences in the quality of infant–caregiver attachment relationships have been linked to later social outcomes, including behavior problems such as aggression in elementary school (e.g., Renken, Egeland, Marvinney, Mangelsdorf, & Sroufe, 1989; Sanson, Smart, Prior, & Oberklaid, 1993).

Another way in which temperament and attachment are similar is that both constructs have behavioral components. For example, temperament researchers investigate behaviors such as reactivity, distress to novelty, inhibition, or soothability. Attachment researchers note similar behaviors, although attention is devoted to the parent–child relationship as the context for such behaviors.

Consider, for example, crying in the first year of life. Temperament researchers would focus on how frequently and how intensely children cry in various contexts, and how easily children are soothed when distressed. Attachment researchers, in contrast, would describe crying as an attachment behavior because it promotes proximity to, or contact with, the caregiver (e.g., S. M. Bell & Ainsworth, 1972; Hubbard & van IJzendoorn, 1991).

Beyond infancy, it remains true that temperament researchers and attachment researchers have often studied similar behaviors in children, but have ascribed these behaviors to either temperament, or to the earlier parent–child attachment relationship. For example, behaviors observed in childhood, such as persistence, compliance, sociability, high positive affect, and low negative affect are considered by attachment researchers to be correlates of attachment security during infancy (e.g., Arend, Gove, & Sroufe, 1979; Matas, Arend, & Sroufe, 1978). In contrast, temperament researchers have attributed these same characteristics to individual differences in temperament (e.g., Thomas & Chess, 1977).

Are temperament and attachment researchers merely using different constructs to describe the same individual differences in behavior? Or are temperament and attachment distinctly different constructs? That is, are these two constructs explaining different individual differences in child behavior? These are the questions we will address in this chapter.

Although temperament and attachment *behaviors* may share commonalities, temperament is viewed as an individual construct, while attachment is a dyadic, or relational construct. Another difference between temperament theorists' and attachment theorists' accounts of early development appears to be the extent to which differences among children are attributed to innate differences in children, that is, their nature, or to basic differences in caregiving or nurture. Psychologists and philosophers alike have long realized that such a dichotomous approach to the study of human behavior is vastly oversimplified. In fact, even John Locke, who is often quoted as a staunch believer in the power of the environment, or "nurture," acknowledged some innate characteristics (R. Q. Bell, 1968). Although R. Q. Bell's (1968) classic article on bidirectional effects in parent–child relationships is widely cited, in most research on parent–child relationships the tendency has been to emphasize the role of either the parent or the child as the primary architect of the child's later social-emotional development.

In order to disentangle whether temperament and attachment researchers are merely using different labels to describe the same construct or whether in fact these two research traditions represent distinct, yet perhaps complementary, approaches to individual differences in social-emotional development, a necessary first step is to define precisely what is meant by each of the two constructs. Thus in the next section, definitional and measurement issues in the two areas are examined.

III. What Is Temperament?

The notion of temperament has been present in some form for over 2000 years, going back at least to the time of Hippocrates, who believed that a person's mental disposition was determined by the four humours: sanguine, choleric, melancholic, and phlegmatic (Rothbart, 1989; Rutter, 1989). Nonetheless, despite the long history of the notion, not everyone has agreed about just what temperament is and is not. For many years, psychologists strongly influenced by psychoanalytic theory neglected the existence of important constitutionally based individual differences among infants, and focused instead on parent–child relationships or parental behavior as the primary determinant of most individual differences in child behavior.

A. THE NEW YORK LONGITUDINAL STUDY: THE FIRST MAJOR
STUDY OF TEMPERAMENT

One of the most serious challenges to the view that parents were the major contributors to children's personality development came in the late 1950s when Thomas, Chess, and their colleagues (Thomas, Chess, & Birch, 1968; Thomas, Chess, Birch, Hertzig, & Korn, 1963) began the New York Longitudinal Study. In this study, 133 middle and upper middle-class children were followed from 2 or 3 months of age through adolescence. Thomas and Chess (1977) approached the study of temperament as an inquiry into the stylistic or "how" component of behavior, rather than the "what" (abilities and content) or the "why" (motivations) components. In other words, according to their view, children differ in *how* intense they are in their emotional reactions (e.g., *how* active, *how* distressed).

From their research, Thomas and Chess concluded that individual differences among infants are indeed relatively stable, and that these differences are evident shortly after birth. To reach this conclusion, parents' descriptions of their children were obtained via interviews and were subsequently scored for the following nine dimensions of temperament: (1) mood, (2) approach-withdrawal (reaction to novelty), (3) adaptability (to changes in routine), (4) intensity, (5) rhythm (e.g., body rhythms in sleep-wake cycles), (6) persistence (extent to which child remains engaged in an activity), (7) threshold, (8) activity, and (9) distractibility (difficulty or ease with which an ongoing activity can be interrupted). On the basis of both qualitative judgments and factor analysis of the nine dimensions, Thomas and Chess identified three temperament types: *Easy, Difficult,* and *Slow-to-Warm-Up.* Easy babies are positive in mood, regular in body functions and habits, and adaptable to new experiences. Their reactions are mild to moderate in intensity. Approximately 40% of the children in the sample were identified as Easy. Difficult babies, by comparison, are negative in mood, active, irregular in cycles and habits, and unadaptable. These babies withdraw in new situations and react with high intensity. Approximately 10% of the children in the study were identified as Difficult. Like the Difficult babies, Slow-to-Warm-Up children also withdraw from new situations. However, children identified as Slow-to-Warm-Up are also low in activity, slow to adapt to new situations, and their reactions are low to moderate in intensity. These children may be labeled as shy by family members and friends. Approximately 15% of the sample were identified as Slow-to-Warm-up. About 35% of the children in the study were not rated as high on any of the nine dimensions; they were identified as *Average.*

The New York Longitudinal Study had significant theoretical and practical implications. For example, some of the children developed behavioral problems such as high anxiety, aggressiveness, sleep difficulties, or extreme passivity later in childhood. These children were likely to have been rated as "Difficult" in infancy (Rutter, Birch, Thomas, & Chess, 1964; Thomas, Chess, & Korn, 1982). Thus, the New York Longitudinal Study raised the possibility that childhood behavioral problems might be predicted from knowledge of temperament at earlier ages.

In addition to predicting behavior problems, earlier measures of temperament predicted, to some extent, later school functioning. Thomas and Chess described individual cases of Slow-to-Warm-Up children who had great trouble with school situations that required them to adapt quickly to new demands (e.g., making new friends, mastering new school subjects). Children with difficulties in persistence and attention span at home were also likely to have difficulties in school, unless their teachers effectively paced their demands to match the students' lessened abilities to concentrate.

This last point illustrates a theoretically significant outcome of the New York Longitudinal Study—the idea of "Goodness of Fit." Prior to the work of Thomas and Chess, most psychologists could be divided into two groups: (a) those who believed that the child's intrinsic personality determined whether or not developmental difficulties would occur; and (b) those who believed that the child's environment, particularly the social ambiance created by the parents, determined whether later behavior would be normal or abnormal. Thomas and Chess were among the first to propose that it was the Goodness of Fit between the child's temperament and the demands of his or her environment that produced favorable or unfavorable outcomes. That is, neither theoretical group was entirely correct; rather a combination of both perspectives was important for understanding development.

To illustrate this point, consider two children—one identified as Difficult in infancy; the other identified as Easy. Which child is more likely to develop behav-

ior problems? Although the Difficult child might be expected to develop more behavior problems than the Easy child, Thomas and Chess pointed out that in the
right environment, the temperament of a Difficult infant need not result in subsequent behavioral disorders. The outcome would be normal if parents of such a child
responded in a manner that helped the child regulate his or her behavior and provided activities (such as athletics) in which the child's traits (e.g., high activity)
were valued. By contrast, Thomas and Chess (Chess & Thomas, 1984) found that
even Easy infants could develop behavioral and psychological problems if their
parents placed excessive demands on them. Problem behaviors may also occur if
parents were unresponsive to the needs of the Easy infants, perhaps because these
children are not as demanding as other children. Thus, although Thomas and Chess
argue for the innate presence of temperament, they do not believe that temperament is impervious to environmental influence. They believe that parent–child
interaction and other aspects of the environment can modify the expression of constitutionally given temperament traits, changing them for better or worse (Goldsmith et al., 1987), and ultimately shaping the child's developmental trajectory.

B. BEYOND THE NEW YORK LONGITUDINAL STUDY: NEW
PERSPECTIVES ON TEMPERAMENT

Since Thomas and Chess' pioneering research in the 1950s, the study of individual differences in temperament has grown substantially. For example, Carey
and colleagues have focused on the same nine dimensions of temperament proposed by Thomas and Chess and have developed standardized questionnaire measures to examine temperament during infancy (e.g., Carey, 1970; Carey & McDevitt, 1978), toddlerhood (Fullard, McDevitt, & Carey, 1984), and later childhood
(Hegvik, McDevitt, & Carey, 1982; McDevitt & Carey, 1978). The development
of these measures has been a significant methodological contribution to the field,
as multiple reports of child temperament can be obtained in an economical and efficient manner. However, as we will discuss below in section II.C, these measures
are also subject to criticism because of their subjective nature.

Other temperament researchers have not identified as many dimensions of temperament as Thomas and Chess did. In general, empirical work has revealed that
Thomas and Chess's nine dimensions are not necessarily independent (for discussion of this issue, see J. E. Bates, 1987; Rothbart & Bates, 1998). In part because
of this, other researchers have taken different approaches to the study of temperament and have defined and assessed temperament in distinct ways. For example,
Rothbart defined temperament as, "relatively stable, primarily biologically based
individual differences in reactivity and self-regulation" (Derryberry & Rothbart,
1984; Rothbart & Derryberry, 1981). Based on the work of Thomas and Chess
(1977), Escalona (1968), and others, Rothbart identified six dimensions of tem-

perament in infancy: (a) activity, (b) smiling and laughter, (c) fear, (d) distress to limitations (frustration), (e) soothability, and (f) duration of orienting (interest) (Rothbart, 1989).

With development, children's behavior becomes increasingly complex and differentiated. Thus, not too surprisingly, in research with older children (ages 3–8 years), Rothbart and her colleagues (Rothbart, Ahadi, & Hershey, 1994) identified 15 dimensions of temperament—a greater number than identified by Rothbart in her research with infants. The dimensions identified in infancy still remained in later childhood, but they often differentiated into more than one dimension. For example, fear differentiated and became fear and shyness. Rothbart et al. found that these 15 dimensions underlie three higher-order broad dimensions of temperament: Surgency/Extroversion, Negative Affectivity, and Inhibitory Control. Surgency/Extroversion reflects high-intensity pleasure, activity, and impulsivity. Negative Affectivity includes discomfort, fear, anger/frustration, and sadness. Inhibitory Control reflects attentional focusing, low-intensity pleasure, and perceptual sensitivity.

Goldsmith and Campos, two other temperament researchers, have focused specifically on affective dimensions and have defined temperament as "individual differences in the probability of experiencing and expressing the primary emotions and arousal" (Goldsmith et al., 1987). Thus they suggest that temperament consists of individual differences in the intensity, frequency, and time parameters. Other temperament researchers, such as Kagan, have focused specifically on the dimensions of inhibition or shyness (e.g., Kagan, 1989; Kagan, Reznick, Clarke, Snidman, & Garcia-Coll, 1984; Kagan, Reznick, & Snidman, 1988), or have focused on constellations of dimensions such as "difficultness" (Bates, 1987). In short, the literature on temperament in young children clearly shows that researchers differ in the number and types of dimensions included in their approaches to the study of temperament.

Aside from definitional issues, temperament researchers also differ in their beliefs about the extent to which nature is a defining feature of temperament. As indicated above, Rothbart said "*primarily* biologically based" (emphasis added), leaving room for nongenetic, but biological influences, such as prenatal factors. Goldsmith and Campos (1982) say that heritability may be more or less influential depending on the dimension of temperament being studied, and on the developmental period under consideration. In contrast, Buss and Plomin (1975) assert that temperament is a set of inherited personality traits that appears early in life. In their early writings on the subject, they focused on emotionality, activity, sociability, and impulsivity as the major dimensions of temperament. However, more recently Buss and Plomin (1986) concluded that the evidence for the inheritance of impulsivity is inadequate and thus, impulsivity has been dropped from their definition of temperament. Having a strict criterion for temperament such as heritability may be useful in some instances. However, an emphasis on the genetic basis of temperament may limit our ability to describe the full range of individual differences in child behavior (Rutter, 1982).

Identifying and integrating these multiple approaches to temperament was a primary goal of a roundtable discussion held in 1985. A number of prominent temperament theorists participated in a discussion of the definitions, dimensions, and influences of temperament. As an outgrowth of this meeting, McCall proposed a synthesis definition of temperament, suggesting that,

> Temperament consists of relatively consistent, basic dispositions inherent in the person that underlie and modulate the expression of activity, reactivity, emotionality, and sociability. Major elements of temperament are present early in life, and those elements are likely to be strongly influenced by biological factors. As development proceeds, the expression of temperament increasingly becomes more influenced by experience and context. (Goldsmith et al., 1987, p. 524)

McCall's definition reflects the dynamic and complex nature of the construct of temperament, but may be unnecessarily limiting by placing developmental constraints on the emergence of dimensions of temperament. According to this definition, certain dimensions of temperament not yet apparent in early infancy but emerging in later childhood and adulthood (e.g., risk-taking behaviors) would not be defined as temperament.

C. HOW IS TEMPERAMENT STUDIED?

Traditionally, child temperament has been studied via parental interviews or parental questionnaires regarding the behavior of infants and children (for comprehensive reviews of such measures, see Hubert, Wachs, Peters-Martin, & Gandour, 1982; Slabach, Morrow, & Wachs, 1991). For example, as discussed above in the New York Longitudinal Study, the investigators relied almost exclusively on parental reports of child temperament. Reliance on parents as the primary reporters of their children's temperaments has been one of the major criticisms of that study, and this methodological approach to the study of temperament continues to create controversy. A number of researchers have documented that parental reports are subject to bias, and have both objective and subjective components. Although parents can describe their children's behavior accurately (Rothbart & Bates, 1998), parental reports can also be influenced by variables such as parents' expectations and personality (e.g., Bates & Bayles, 1984; Diener, Goldstein, & Mangelsdorf, 1995).

In response to these criticisms, researchers have begun to include observational measures of temperament in addition to parent report measures. For example, temperament researchers have developed standardized laboratory-based assessments for use in conjunction with parental reports (e.g., Goldsmith & Rothbart, 1991; Matheny & Wilson, 1981). Occasionally, but far less commonly, researchers have also conducted naturalistic observations of temperament (e.g., J. E. Bates & Bayles, 1984; Seifer, Sameroff, Barrett, & Krafchuck, 1994). But, in all cases, regardless of whether the temperament measures are questionnaires, interviews, or home or laboratory-based observations, temperament dimensions are usually examined on a continuum. Infants and children are typically rated as low, moderate, or high on various temperament dimensions such as emotional tone, soothability, positive affect, intensity, and activity. Such an assessment strategy is quite different from the categorical approach typically used when describing infant–parent attachment relationships.

D. CONCURRENT AND PREDICTIVE VALIDITY OF TEMPERAMENT

Individual differences in temperament during infancy and early childhood have been examined both as correlates and as predictors of later socioemotional functioning. Studies of the concurrent correlates of psychiatric disorders among preschool children have shown that activity level is positively associated with various forms of psychiatric disturbance, and persistence is negatively associated with psychiatric disturbance. Specifically, more active and less persistent children are likely to display externalizing problems as preschoolers; less active children are likely to display internalizing problems (Lavigne et al., 1996).

Researchers have also found infant temperament to be a useful predictor of later behavior problems. For example, as mentioned earlier, Thomas and Chess (Chess & Thomas, 1984) found that of the children who developed behavior problems in elementary school, most had been rated as "Difficult" in infancy. In fact, measures of children's temperament from as early as 12 to 24 months of age were significant predictors of psychiatric problems by age 7 years (Rutter et al., 1964). However, no single temperament dimension predicted later problems; rather, the *pattern* of temperament characteristics mattered. The clinical cases were significantly more irregular, nonadaptable, and intense and negative in mood during infancy, than the children not presenting.

Subsequently, other researchers have replicated this finding; temperamental difficulty in infancy predicts later behavior problems. For example, Bates and colleagues (J. Bates, Maslin, & Frankel, 1985) found that measures of infant difficultness at 6 and 13 months of age predicted child behavior problems at 3 years of age. Specifically, both mothers' and observers' ratings of infant fearfulness predicted children's anxiety problems at age 3 and reports of early activity management problems predicted "acting-out" or externalizing behavior problems. Similarly, Shaw and Vondra (1995) found that difficult temperament assessed in infancy was predictive of both internalizing and externalizing behavior problems in preschool-age girls. This finding, in part, may be due to the fact that internalizing and externalizing problems are highly correlated in very young children and become more differentiated in later childhood (Achenbach, 1991, 1992).

As mentioned earlier, Sanson and colleagues (1993) found that temperament in infancy, particularly difficult temperament in infancy and early childhood, predicted later behavior problems, especially aggression in elementary school. From a related perspective, Caspi, Elder, and Bem (1987) found that explosive behavior in childhood predicted "explosive behavior" in adulthood. Although Caspi and colleagues did not describe explosive children in terms of temperament per se, an explosive child was one who is negative in mood, high in intensity, and low on adaptability. Recall that these characteristics are similar to those included in Thomas and Chess's description of a Difficult child.

Other researchers have found that dimensions of temperament other than difficultness in infancy are predictive of behavior problems in school-age children. For example, Rende (1993) found in a 7-year longitudinal study that emotionality assessed in infancy and early childhood was predictive of anxiety and depression at age 7 years. An important point is that Rende used the Colorado Child Temperament Inventory (Rowe & Plomin, 1977) to assess temperament and the only type of emotionality assessed via that questionnaire is actually *negative* emotionality; positive emotionality is not assessed. As negative emotionality is a central component of the "Difficult" constellation, these results are consistent with those of researchers using Thomas and Chess's typology.

In addition to demonstrating the short-term predictive validity of early temperament measures, the predictive validity of these measures has also been shown over the course of nearly two decades. In a longitudinal study, Caspi and colleagues (Caspi, Moffitt, Newman, & Silva, 1996; Caspi & Silva, 1995) found that dimensions of temperament assessed at 3 years of age via behavioral observations were meaningfully related to later personality and adult psychiatric disorders at age 21. For example, children identified as "undercontrolled" (i.e., exhibiting a pattern of impulsive, restless, and distractible behavior) at age 3 years score higher on measures of impulsivity, danger seeking, aggression, and social potency at age 18 than children classified as average. They also found that adults who have been classified as "undercontrolled" at age 3 years were more likely than a comparison group of adults, classified as average during the preschool years, to meet diagnostic criteria for antisocial personality disorder and to be involved in crime. By comparison, adults who had been classified as "inhibited" (i.e., shy, fearful, and easily upset) at age 3 years were more likely to be diagnosed as depressed than adults who had been classified as average during childhood. Both the "undercontrolled" and the "inhibited" groups were more likely than the control group to attempt suicide, and men from both the undercontrolled and the inhibited groups were more likely than the comparison men to have alcohol-related problems. Caspi et al. noted that the undercontrolled group is behaviorally similar to Thomas and Chess's "Difficult" temperament type and the "inhibited" group is similar to Thomas and Chess's "Slow-to-Warm-Up" group. Thus, although the labels researchers apply to groups of children who exhibit certain dimensions of temperament may differ, similarities in the behaviors included are often quite apparent.

In summary, evidence indicates that early temperament is related to concurrent and later behavior problems. Specifically, certain temperament characteristics, such as high activity and impulsivity, are related to subsequent externalizing problems, and other characteristics, such as fearfulness and proneness to distress, are related to later internalizing problems. An important point, however, is that many of these findings were based on maternal reports of *both* child temperament and child behavior problems, thereby possibly inflating the appearance of stability over time. However, the work of Caspi et al. (1996), using behavioral observations of temperament in early childhood to predict psychiatric problems in adulthood, is an important addition to this literature and provides evidence consistent with the research based on maternal reports.

IV. What Is Attachment?

Although the term *attachment* is often used in society to describe a range of behaviors and preferences, such as a child's unwavering preference for a particular toy, attachment in the psychological literature generally refers to relationships between people. Mary Ainsworth, a pioneer in the field, defined attachment as "an affectional tie that one person forms to another specific person, binding them together in space and enduring over time" (Ainsworth, 1973, p. 1).

Bowlby asserted that all human infants are strongly predisposed to form an attachment with their caregivers, and that all infants become "attached" to the people who care for them. He posited that humans have an innate need for social interaction that becomes focused on specific caregivers over the course of the first year of life. According to Bowlby (1982), attachment behaviors (e.g., crying, proximity seeking) and the attachment relationships infants form with their caregivers derive from our biological make-up as mammals and primates. These attachment relationships have evolutionary significance in that they offer survival value for the species. If infants are attached to specific caregivers and seek to maintain proximity with them, infants will then be protected from predators.

Infant–caregiver attachments form gradually over the course of the first year of the child's life and are manifested behaviorally in a number of related ways during the second half of the first year. For example, the infant will seek proximity and contact with the caregiver when distressed, generally exhibit distress at separations from the caregiver (referred to as separation anxiety or separation protest), and may manifest wariness when interacting with strangers (referred to as stranger anxiety). In addition, during the course of exploration in a novel setting, the child may show toys to the caregiver or exchange looks and vocalize when at a distance.

In particular, when a child encounters something unfamiliar, he or she may look to the caregiver for additional information (social referencing). Central to attachment is *secure-base* behavior, or the infant's ability to balance proximity to the caregiver with distance or exploration (Seifer & Schiller, 1995). Secure-based behavior ensures that the infant will be able to learn about the physical environment while maintaining a sense of "felt security."

Bowlby asserted that by age 12 months virtually all infants will be attached to the person(s) who care for them, regardless of the quality of care they receive. However, he also stated that the quality of care the infant receives will be related to the quality of the attachment relationship. Thus, although virtually all infants become attached, not all infants share the same quality of attachment relationship with their caregivers. For example, more sensitive or responsive caregivers are likely to have children who feel more secure in their attachment relationships than children whose caregivers are less sensitive. This point, that quality of care is related to quality of attachment, has been examined empirically.

A. THE BALTIMORE STUDY: A LANDMARK STUDY OF ATTACHMENT

The first major study of infant–mother attachment was conducted by Ainsworth (1973) in Baltimore, Maryland. She studied 26 middle-class mother–infant dyads over the course of the first year of life. Extensive observations of infant behavior and mother–child interaction were conducted; 4-h observations were made every 3 weeks from birth to 54 weeks. Ainsworth noted vast individual differences in mother–child relationships as observed in the home. She observed differences in mothers' behavior towards their infants; for example, some mothers were more sensitive and responsive to their babies' cues than other mothers. Similarly, she noted that children differed in how much they sought proximity and contact with their mothers, how much they explored the environment, and how they responded to separations and reunions with their mothers. However, Ainsworth was also interested in whether these differences would be present in environments other than the home—that is, she asked whether infants' behaviors in the home reflected something specific about the security of their relationship with their caregiver, or about their security with their familiar home environment.

B. HOW IS ATTACHMENT STUDIED?

1. The Strange Situation Procedure

In order to investigate whether infant behavior would be consistent across contexts, Ainsworth observed the infant–mother dyads in a standardized, laboratory-based context when the infants were 51 weeks of age. The goal of this procedure, known as the "Strange Situation," was to systematically examine individual differences in the quality of attachment relationships (Ainsworth, Blehar, Waters, & Wall, 1978). Through subsequent analyses, Ainsworth and her colleagues noted that infant behavior was meaningfully related across the home and laboratory contexts; responding positively to being picked up and held by the mother at home and "sinking in" were positively associated with both proximity seeking and contact maintaining observed in the laboratory. Ainsworth identified three groups of dyads that differed in terms of the patterning of behavior that they exhibited during the laboratory observation (these patterns are described in section III.C). Moreover, Ainsworth identified characteristics of mothers' behavior observed in the home that related to the kinds of attachment relationship that infants formed with their caregivers; the clearest intergroup differences were in the area of sensitivity. Specifically, mothers of securely attached infants were significantly more sensitive, accepting, cooperative, and psychologically accessible to their infants than mothers of avoidant or resistant infants (Ainsworth et al., 1978).

Since Ainsworth's pioneering work on the associations between maternal behavior and the quality of the infant–mother attachment relationship, extensive research in this area has supported and extended the findings from the Baltimore study; sensitive parenting is significantly associated with security of attachment (e.g., Ainsworth et al., 1978; Belsky, Rovine, & Taylor, 1984; DeWolff & van IJzendoorn, 1997; Egeland & Farber, 1984; Isabella, 1993; Isabella & Belsky, 1991). Thus, as Bowlby hypothesized, attachment relationships vary as a function of the quality of care the child receives.

The "Strange Situation" laboratory procedure that Ainsworth developed has been widely used in attachment research. The Strange Situation procedure is typically conducted with infants 12 to 18 months old and consists of a series of eight episodes involving interactions with a stranger and separations and reunions with the mother.[1] The Strange Situation procedure gradually escalates the amount of stress the infant is experiencing. Here, the idea is that under stress, individual differences in attachment security will be more readily observable. That is, the attachment system will be "activated" during times of stress. The child's exploratory behavior, responses to a stranger, and reactions during separations and reunions with the caregiver are all noted. Specific behaviors scored include the child's proximity seeking, contact maintaining, avoidance and resistance of contact, and crying. The child is then given one of three major classifications (each

[1]Although the Strange Situation has been predominantly used to assess attachment in infant–mother dyads, a number of studies have investigated infant–father attachment, as well as infants' attachments to other individuals. For the purposes of this discussion, however, we restrict our focus to the infant–mother dyad, as Ainsworth did in her Baltimore study. Moreover, although infants are described in terms of secure or insecure attachment, attachment researchers are referring to the infants' relationship with a particular caregiver. Thus infant attachment is seen as a dyadic construct.

with two to four subgroups, described in section VI.D): (a) secure, (b) insecure-avoidant, or (c) insecure-resistant (often referred to as ambivalent). These classifications are determined by examining the organization of the child's behavior across the episodes of the Strange Situation procedure.

The securely attached infant explores freely in the mother's presence and is often visibly upset when separated from the mother, but greets her warmly at reunion. Insecure-avoidant infants show little if any distress when separated from their mother, and tend to turn away from and avoid contact with her at reunion. Insecure-avoidant infants are not wary of strangers and sometimes show more positive interactions with strangers than with their mothers. Insecure-resistant infants, in contrast, are thoroughly distressed by separations and are difficult to soothe upon reunion. In addition, insecure-resistant infants often mix proximity-seeking behaviors with angry ones and resist contact even though they have sought it out. This mixture of anger and resistance in the context of contact suggests the infants' ambivalence about the caregiver.

Approximately 65% of infants assessed in a sample of middle-class infants in the United States are likely to be classified as secure, 10% as resistant, and 25% as avoidant. However, this distribution has been found to differ in other countries. For example, researchers using the Strange Situation in Northern Germany classified a greater proportion of children as insecure-avoidant than in the United States (Grossmann, Grossmann, Spangler, Suess, & Unzner, 1985). Children in Israel and Japan, by comparison, are more likely to be classified as insecure-resistant than U.S. children (Miyake, Chen, & Campos, 1985; Sagi et al., 1985). In a meta-analysis of almost 2000 Strange Situations obtained in eight different countries it was found that although substantial intracultural similarities were noted, there were also cross-cultural differences. Specifically, a higher percentage of insecure-avoidant infants were found in northern European countries, and a higher percentage of insecure-resistant infants were found in Israel and Japan (van IJzendoorn & Kroonenberg, 1988) than in the United States.

In addition to the three groups that Ainsworth identified, Main and Solomon (1986, 1990) identified a fourth pattern, Disorganized. According to Main and Solomon, children classified as Disorganized may simultaneously display contradictory behaviors such as approaching the caregiver with their head averted. Disorganized infants may also display incomplete or undirected movements and expressions and may exhibit indices of confusion and apprehension, such as displaying strong fear of their parent, covering their face when the parent returns, or falling prone on floor. This pattern has been found to be more prevalent in samples of abused and neglected children and in children whose mothers have affective disorders (Crittenden, 1985, 1988; Radke-Yarrow, Cummings, Kuczynski, & Chapman, 1985; Spieker & Booth, 1988). Prior to Main and Solomon's identification of the Disorganized pattern, these infants were generally considered unclassifiable.

2. The Attachment of Q-Set: An Alternative Measure of
Attachment Security

In the 1980s, Everett Waters and his student Katherine Deane developed a 100-item Attachment Q-set (Waters & Deane, 1985) that enabled researchers to examine attachment security as a continuous variable by having parents or trained observers rate child behavior on a continuum ranging from "most like" to "least like". A modified and revised version—the 90-item Attachment Q-Set (Waters, 1987, 1995)—is designed to assess attachment and attachment-relevant behaviors of children from the ages of 12 months to $3\frac{1}{2}$ years. An overall security score is derived by correlating parents' or trained observers' sorts with a criterion sort that was developed by a team of experts in the area of attachment. The criterion sort reflects the behavior of the prototypical secure child. Unlike the categorical approach used with the Strange Situation procedure, with the Attachment Q-set, children are described as more or less secure depending on their overall security score. A number of studies have demonstrated associations between attachment security as assessed by the Strange Situation and Attachment Q-Set security scores (e.g., Seifer, Schiller, Sameroff, Resnick & Riordan, 1996; B. E. Vaughn & Waters, 1990), but this association has not been found in other investigations (e.g., Mangelsdorf et al., 1996; van Dam & van IJzendoorn, 1988). These disparate results may reflect methodological or sample differences.

C. CONCURRENT AND PREDICTIVE VALIDITY OF ATTACHMENT

1. Predictive Validity of Attachment as Assessed in the
Strange Situation

According to attachment theory, the attachment relationship serves an important role in young children's development and provides a context for learning about the environment; specifically, it has been proposed that the quality of the attachment relationship lays the foundation for the child's developing personality and sense of self (Sroufe, 1996). In order to empirically examine the hypothesis that early attachment relationships have implications for later social-emotional development, a number of investigators have explored the predictive validity of attachment classifications from the Strange Situation. Those who have examined the period between infancy and toddlerhood have found that infants classified as securely attached develop into 2-year-olds who are more enthusiastic, demonstrate more positive affect, and show greater persistence in problem solving than infants classified as insecurely attached (both avoidant and resistant children). The latter infants develop into 2-year-olds who are easily frustrated, negativistic, and noncompliant (Matas et al., 1978; replicated by Frankel & Bates, 1990). In addition, 2-year-olds classified as securely attached at 18 months are more sociable during play with their mothers and peers in a play situation than 2-year-olds who were insecurely attached at 18 months of age (Pastor, 1981).

Attachment as assessed in the Strange Situation also has predictive validity between infancy and the preschool years. Securely attached 12- and 18-month-olds become preschoolers who (a) are rated by their preschool teachers (who are unaware of their attachment histories) as higher on positive and lower on negative affect (Sroufe, Schork, Motti, Lawroski, & LaFreniere, 1984), (b) are more empathic (Kestenbaum, Farber, & Sroufe, 1989; Waters, Wippman, & Sroufe, 1979), and (c) are more compliant (Waters et al., 1979). Preschoolers with a history of secure attachment during infancy also score higher on ego resiliency and social competence (Arend et al., 1979), have higher self-esteem (Waters et al., 1979), and display fewer behavior problems (Shaw & Vondra, 1995) than preschoolers who were insecurely attached during infancy. In later childhood, attachment insecurity as assessed in infancy is predictive of high levels of aggression in elementary school age boys (Renken et al., 1989), and attachment security is predictive of self-confidence and social skills with peers in 10 and 11 year olds (Elicker, Englund, & Sroufe, 1992). Thus, these and other studies have generally indicated that secure attachment in infancy predicts positive outcomes in later childhood; insecure attachment predicts poorer outcomes.

2. Correlates of Attachment Security as Assessed by the Attachment Q-Set

Like attachment security assessed with the Strange Situation, attachment security assessed with the Attachment Q-Set (Waters, 1987, 1995) has been associated with more optimal social-emotional development in children. However, far more research has been done on the contemporaneous correlates and predictive validity of attachment security as assessed with the Strange Situation, than as assessed with the Attachment Q-Set. Moreover, although parenting behavior, particularly maternal sensitivity, has been associated with attachment security as assessed with the Strange Situation, the parenting correlates of security as assessed with the Attachment Q-Set remain largely unknown.

Two notable exceptions are investigations by Pederson et al. (1990) and Teti, Nakagawa, Das, and Wirth (1991). Pederson et al. (1990) demonstrated associations between infant–mother attachment as assessed by mothers' and observers' sorts of the Attachment Q-Set and maternal sensitivity as assessed by the Maternal Behavior Q-Set (Pederson et al., 1990) and Ainsworth's (Ainsworth et al., 1978) maternal sensitivity scale. Specifically, mothers of infants scoring higher on attachment security were more attuned to and responsive to their infants' signals.

Teti et al. (1991) investigated the associations among security of attachment, social interaction, and parenting stress. Attachment security scores were obtained from mothers' sorts of the Attachment Q-Set. In addition, mothers completed a measure of parenting stress, and mother–preschooler dyads were observed during free-play. Teti et al. found that greater security was associated with more sensitive, flexible, and affectively appropriate maternal behavior. Greater security was also related to preschoolers' affectivity: more secure preschoolers exhibited less negative affect toward their mothers and greater sociability in the laboratory. Mothers of less secure children also reported more parenting stress, particularly with respect to characteristics of their children, than mothers of more secure preschoolers.

Other research by Teti and Ablard (1989) indicated that greater security as assessed by the Attachment Q-Set was associated with the caregiving behavior of older siblings toward their infant siblings. Park and Waters (1989) found that best-friend dyads composed of two secure preschoolers were less controlling during play than secure–insecure dyads. In addition, Bost, Vaughn, Washington, Cielinski, and Bradbard (1998) found that preschoolers' social competence could be predicted from security of attachment as assessed with the Attachment Q-Set and characteristics of children's social support networks.

Although most investigations have considered the Attachment Q-Set with respect to the infant–mother attachment, we have explored the use of this measure with fathers in our investigation of child–parent attachment and preschoolers' socioemotional functioning (Frosch & Mangelsdorf, 1999). Mothers and fathers independently completed the Attachment Q-Set during a home observation and completed measures of their children's internalizing and externalizing behaviors. Observers also reported on preschoolers' externalizing behavior following the home visit, and preschool teachers or childcare providers reported on children's externalizing behaviors and social behavior with peers. The results indicated that higher security scores were associated with parents' reports of fewer internalizing and externalizing problems in their 3-year-old children. Security of attachment to both mother and father was also associated with observers' ratings of fewer externalizing problems. In addition, security of attachment to mother, but not father, was negatively associated with preschool teachers' or daycare providers' reports of shy/withdrawn child behavior.

Taken together, these studies indicate that security of attachment as assessed with the Attachment Q-Set is related to more optimal parenting behavior and aspects of child functioning, including fewer behavior problems and more positive interactions with siblings, parents, and peers. Examination of the predictive validity of attachment as assessed with the Attachment Q-Set, however, appears to be a necessary and important topic for future research.

V. How Are Temperament and Attachment Related?
A Theoretical Debate

We now turn our attention to considering if, and how, these two constructs are related. This very issue has generated considerable debate among researchers, and widespread disagreement ensues about how temperament and attachment are related. One stance is that temperament and attachment are orthogonal constructs (e.g., Sroufe, 1985); another is that the two are one and the same. The perspective taken by many temperament researchers is that the Strange Situation measures variability in temperament (e.g., Buss & Plomin, 1986; Kagan, 1982), rather than something specific about the quality of the relationship between child and caregiver. In contrast, attachment researchers suggest that individual differences in early social-emotional development, such as affectivity and persistence, are due to differences in the quality of the parent–child attachment relationship (e.g., Matas et al., 1978) rather than to temperament. An alternative to these perspectives is that the association between temperament and attachment is best understood from a transactional or "goodness-of-fit" approach. In other words, we must look at how individual differences in child temperament may interact with social-contextual factors to predict the quality of the parent–child attachment relationship (e.g., Crockenberg, 1981; Mangelsdorf, Gunnar, Kestenbaum, Lang, & Andreas, 1990). In the following section we will examine each of these perspectives in turn.

A. PARENTING VERSUS TEMPERAMENT: WHICH MATTERS MORE?

In general, the position presented by most attachment researchers is that individual differences in temperament among infants are overwhelmed by differences among caregivers in the development of infant–parent attachment relationships. In fact, the very notion of "sensitive parenting" implies that the parent is attuned to the needs of the individual child, whatever these needs may be. Moreover, this suggestion implies that the sensitive parents should be capable of being sensitive to all children; adapting their parenting behavior to meet the needs of particular children.

Attachment theorists, therefore, posit that the truly sensitive parent should be able to overcome obstacles in parenting presented by infants of different temperaments (e.g., Ainsworth, 1982). Attachment theorists such as Sroufe (1985) have argued that the history of attachment security between caregiver and child completely transforms constitutional temperament variations such that temperament makes little or no contribution to security of attachment. However, Sroufe acknowledges that this is a radical position and suggests that it is also possible that attachment and temperament may be orthogonal constructs which are at different levels of analysis (i.e., dyadic vs. individual). He also suggests that temperament might influence the type of insecurity (avoidant or resistant) the child exhibits, but not whether or not the child is securely attached. Thus, according to attachment theorists, sensitivity of parental care is primarily responsible for individual differences in attachment security, not temperament.

B. TEMPERAMENT CONTRIBUTIONS TO ATTACHMENT

Other researchers, however, have emphasized the crucial role played by infant temperament, and have proposed a number of ways in which temperament might influence the infant–caregiver attachment relationship (Goldsmith et al., 1986; Lamb, Thompson, Gardner, & Charnov, 1985). Temperament researchers such as Kagan (1982, 1984) have asserted that individual differences observed in the Strange Situation are probably due to endogenous differences in infants rather than to variations in the quality of caregiving as attachment theorists propose (e.g., Ainsworth et al., 1978). Kagan asserted that an infant's behavior in the Strange Situation is determined by the child's threshold for distress. That is, infants classified as insecure-avoidant are temperamentally calm, thereby accounting for their lack of distress during separations and their failure to seek contact at reunions. Insecure-resistant infants, in contrast, are easily distressed and thus become quite distraught in the Strange Situation. Finally, Kagan has suggested that securely attached infants are between the insecure-avoidant and insecure-resistant infants on proneness-to-distress and thus, they exhibit less extreme patterns of behavior than either type of insecurely attached infants.

Similarly, Buss and Plomin (1986) viewed attachment security as merely a measure of temperament, and they ascribed differences in attachment classifications to differences in two dimensions of temperament, namely sociability and emotionality. They maintained that secure infants are likely to be at least moderately sociable and not especially emotional. Furthermore, they argued that insecure-avoidant infants are likely to be unsociable and unemotional, playing less with the stranger[2] and showing little interest in the mother when she returns. Insecure-resistant infants, in contrast, are likely to be emotional throughout the procedure, showing fear of the stranger, distress upon separation, and anger upon their mothers' return.

Buss and Plomin cited two sets of findings as evidence supporting their hypothesis: (a) Insecure-resistant infants cry nearly twice as much as securely attached infants as early as the first few months of life (Ainsworth et al., 1978), and (b) securely attached infants are more sociable with peers (Easterbrooks & Lamb, 1979; Lieberman, 1977; Pastor, 1981; Waters et al., 1979). In fact, securely attached infants are more sociable and less shy with strange adults (e.g., Thompson & Lamb, 1983). A noteworthy point about the attachment versus temperament perspectives is that attachment researchers (e.g., Sroufe, 1985, 1996) claim that differences in sociability are due to environmental effects. That is, attachment security leads to sociability, or stated another way, sociability is a *consequence* of attachment security. Buss and Plomin, however, did not see sociability as a consequence of attachment security, but rather as one of the *determinants* of whether an infant will be classified as securely attached. They stated, "[O]ur approach leads to a different interpretation: Children differ initially in sociability and emotionality and these temperaments affect social interaction with both mother and stranger" (Buss & Plomin, 1986, p. 69).

---

[2]Recall that unlike Buss and Plomin, Ainsworth noted that insecure-avoidant infants are often more sociable with the stranger in the Strange Situation procedure. This finding of an association between insecure-avoidant attachment and sociability with the stranger continues to be supported in studies of infant–parent attachment.

One other response to the question of whether certain temperament characteristics may predispose children to form insecure attachments was proposed by Fox
(1992). He suggested that

> There is a particular type of infant temperament that in interaction with maternal care-
> giving style produces a pattern of behavior in the Strange Situation that is classified as
> insecure. But it seems that whether the infant is classified as avoidant or resistant de-
> pends more on that pattern of mothering than on infant characteristics. (p. 41)

Fox's view, therefore, can be seen as a variant of the temperament perspectives
proposed by other researchers (e.g., Buss & Plomin, 1986; Kagan, 1982). As noted
earlier, both Buss and Plomin and Kagan proposed that temperament predicts
whether a child will be secure, insecure-avoidant, insecure-resistant, and that
caregiving is irrelevant for predicting attachment classifications. In contrast, Fox
(1992) proposed that temperament predicts whether or not a child will have an insecure attachment, but parenting predicts the type of insecurity the child will manifest. Thus Fox's position, unlike the positions of other strictly temperament theorists, does acknowledge that parenting contributes to the type of attachment
relationships children will form with their parents.

C. GOODNESS-OF-FIT AND TRANSACTIONAL MODELS

In addition to the two perspectives on temperament and attachment described
earlier, that attachment security obscures individual differences in temperament
(Sroufe, 1985) or that individual differences in attachment security and temperament are one and the same (Buss and Plomin, 1986; Kagan, 1982, 1948), a third
perspective merits discussion. The third perspective is that individual differences
in temperament may make some infants more or less difficult to parent (Waters &
Deane, 1982). For example, parents may have more difficulty in responding sen-
sitively to a highly irritable or "difficult" baby, and this problem may then result
in an insecure attachment relationship. Thus, irritable or difficult babies are more
likely to be insecurely attached because of the demands placed on their parents.
Some evidence supports this perspective when behavioral evaluations of newborns
(rather than parental reports) are used (Belsky & Isabella, 1988).

This third perspective can be discussed as a "goodness-of-fit" model or transactional model (Crockenberg, 1986; Sameroff & Chandler, 1975; Sameroff &
Fiese, 1990). Drawing upon Thomas and Chess's goodness-of-fit model described
earlier, such a perspective assumes that the *fit* between child temperament characteristics and parental personality determines the security of attachment relationships and other outcomes. Likewise, transactional models imply that developmental outcomes are not solely a function of an individual (temperament of the
child) nor of the experiential context (sensitive parenting). Rather, outcomes are a
product of the combination of an individual *and* his or her experience.

A goodness-of-fit or transactional model suggests that we need to examine how infant and parent characteristics interact or work together to predict secure versus insecure attachments. For example, parents will be differentially sensitive to particular temperament characteristics in their infants and in fact, some parents may be better able to tolerate irritable or "difficult" children than others. This interchange between parent and child will contribute to whether a secure or insecure attachment relationship results.

An implication of a transactional or "goodness-of-fit" approach to the study of temperament and attachment is that one would be unlikely, except perhaps in extreme cases, to find major effects of either infant characteristics or parental characteristics on security of attachment. However, research has shown such major effects in the case of extreme irritability in infants (e.g., van den Boom, 1989) or maternal psychopathology (e.g., DeMulder & Radke-Yarrow, 1991; Radke-Yarrow et al., 1985). A transactional model is consistent with attachment theory in that it takes into account the evidence that consistent and sensitive maternal behavior is associated with secure attachment relationships (e.g., Ainsworth et al., 1978; Belsky et al., 1984; De Wolf & van IJzendoorn, 1997; Egeland & Farber, 1984; Isabella, 1993; Isabella & Belsky, 1991).

D. WHAT DO INDIVIDUAL DIFFERENCES IN THE STRANGE SITUATION REALLY MEAN?

Children's behavior within the Strange Situation differs markedly. For example, some children cry a great deal when separated from their caregiver, while other children show no overt distress in response to separation. As noted earlier, temperament researchers believe that these differences in response to separation are due to differences in temperament. Attachment researchers believe that these differences could be due to either differences in temperament, or to differences in the caregiving environment, yet they emphasize that these differences in reactivity need not predict overall attachment security. That is, both of these children could be securely attached.

As stated earlier, temperament researchers such as Kagan (1982, 1984) argue that individual differences in attachment patterns manifested in the Strange Situation are due to endogenous differences in temperament. Attachment researchers (e.g., Sroufe, 1985) have disputed this argument, pointing out that it is the *organization* of infants' behaviors across episodes of the Strange Situation that results in a particular attachment classification, rather than the absolute frequency of behaviors such as crying. For example, two different children could receive the same score for crying during a reunion episode with the caregiver, yet one child could be classified as securely attached; the other as insecurely attached. Specifically, one child could be distressed and crying upon the caregiver's return yet settle over the course of the reunion episode. This pattern, marked by a decrease in crying upon reunion with the caregiver, suggests a secure attachment relationship. The second child could show no distress prior to the caregiver's return, but when reunited with the caregiver, shows increasing distress and crying across the episode. This pattern, marked by an increase in crying upon reunion with the caregiver, suggests an insecure attachment relationship. Thus, it was the organization of crying that contributed to the overall classification, not the absolute frequency of crying. The organization of other behaviors in the Strange Situation, for example proximity seeking or avoidance, also differs both between and within secure and insecure groups. In fact, Sroufe pointed out that crying and proximity seeking vary as much within the secure group as between the secure and insecure groups (Ainsworth et al., 1978). Sroufe (1985) suggested that temperament can influence the subgroup classification a child receives in the Strange Situation, but that temperament will not affect security of attachment. In other words, although characteristics of the caregiver's behavior—for example, sensitivity—would influence security or insecurity, temperament may influence the type of insecurity (avoidant versus resistant).

VI. Empirical Evidence on the Relations between Temperament and Attachment

A. PARENTS' REPORTS OF TEMPERAMENT

The empirical literature reveals little evidence for effects of parents' reports of infant temperament on security of attachment. One exception is an investigation by Calkins and Fox (1992) which indicated that maternal ratings of high infant activity level at 5 months of age were predictive of insecure-avoidant attachment at 14 months of age. More often, maternal reports of certain aspects of infant temperament have been found to predict similar infant behaviors in the Strange Situation. For example, Bates et al. (1985) found that although overall ratings of attachment security were unrelated to temperament, early measures of temperament predicted infant contact maintenance in the reunion episodes of the Strange Situation. They concluded that Strange Situation classifications were largely independent of both mothers' and observers' ratings of temperament. However, infant temperament measures were modestly correlated with specific reunion behavior ratings during the Strange Situation. Likewise, Vaughn, Lefever, Seifer, and Barglow (1989) found that mothers' ratings of infants' negative emotionality or "difficult temperament" were significantly related to observed negative emotionality during the separation episodes of the Strange Situation. However, temperament ratings alone did not predict negative emotionality during the reunion episodes with the caregiver, nor did they relate to overall attachment classifications. Just as Vaughn et al. found associations between difficult temperament and infants' behaviors during separation, Weber, Levitt, and Clark (1986) found that infant temperament variables showed a stronger relation to stranger-directed behaviors during separations than to mother-directed behaviors during the reunions. However, they also reported that infant "difficultness" was related to infants' resistance toward their mothers during the reunion episodes of the Strange Situation. Similar to Vaughn et al., Weber et al. found that temperament was not related to overall attachment classifications.

Similar findings concerning an association between temperament and behaviors within the Strange Situation, but not to overall attachment classifications were noted by Goldsmith and Alansky (1987). The authors identified 18 studies that included measures of both proneness-to-distress temperament and parent–child attachment for which an effect size could be derived. The majority of the studies they examined used maternal reports of infant temperament. They found that proneness-to-distress temperament significantly predicted resistant *behavior* in the Strange Situation, but did not predict insecure-resistant attachment. Thus, with the exception of the Calkins and Fox (1992) study, investigators using maternal reports of infant temperament have failed to find a direct association between temperament and attachment security.

B. MULTIMETHOD APPROACHES

However, studies involving observational measures of temperament have yielded slightly different evidence. For example, in the Mother–Child project conducted at the University of Minnesota, newborn infants were rated on Brazelton's Neonatal Assessment Scale (Waters, Vaughn, & Egeland, 1980). Waters et al. found a direct association between scores on this scale and later insecure-resistant attachment. Specifically, infants later classified as insecure-resistant were less responsive, less motorically mature, and less well regulated as newborns. In a later investigation of the same sample, Egeland and Farber (1984) reported that nurses' ratings of low alertness and high activity in newborns predicted later insecure-resistant attachment. In addition, insecure-resistant and insecure-avoidant infants were rated as more difficult to care for than secure infants. In a more recent analysis of the same data set using logistic regression, Susman-Stillman, Kalkoske, Egeland, and Waldman (1996) predicted later attachment security from infant temperament, as assessed by observation and maternal report at 3 and 6 months. They found a modest direct effect of infant irritability during the first year of life on later insecure-resistant attachment. Other notable findings were that maternal sensitivity predicted attachment security, and temperament predicted type of insecurity and subgroup classification. This finding is discussed in more detail below in section VI.

In another study with observational measures of temperament from early infancy, Calkins and Fox (1992) found that infants who cried more during pacifier withdrawal at 2 days of age were more likely to be classified as insecurely attached at 14 months of age. However, no differences were found between infants later classified as insecure-avoidant and those later classified as insecure-resistant. Thus, although neonatal reactivity was associated with insecurity, reactivity did not distinguish types of insecurity.

Observers' ratings of infant temperament were also used in an investigation by Seifer and colleagues (1996) and were aggregated across multiple home observations; maternal ratings of temperament were also obtained. Temperament, either as observed in the home or as reported by mothers, was largely unrelated to Strange Situation classifications, although insecure-resistant infants tended to be rated by their mothers as higher on fussy-difficultness than infants in the insecure-avoidant or secure attachment groups.

Gunnar, Mangelsdorf, Larson, and Hertsgaard (1989) found that proneness-to-distress, as assessed by both maternal reports and observational assessments at 9 months of age, predicted infants' distress in the Strange Situation at 13 months. However, proneness-to-distress was not related to overall attachment classifications. Infants high on proneness-to-distress were no more likely to be classified as insecurely attached than infants low on proneness-to-distress (Mangelsdorf, Gunnar et al., 1990).

Other research conducted in our laboratory (Mangelsdorf, Diener, McHale, & Pilolla, 1993; Mangelsdorf, McHale, Diener, & Lehn, 1993) has also indicated associations between temperament (as rated by parents and as assessed in the laboratory) and infants' behaviors in the Strange Situation (e.g., crying, proximity seeking, avoidance), but not to the overall attachment classifications. In addition to these associations, we found that infants who were rated as more sociable with a stranger during a laboratory temperament assessment (Goldsmith & Rothbart, 1990) were likely to be more avoidant of the mother during the Strange Situation. But, despite the fact that these infants displayed more avoidant *behavior,* they were no more likely to get an overall classification of insecure-avoidant. Hence, our research and the research of a number of other investigators indicates that although some stability in infants' behavior can be found across different contexts (i.e., home, laboratory), this stability in and of itself does not predict the security of infant–caregiver attachment relationships. Rather, as discussed below, the attachment relationship emerges out of a complex interaction among a variety of factors, including but not limited to infant temperament, maternal personality, and maternal social support.

C. EXAMINING EXTREME GROUPS

In research in which infants have been selected specifically on the basis of extreme scores (top 17%) on proneness-to-distress or irritability during the newborn period, higher rates of insecurity have been found than in other samples (van den

Boo, 1989, 1994). For example, van den Boom (1994) found that extreme irritability was associated with increased rates of insecure attachment. In fact, 78% of highly irritable infants whose mothers did not receive any form of parenting intervention were classified as insecurely attached, in contrast to most normal unselected samples in which about 30% of infants are classified as insecure. Thus, van den Boom's study suggests that when extreme groups are examined, temperament may exert stronger direct effects on attachment security than when other samples are used. However, a substantial body of empirical research on unselected, or nonextreme samples has failed to support Kagan's hypothesis that individual differences in temperament explain all of the variance in attachment classifications. This lack of support does not imply that temperament has no effect on Strange Situation classifications—temperament does seem to be related to behavior in the Strange Situation and may affect the *type* of insecurity a child manifests. Temperament theorists have suggested that failure to find effects of temperament on attachment security may be due to inadequate statistical power associated with small sample sizes (Goldsmith et al., 1986). Given the distribution of secure, insecure-avoidant, and insecure-resistant infants in normal populations (65%, 25%, 10% respectively), significant differences may be hard to find when comparisons are made between attachment categories with small numbers of subjects in each group, as is typically true of the insecure-resistant and insecure-avoidant groups (Fox, 1992).

D. THE REACTIVITY DISTINCTION

As indicated in our earlier discussion of attachment, each of the three Strange Situation classifications has from two to four subgroups. There are two subgroups of insecure-avoidant infants (A1, A2), four subgroups of secure infants (B1, B2, B3, B4), and two subgroups of insecure-resistant infants (C1, C2). These subgroups differ in terms of their patterns of crying, proximity seeking and contact maintaining, avoidance, and resistant to contact (see Ainsworth et al., 1978, for a detailed description of each of these subgroups).

Some researchers examining the contributions of temperament to attachment have explored how the eight attachment subgroups may differ in terms of temperament. For example, Frodi and Thompson (1985) reported that two subgroups of secure infants (B1 and B2) were more similar to avoidant infants in their display and regulation of distress than they were to other secure infants (B3 and B4) infants, but B3 and B4 infants were more similar to resistant infants in terms of proneness-to-distress. Thus, Frodi and Thompson suggested that an affect continuum might underlie certain Strange Situation behaviors. Infants classified as insecure-avoidant (A1 or A2) or as the B1 or B2 subgroups of secure attachment are considered to be less reactive than the other two subgroups of secure infants (B3, B4), or the insecure-resistant infants (C1 or C2). Low reactive subgroups tend to show little distress during separations and are less likely to seek physical contact with their caregiver following separation. In contrast, the high reactive infants show greater distress and are more likely to seek physical contact.

Following up on the suggestion that an affect continuum might underlie infants' behaviors in the Strange Situation, Belsky and Rovine (1987) examined Sroufe's (1985) hypothesis that temperament would influence the *type* of insecurity manifested, rather than overall security or insecurity, by examining differences in low versus high reactive groups. Specifically, Belsky and Rovine explored whether infants who were classified as A1-B2 (low reactive) and B3-C2 (high reactive) in the Strange Situation at 12 and 13 months of age differed in their temperaments earlier in infancy. They found that infants classified as low reactive at 12 months with their mothers and at 13 months with their fathers had displayed greater autonomic stability during the administration of the Neonatal Behavioral Assessment Scale during the newborn period, than those classified as high reactive at 12 and 13 months. In addition, infants subsequently classified as low reactive were consistently rated by their mothers as having "easier" temperaments at 3 months of age than those infants later classified as high reactive. An additional investigation examining infant-proneness-to-distress (based on both observational assessment and maternal report) at 9 months and security of attachment at 13 months failed to replicate this reactivity split (Mangelsdorf, Gunnar et al., 1990). Perhaps the different findings obtained in these two investigations are partially due to age differences in the assessment of proneness-to-distress. Irritability in the neonatal period may have a different association with Strange Situation classifications than irritability or proneness-to-distress assessed later in the first year of life.

Additional empirical evidence supporting the notion of a reactivity dimension underlying individual differences in Strange Situation behavior comes from the work of Susman-Stillman et al. (1996). They found that infants high on sociability at 3 months (based on both mothers' and observers' ratings) were more likely to be classified as low reactive than as high reactive in the Strange Situation at 12 months of age. In contrast, infants high on irritability were more likely to be classified as high reactive than as low reactive. This pattern is consistent with the position that temperament may influence behavior within the Strange Situation, and hence subclassifications, but not overall attachment security (Belsky & Rovine, 1987; Sroufe, 1985). Also consistent with this view are the results of research by Braungart and Stifter (1991) on infant emotional reactivity and emotion regulation within the Strange Situation. They noted patterns of reactivity that were consistent with the reactivity continuum (Belsky & Rovine, 1987; Frodi & Thompson, 1985), with insecure-avoidant (both A1 and A2), secure-B1, and secure-B2 infants being less reactive than secure-B3, secure-B4, and insecure-resistant (both C1 and C2) infants. However, they also identified patterns of regulation that distinguished insecure from secure infants. For example, insecure-avoidant infants were more object-oriented and more likely to engage in self-comforting behaviors than other infants.

Further evidence supporting the notion of a reactivity dimension underlying behavior within the Strange Situation is found in a meta-analysis conducted by Fox, Kimmerly, and Schafer (1991). Eleven studies of the concordance of mother–infant and father–infant attachment were included in the analysis. Fox et al. found significant associations between attachment classifications for infant–mother and infant–father dyads, particularly when the reactivity dimension was examined. In fact, over 75% of the infants exhibited concordance on the reactivity dimension. In other words, infants who were high reactive in the Strange Situation (B3 to C2), with one parent were unlikely to be low reactive in the Strange Situation (A1 to B2) with the other parent. Moreover, if infants were insecure with both parents, they tended to manifest the same type of insecurity with each parent. For example, 63% of infants who were insecurely attached with both parents were insecure-avoidant with both; 25% were insecure-resistant with both. Similarity in attachments to both mother and father cannot be attributed solely to child characteristics, as spouses tend to be similar on measures of personality, relationship history, self-esteem (e.g., Frosch, Mangelsdorf, & McHale, 1998), and parenting (e.g., Belsky & Volling, 1987). However, these results do suggest that certain temperament characteristics may predispose the child to manifest one particular type of insecurity or the other. That is, fussiness or proneness-to-distress may predispose a child toward insecure-resistant attachment, and sociability may predispose a child toward insecure-avoidant attachment.

E. EVIDENCE OF GOODNESS-OF-FIT

In support of a Goodness-of-Fit model, Crockenberg (1981) reported that irritable temperament during the newborn period is predictive of insecure attachment only in conjunction with low maternal social support. That is, neither infant temperament nor maternal support exerted a main effect on attachment. Instead, the *interaction* between these two variables predicted insecure attachment. Similarly, Mangelsdorf, Gunnar, et al. (1990) found that security of attachment, as assessed at 13 months in the Strange Situation, could be predicted by an interaction between infants' proneness-to-distress temperament measured at 9 months in a standardized laboratory temperament assessment (Matheny & Wilson, 1981) and maternal personality. Mothers who scored high on the Constraint scale of Tellegen's (1982) Multidimensional Personality Questionnaire and who had infants who scored high on proneness-to-distress at 9 months were also likely to have insecurely attached infants at 13 months. As in the Crockenberg (1981) study, temperament or maternal personality had no significant main effects. Rather, the interaction between the two variables predicted insecure attachment. One can easily imagine how the combination of a fearful and rigid mother (i.e., the profile of high scorers on the Multidimensional Personality Questionnaire dimension, Constraint) coupled with an easily distressed infant could result in a less than optimal relationship. Such interactive effects have also been found by Bohlin and colleagues (Bohlin, Hagekull, Germer, Andersson, & Lindberg, 1989). Although infant temperament measures

did not predict later insecure attachment, the interaction of maternal physical contact and infant intensity/activity significantly predicted insecure-avoidant attachment. In other words, highly intense and active infants who received little emotional physical contact from their mothers appeared to be at risk for developing
avoidant relationships.

Thus, the findings from these studies provide empirical support for a goodness-
of-fit or transactional model (Crockenberg, 1986; Sameroff & Chandler, 1975;
Sameroff & Fiese, 1990). Remaining to be examined, however, are the parameters
of such a model. Some infant characteristics, such as irritability or proneness-to-
distress seem more likely to contribute to insecure attachment than others. Similarly, specific parental characteristics may be particularly important to attachment
relationships, and certain forms of social support, particularly marital support, may
be particularly important for predicting sensitive parenting (Goldstein, Diener, &
Mangelsdorf, 1996). In fact, an extensive body of literature documents the association between the quality of the marital relationship and multiple aspects of parenting behavior, including sensitivity, negativity, and intrusiveness (e.g., Belsky,
Youngblade, Rovine, & Volling, 1991; Cox, Owen, Lewis, & Henderson, 1989;
Cox, Paley, Payne, & Burchinal, 1999; Frosch & Mangelsdorf, 1999; Miller, Cowan, Cowan, Hetherington, & Clingempeel, 1993; see also Erel & Burman, 1995).
Future researchers should examine more thoroughly the particular variables that
contribute to the "fit" between infant and parental characteristics. In addition, researchers should further explore how paternal and child characteristics interact to
predict *father*–child relationship outcomes.

Although thus far in this chapter, attachment security has been examined as the
outcome measure, "goodness-of-fit" is a concept that continues to be useful for examining the constructs of temperament and attachment after the formation of the
infant–parent attachment relationship. Nachmias, Gunnar, Mangelsdorf, Parritz,
and Buss (1996) assessed the relation of temperament and attachment to physiological stress reactivity in 18-month-olds. We found that the goodness-of-fit between the child's needs and the attachment relationship with the mother predicted
the child's physiological stress reactivity. Specifically, behaviorally inhibited toddlers (as assessed in the laboratory) exhibited increases in salivary cortisol (a physiological indicator of stress reactivity) both during a stressful laboratory procedure
and during the Strange Situation. However, these increases were observed *only* for
inhibited toddlers who were insecurely attached to their mothers. Inhibited toddlers who were securely attached did not show such increases. In other words, a
secure relationship with their mother helped to buffer the inhibited child from the
stresses of the laboratory procedures. Thus in this study, temperament and attachment security interacted to predict how children would respond to stressful events.
These findings highlight the importance of examining both temperament and attachment in studies of stress reactivity and emotional development.

Kochanska (1991, 1995) has documented similar interactive effects of temperament and attachment security in the prediction of preschoolers' conscience development. Specifically, for wary or fearful children, only gentle maternal discipline that de-emphasizes power seems to be necessary for children's internalization of moral values and compliance. For relatively fearless children, in contrast, gentle discipline was ineffective, but security of attachment was predictive of internalization. Kochanska (1995) suggested that gentle discipline, which may evoke mild anxiety, is simply not sufficient for fearless children to encode a rule. However, fearless children will comply in order to please their mothers if their affective relationship is close. In other words, internalization has alternative pathways: one emphasizes mild fear and anxiety, and the other builds on the positive relationship between mother and child. Importantly, these two pathways appear to be differentially effective for children of varying temperaments.

F. SUMMARY OF METHODOLOGICAL ISSUES

Little research has revealed main effects of temperament on attachment security as assessed in the Strange Situation, perhaps in part because of the methodology used. We alluded to methodological differences earlier, but a main difference is that the constructs of temperament and attachment have been assessed in very different ways. Temperament has generally been assessed with questionnaires, and only more recently have standardized laboratory-based assessments been used. With both methodologies—self-report and standardized observations—temperament characteristics are usually examined as continuous dimensions. In contrast, most attachment researchers have relied almost exclusively on the use of the Strange Situation, which results in a categorical rating of secure, insecure-avoidant, or insecure-resistant. Despite the categorical nature of Strange Situation classifications, a few investigations have attempted to place attachment subclassifications along a continuum, ranging from most secure to least secure, although this continuum has varied across studies, and there is no consensus about whether certain subgroups are more or less secure than others. Despite these attempts to create a continuum of attachment security as assessed in the Strange Situation, the three-category approach (or four, if Disorganized attachment is included) remains the most common methodological approach to examining Strange Situation data. Thus, failure to find consensus across multiple studies assessing both temperament and attachment may be due to differences in how the constructs are defined and measured.

G. ATTACHMENT Q-SET AND MEASURES OF TEMPERAMENT

Thus far, relatively few investigators have explored the associations among temperament and attachment using the Attachment Q-Set instead of the Strange Situation. One notable exception was a large-scale investigation conducted by Vaughn and his colleagues (1992). In their investigation, data were pooled from six different studies involving both Q-set measures of attachment security and ratings of child temperament (total $N = 555$). They found, using different measures of child temperament and different raters, an increasing convergence over time between Q-set ratings of security and temperament ratings from 12 to 42 months of age. The magnitude of the correlation between greater negative reactivity and lower attachment security was substantially greater for older children than for infants and toddlers. Apparently, with increasing age, the two measures look increasingly more similar.[3] However, even in the samples of the older children in which mothers completed measures of both temperament and attachment, these measures shared less than 25% of the variance. Thus, although the Vaughn et al. investigation provides evidence that temperament and attachment are increasingly related with development, the results certainly do not indicate that the two constructs are one and the same.

Wachs and Desai (1993) reported similar findings in a smaller sample. They found that security in the infant–parent attachment relationship as assessed with the Attachment Q-Set was related to five different temperament dimensions using Carey's Toddler Temperament Scale. Specifically, they found that greater attachment security was associated with less activity, more rhythmicity, more adaptability, milder intensity, and more positive mood in 2-year-olds.

Seifer et al. (1996) also found that infant temperament was significantly associated with security of attachment as assessed with observers' sorts of the Attachment Q-Set, but not with attachment security as assessed in with Strange Situation. For example, mothers' reports of infant difficultness, distress to limitations, fussiness, and emotionality at 12 months were negatively associated with the Attachment Q-Set security scores at 12 months. The results of the Teti et al. (1991) investigation described earlier are also relevant. Recall that they found associations between mothers' sorts of the Attachment Q-Set and their reports of parenting stress, particularly regarding child characteristics. Frosch and Mangelsdorf (1999) also found associations between the security of preschooler–parent attachment as assessed with the Attachment Q-Set and parents' reports of temperament as assessed with the Toddler Behavior Questionnaire (TBAQ; Goldsmith, 1988). Specifically, more secure child–mother and child–father attachment relationships were associated with greater inhibitory control, soothability, and interest, and less anger and sadness. Thus, taken together, these results suggest that associations between temperament and security of attachment may be stronger when the Attachment Q-Set is used as a measure of attachment than when the Strange Situation is used. Given that the Strange Situation assesses behavior under duress and the Attachment Q-Set assesses a wider repertoire of behaviors under a variety of more normal circumstances, these results are not particularly surprising.

---

[3]This is not surprising given that attachment theorists such as Bowlby (1969; 1982) argue that the quality of infant–parent attachment influences personality development and many temperament measures assess more stable, personality-like characteristics.

In our research, we have used the Attachment Q-Set quite successfully to examine "temperament-like" characteristics. In one investigation, two trained observers conducted home observations when the infants were 14 months old ($+/-$ 3 weeks). Two observations, each lasting $1\frac{1}{2}$ hours, were conducted for each family. Following each home visit, the observers independently completed the 90-item Attachment Q-Set. The two raters' sorts were averaged across visits, and then averaged across raters, to create a composite Q-sort for each child. An overall security score was calculated for each child by correlating the composite Q-sort with a criterion security sort developed by Waters (1987).

To develop scales for examining temperament with the Attachment Q-Set, two raters who were unaware of data collected during the home observation, independently grouped Q-Set items into conceptually related categories (Mangelsdorf, Berlin, Dedrick, & Sussell, 1990). The raters then met to discuss these categories and develop scales that captured a variety of dimensions of temperament such as sociability, frustration tolerance, reaction to novelty, and positive/negative affect, as well as attachment behaviors such as resistance, contact seeking, and secure-base behavior.

Parents also completed Bates' Infant Characteristics Questionnaire when their infants were 8 and 19 months of age. When the major temperament factors from the Bates—fussy and unadaptable—were correlated with the 14-month Q-sort scores, significant but low-level associations emerged (see Table I). However, given that the Infant Characteristic Questionnaire and the Attachment Q-set are quite different and that various raters (observers vs. mothers) completed these measures at intervals separated in time by 5 and 6 months, the fact that any convergence at all occurred is noteworthy. Moreover, it is noteworthy that temperament ratings

TABLE I

Associations between Infant Characteristics Questionnaire Factors at 8 and 19 Months
and Attachment Q-Set Scales (14 Months)

	8 months		19 months	
	Fussy	Unadaptable	Fussy	Unadaptable
Security criterion	.14	−.12	−.31	−.21*
Reaction to novelty	.14	.32*	.24*	.29*
Frustration tolerance	−.24*	−.35**	−.34**	−.33**
Separation distress	.37**	.32**	.36**	.33**
Positive affect	−.23	−.30*	−.29*	−.28*
Resistance	.26*	.13	.28*	.11
Contact seeking	.10	.31*	.04	.13
Secure base	.24*	.30*	−.01	.21

$*= p < .05.$ $**= p < .01.$

TABLE II

Correlations between Attachment Q-Set Scales at 14 months and Interactive Behavior
in the Strange Situation at 19 Months[a]

	Q-set scales		
	Reaction to novelty	Activity	Sociability
Proximity seeking	.47**	−.22	−.63***
Contact maintaining	.35*	−.29	−.29
Avoidance	−.54**	.40*	.59***
Resistance	.07	-.07	−.09

[a]Strange Situation Behaviors coded are averaged across the two reunion episodes (episodes 5 and 8).
$*= p < .05.$ $**= p < .01.$ $***= p < .001.$

and Q-sort security criterion scores were significantly associated at 19 months, but not at 14 months. This finding is consistent with the research of Vaughn and colleagues (1992) showing developmental increases in convergence between Q-Set ratings of security and temperament ratings.

When we (Mangelsdorf, Berlin, et al., 1990) examined the associations between our Q-Set scales (as opposed to overall security scores) and infants' behavior in the Strange Situation, the correlations were more robust (see Table II). The association between infant sociability and avoidance in the Strange Situation is one we described earlier—positive affect during interaction with a stranger at 8 months (in a laboratory temperament assessment) is associated with more avoidance of the mother in the Strange Situation, but *not* with the overall classification of insecure-avoidant. This finding of an association between sociability and avoidance of mother is inconsistent with Buss and Plomin's hypothesis that insecure-avoidant children are those who are low on sociability, but is consistent with the findings of other investigations showing that avoidance of mother is associated with positive temperament characteristics including sociability (e.g., Goldsmith et al., 1986; Susman-Stillman et al., 1996).

Other researchers have also used the Attachment Q-Set to examine temperament characteristics. For example, much as we did, Pederson and Moran (1995; Moran & Pederson, 1997) developed scales from the Attachment Q-Set to examine infant temperament characteristics such as fussiness and compliance, and infant attachment behaviors such as secure-base behavior. Infants who scored higher on the Fussy/Difficult scale derived from the Attachment Q-set were also rated as more Fussy/Difficult on the Infant Characteristics Questionnaire. In addition, Moran and Pederson (1997) found that insecure-resistant infants scored higher on both measures of Fussy/Difficult behavior. These results are consistent with other investigations and indicate modest but significant associations between fussiness or negative affectivity and resistance (e.g., Goldsmith & Alansky, 1987; Susman-Stillman et al., 1996).

VII. Summary and Conclusions

In this chapter we described the constructs of temperament and attachment and have discussed similarities and differences between the two. We addressed the issue of whether temperament contributes to overall attachment security or to the specific *type* of attachment that children display. We conclude that although temperament may influence the *type* of secure and insecure attachment relationship children form with their parent, temperament alone will not determine if a child is classified as securely or insecurely attached. We presented evidence suggesting that certain dimensions of temperament, specifically negative emotionality, may be associated with infants' behavior during the Strange Situation, such as proneness-to-distress during separations. However, we noted that these temperament dimensions do not predict overall security of attachment. It is likely that although no single temperament characteristic, such as proneness-to-distress, in and of itself determines overall attachment security, it is possible that a constellation of temperament characteristics may be more strongly related to attachment security. The examination of constellations of temperament characteristics may be particularly useful for furthering our understanding of individual differences within attachment classifications. Such an approach may elucidate the reasons why infants are classified into one subgroup of secure, insecure-avoidant, or insecure-resistant attachment versus another subgroup.

Furthermore, we suggest that the collection of findings regarding temperament and attachment not only underscores the importance of a transactional approach to early social-emotional development, but emphasizes that temperament and attachment can make unique and interactive contributions to children's social emotional functioning. That is, the goodness-of-fit between infant and parent characteristics may best predict security of attachment. Although child characteristics clearly contribute to the development of the parent–child relationship, we believe that the effects of infant temperament on infant–caregiver attachment may well be indirect, and may be moderated by such variables as maternal personality and social support. Thus, taken together, a growing literature clearly indicates that although temperament and attachment security are interrelated, they are by no means interchangeable constructs. To return to our guiding question, "Temperament and attachment: One construct or two?" We reply, "two."

ACKNOWLEDGMENTS

While preparing this chapter, Cynthia A. Frosch was supported by a National Institute of Child Health and Human Development postdoctoral fellowship through the Carolina Consortium on Human Development at the Center for Developmental Science at the University of North Carolina at Chapel Hill and by the National Center for Early Development and Learning (Department of Education, Grant No. R307A6004). We thank Hayne Reese and Ariana Shahinfar for thoughtful comments regarding an earlier version of this chapter.

214 *Sarah C. Mangelsdorf and Cynthia A. Frosch*

REFERENCES

Achenbach, T. M. (1991). *Manual for the Child Behavior Checklist/4-18 and 1991 Profile*. Burlington: University of Vermont, Department of Psychiatry.

Achenbach, T. M. (1992). *Manual for the Child Behavior Checklist/2-3 and 1992 Profile*. Burlington: University of Vermont, Department of Psychiatry.

Ainsworth, M. D. S. (1973). The development of infant–mother attachment. In B. M. Caldwell & H. N. Ricciuti (Eds.), *Review of child development research* (Vol. 3, pp. 1–94). Chicago: University of Chicago Press.

Ainsworth, M. D. S. (1982). Attachment: Retrospect and prospect. In C. M. Parkers & J. Stevenson-Hinde (Eds.), *The place of attachment in human behavior* (pp. 3–30). New York: Basic Books.

Ainsworth, M. D. S., Blehar, M., Waters, E., & Wall, S. (1978). *Patterns of attachment*. Hillsdale, NJ: Erlbaum.

Arend, R., Gove, F. L., & Sroufe, L. A. (1979). Continuity of individual adaptation from infancy to kindergarten: A predictive study of ego-resiliency and curiosity in preschoolers. *Child Development, 50,* 950–959.

Bates, J. E., Maslin, C. A., & Frankel, K. A. (1985). Attachment security, mother-child interaction, and temperament as predictors of behavior problem ratings at age three years. *Monographs of the Society for Research in Child Development, 50*(1–2, Serial No. 209).

Bates, J. E. (1987). Temperament in infancy. In J. Osofsky (Ed.), *Handbook of infant development* (pp. 1101–1149). New York: Wiley.

Bates, J. E., & Bayles, K. (1984). Objective and subjective components in mothers' perceptions of their children from age 6 months to 3 years. *Merrill-Palmer Quarterly, 30,* 111–130.

Bell, R. Q. (1968). A reinterpretation of the direction of effects in studies of socialization. *Psychological Review, 75,* 81–95.

Bell, S. M., & Ainsworth, M. D. S. (1972). Infant crying and maternal responsiveness. *Child Development, 43,* 1171–1190.

Belsky, J., & Isabella, R. (1988). Maternal, infant, and social-contextual determinants of attachment security. In J. Belsky & R. Isabella (Eds.), *Clinical implications of attachment* (pp. 41–94). Hillsdale, NJ: Erlbaum.

Belsky, J., & Rovine, M. (1987). Temperament and attachment security in the Strange Situation: An empirical rapprochement. *Child Development, 58,* 787–795.

Belsky, J., Rovine, M., & Taylor, D. G. (1984). The Pennsylvania infant and family development project. III. The origins of individual differences in infant-mother attachment: Maternal and infant contributions. *Child Development, 55,* 718–728.

Belsky, J., & Volling, B. L. (1987). Mothering, fathering, and marital interaction in the family triad during infancy: Exploring family system's processes. In P. Berman & F. Pederson (Eds.), *Men's transition to parenthood* (pp. 37–63). Hillsdale, NJ: Erlbaum.

Belsky, J., Youngblade, L., Rovine, M., & Volling, B. (1991). Patterns of marital change and parent-child interaction. *Journal of Marriage and the Family, 53,* 498–498.

Bohlin, G., Hagekull, B., Germer, M., Andersson, K., & Lindberg, L. (1989). Avoidant and resistant reunion behaviors as predicted by maternal interactive behavior and infant temperament. *Infant Behavior and Development, 12,* 105–117.

Bost, K., Vaughn, B. E., Washington, W. N., Cielinski, K. L., & Bradford, M. R. (1998). Social competence, social support, and attachment: Demarcation of construct domains, measurement, and paths of influence for preschool children attending Head Start. *Child Development, 69,* 193–218.

Bowlby, J. (1982). *Attachment and loss: Vol. 1. Attachment* (2nd ed.). New York: Basic Books.

Braungart, J. M., & Stifter, C. A. (1991). Regulation of negative reactivity during the Strange Situation: Temperament and attachment in 12-month-old infants. *Infant Behavior and Development, 14,* 349–364.

Buss, A. H., & Plomin, R. (1975). *A temperament theory of personality development.* New York: Wiley.

Buss, A. H., & Plomin, R. (1986). The EAS approach to temperament. In R. Plomin & J. Dunn (Eds.), *The study of temperament: Changes, continuities, and challenges* (pp. 67–79). Hillsdale, NJ: Erlbaum.

Calkins, S. D., & Fox, N. A. (1992). The relations among infant temperament, security of attachment, and behavioral inhibition at 24 months. *Child Development, 63,* 1456–1472.

Carey, W. B. (1970). A simplified method for measuring infant temperament. *Journal of Pediatrics, 77,* 188–194.

Carey, W. B., & McDevitt, S. (1978). Revision of the infant temperament questionnaire. *Pediatrics, 61,* 735–739.

Caspi, A., Elder, G. H., Jr., & Bem, D. J. (1987). Moving against the world: Life-course patterns of explosive children. *Developmental Psychology, 23,* 308–313.

Caspi, A., Moffitt, T. E., Newman, D. L., & Silva, P. A. (1996). Behavioral observations at age 3 years predict adult psychiatric disorders. *Archives of General Psychiatry, 53,* 1033–1039.

Caspi, A., & Silva, P. A. (1995). Temperamental qualities at age three predict personality traits in young adulthood: Longitudinal evidence from a birth cohort. *Child Development, 66,* 486–498.

Chess, S., & Thomas, A. (1984). *Origins and evolution of behavior disorders.* New York: Brunner/Mazel.

Cox, M. J., Owen, M. T., Lewis, J. M., & Henderson, V. K. (1989). Marriage, adult adjustment, and early parenting. *Child Development, 69,* 1015–1024.

Cox, M. J., Paley, B., Payne, C. C., & Burchinal, M. (1999). The transition to parenthood: Marital conflict and withdrawal and parent-infant interaction. In M. Cox & J. Brooks-Gunn (Eds.), *Conflict and cohesion in families: Causes and consequences* (pp. 87–104). Mahwah, NJ: Erlbaum.

Crittenden, P. (1985). Maltreated infants: Vulnerability and resilience. *Journal of Child Psychology and Psychiatry, 26,* 85–96.

Crittenden, P. (1988). Relationships at risk. In J. Belsky & T. Nezworski (Eds.), *Clinical implications of attachment* (pp. 136–174). Hillsdale, NJ: Erlbaum.

Crockenberg, S. B. (1981). Infant irritability, mother responsiveness, and social support influences on the security of infant-mother attachment. *Child Development, 52,* 857–867.

Crockenberg, S. B. (1986). Are temperamental differences in babies associated with predictable differences in care giving? *New Directions for Child Development, 31,* 53–73.

DeMulder, E. K., & Radke-Yarrow, M. (1991). Attachment with affectively ill and well mothers: Concurrent behavioral correlates. *Development and Psychopathology, 3,* 227–242.

Derryberry, D., & Rothbart, M. K. (1984). Emotion, attention, and temperament. In C. E. Izard, J. Kagan, & R. B. Zajonc (Eds.), *Emotion, cognition, and behavior* (pp. 132–166). Cambridge, England: Cambridge University Press.

DeWolff, M., & van IJzendoorn, M. H. (1997). Sensitivity and attachment: A meta-analysis on parental antecedents of infant attachment. *Child Development, 68,* 571–591.

Diener, M. L., Goldstein, L. H., & Mangelsdorf, S. C. (1995). The role of prenatal expectations in parents' reports of infant temperament. *Merrill-Palmer Quarterly, 41,* 172–190.

Easterbrooks, M. A., & Lamb, M. E. (1979). The relationship between quality of infant-mother attachment and infant competence in initial encounters with peers. *Child Development, 50,* 380–387.

Egeland, B., & Farber, E. (1984). Infant-mother attachment: Factors related to its development and changes over time. *Child Development, 55,* 753–771.

Elicker, J., Englund, M., & Sroufe, L. A. (1992). Predicting peer competence and peer relationships in childhood from early parent-child relationships. In R. D. Parke & G. W. Ladd (Eds.), *Family-peer relationships: Modes of linkage* (pp. 77–106). Hillsdale, NJ: Erlbaum.

Erel, O., & Burman, B. (1995). Interrelatedness of marital relations and parent-child relations: A meta-analytic review. *Psychological Bulletin, 118,* 108–132.

Escalona, S. E. (1968). *The roots of individuality.* Chicago: Aldine.

Fox, N. A. (1992). The role of individual differences in infant personality in the formation of attachment relationships. In E. J. Susman, L. V. Feagans, & W. J. Ray (Eds.), *Emotions, cognition, health and development in children and adolescents* (pp. 31–52). Hillsdale, NJ: Erlbaum.

Fox, N. A., Kimmerly, N. L., & Schafer, W. D. (1991). Attachment to mother/attachment to father: A meta-analysis. *Child Development, 62,* 210–225.

Frankel, K. A., & Bates, J. E. (1990). Mother-toddler problem solving: Antecedents in attachment, home behavior, and temperament. *Child Development, 61,* 810–819.

Frodi, A., & Thompson, R. (1985). Infants' affective responses in the Strange Situation: Effects of prematurity and of quality of attachment. *Child Development, 56,* 1280–1290.

Frosch, C. A., & Mangelsdorf, S. C. (1999). Predicting multiple reports of preschoolers' behavior problems from marital behavior: Does child gender moderate and parenting behavior mediate? Manuscript under review.

Frosch, C. A., & Mangelsdorf, S. C. (1999). Behavioral correlates of mother-child and father-child attachment during the preschool years. Manuscript in preparation.

Frosch, C. A., Mangelsdorf, S. C., & McHale, J. L. (1998). Correlates of marital behavior at six months post-partum. *Developmental Psychology, 34,* 1438–1449.

Fullard, W., McDevitt, S. C., & Carey, W. B. (1984). Assessing temperament in one- to three-year old children. *Journal of Pediatric Psychology, 9,* 205–216.

Goldsmith, H. H. (1988). *Preliminary manual for the Toddler Behavior Assessment Questionnaire* (Tech. Rep. No. 88-04). Oregon Center for the Study of Emotion.

Goldsmith, H. H., & Alansky, J. A. (1987). Maternal and infant temperamental predictors of attachment: A meta-analytic review. *Journal of Consulting and Clinical Psychology, 55,* 805–816.

Goldsmith, H. H., Bradshaw, D. L., & Reisser-Danner, L. A. (1986). Temperament as a potential developmental influence on attachment. *New Directions for Child Development, 31,* 5–34.

Goldsmith, H. H., Buss, A., Plomin, R., Rothbart, M. K., Thomas, A., Chess, S., Hinde, R. A., & McCall, R. B. (1987). Roundtable: What is temperament? Four approaches. *Child Development, 58,* 505–529.

Goldsmith, H. H., & Campos, J. J. (1982). Toward a theory of infant temperament. In R. N. Emde & R. J. Harmon (Eds.), *The development of attachment and affiliative systems* (pp. 161–193). New York: Plenum.

Goldsmith, H. H., & Rothbart, M. (1990). *The laboratory temperament assessment battery.* Unpublished manuscript, University of Oregon, Eugene.

Goldsmith, H. H., & Rothbart, M. K. (1991). Contemporary instruments for assessing early temperament by questionnaire and in the laboratory. In J. Strelau & A. Angleitner (Eds.), *Explorations in temperament: International perspectives on theory and measurement* (pp. 249–272). New York: Plenum.

Goldstein, L. H., Diener, M. L., & Mangelsdorf, S. C. (1996) Maternal characteristics and social support across the transition to motherhood: Associations with maternal behavior. *Journal of Family Psychology, 10,* 60–71.

Grossmann, K., Grossmann, K. E., Spangler, G., Suess, G., & Unzner, L. (1985). Maternal sensitivity and newborns' orientation responses as related to quality of attachment in northern Germany. *Monographs of the Society for Research in Child Development, 50,*(1–2, Serial No. 209).

Gunnar, M. R., Mangelsdorf, S. C., Larson, M., & Hertsgaard, L. (1989). Attachment, temperament, and adrenocortical activity in infancy. *Developmental Psychology, 25,* 355–363.

Hegvik, R. L., McDevitt, S. C., & Carey, W. B. (1982). The Middle Childhood Temperament Questionnaire. *Developmental and Behavioral Pediatrics, 3,* 197–200.

Hubbard, F. O. A., & van IJzendoorn, M. H. (1991). Maternal responsiveness and infant crying across the first 9 months: A naturalistic longitudinal study. *Infant Behavior and Development, 14,* 299–312.

Hubert, N. C., Wachs, T. D., Peters-Martin, P., & Gandour, M. J. (1982). The study of early temperament: Measurement and conceptual issues. *Child Development, 53,* 571–600.

Isabella, R. A. (1993). Origins of attachment: Maternal interactive behavior across the first year. *Child Development, 64,* 605–621.

Isabella, R. A., & Belsky, J. (1991). Interactional synchrony and the origins of infant-mother attachment: A replication study. *Child Development, 62,* 373–384.

Kagan, J. (1982). *Psychological research on the human infant: An evaluative summary.* New York: Grant Foundation.

Kagan, J. (1984). *The nature of the child.* New York: Basic Books.

Kagan, J. (1989). Temperamental contributions to social behavior. *American Psychologist, 44,* 668–674.

Kagan, J., Reznick, J. S., Clarke, C., Snidman, N., & Garcia-Coll, C. (1984). Behavioral inhibition to the unfamiliar. *Child Development, 55,* 2212–2225.

Kagan, J., Reznick, J. S., & Snidman, N. (1988). Biological bases of childhood shyness. *Science, 240,* 167–171.

Kestenbaum, R., Farber, E. A., & Sroufe, L. A. (1989). Individual differences in empathy among preschoolers: Relation to attachment history. *New Directions for Child Development, 44,* 51–64.

Kochanska, G. (1991). Socialization and temperament in the development of guilt and conscience. *Child Development, 62,* 1379–1392.

Kochanska, G. (1995). Children's temperament, mothers' discipline, and security of attachment: Multiple pathways to emerging internalization. *Child Development, 66,* 597–615.

Lamb, M. E., Thompson, R. A., Gardner, W., & Charnov, E. L. (1985). *Infant-mother attachment: The origins and developmental significance of individual differences in Strange Situation behavior.* Hillsdale, NJ: Erlbaum.

Lavigne, J. V., Gibbons, R. D., Christoffel, K. K., Arend, R., Rosenbaum, D., Binns, H., Dawson, N., Sobel, H., & Isaacs, C. (1996). Rates and correlates of psychiatric disorders among preschool children. *Journal of the American Academy of Child and Adolescent Psychiatry, 35,* 204–214.

Lieberman, A. F. (1977). Preschoolers' competence with a peer: Influence of attachment and social experience. *Child Development, 48,* 1277–1287.

Main, M., & Solomon, J. (1986). Discovery of a new, insecure-disorganized/disoriented attachment pattern. In T. B. Brazelton & M. Yogman (Eds.), *Affective development in infancy* (pp. 95–124). Norwood, NJ: Ablex.

Main, M., & Solomon, J. (1990). Procedures for identifying infants as disorganized/disoriented during the Ainsworth Strange Situation. In M. Greenberg, D. Cicchetti, & M. Cummings (Eds.), *Attachment in the preschool years: Theory, research, and intervention* (pp. 121–160). Chicago: University of Chicago Press.

Mangelsdorf, S., Berlin, S., Dedrick, C., & Sussell, A. (1990, April). *The relation between temperament ratings and attachment Q-sort scores.* Paper presented in a symposium at the International Conference on Infant Studies, Montreal, Canada.

Mangelsdorf, S., Diener, M. L., McHale, J. L., & Pilolla, L. (1993, June). *Temperament and attachment: Individual differences in emotionality and infant-caregiver attachment.* Paper presented at the meeting of the American Psychological Society, Chicago.

Mangelsdorf, S., Gunnar, M., Kestenbaum, R., Lang, S., & Andreas, D. (1990). Infant proneness-to-distress temperament, maternal personality, and mother-infant attachment: Associations and goodness-of-fit. *Child Development, 61,* 820–831.

Mangelsdorf, S., McHale, J. L., Diener, M. L., & Lehn, L. (1993, March). *Infant attachment: Contributions of infant temperament and maternal personality.* Paper presented at the meeting of the Society for Research in Child Development, New Orleans, LA.

Mangelsdorf, S., Plunkett, J. W., Dedrick, C. F., Berlin, M., Meisels, S. J., McHale, J. L., &

Dichtelmiller, M. (1996). Attachment security in very low birth weight infants. *Developmental Psychology, 32,* 914–920.

Matas, L., Arend, R., & Sroufe, L. A. (1978). Continuity of adaptation in the second year: The relationship between quality of attachment and later competence. *Child Development, 49,* 547–556.

Matheny, A. P., & Wilson, R. S. (1981). Developmental tasks and rating scales for laboratory assessment of infant temperament. *JSAS Catalog of Selected Documents in Psychology, 11*(MS. No. 2367).

McDevitt, S. C., & Carey, W. B. (1978). Measurement of temperament in 3- to 7-year-old children. *Journal of Child Psychology and Psychiatry and Allied Disciplines, 19,* 245–253.

Miller, N. B., Cowan, P. A., Cowen, C. P., Hetherington, E. M., & Clingempeel, W. G. (1993). Externalizing in preschoolers and early adolescents: A cross-study replication of a family model. *Developmental Psychology, 29,* 3–18.

Miyake, K., Chen, S., & Campos, J. J. (1985). Infant temperament, mother's mode of interaction, and attachment in Japan: An interim report. *Monographs of the Society for Research in Child Development, 50*(1–2, Serial No. 209).

Moran, G., & Pederson, D. R. (1997, April). *Proneness to distress and ambivalent relationships observed in the home.* Paper presented at the meeting of the Society for Research in Child Development, Washington, DC.

Nachmias, M., Gunnar, M., Mangelsdorf, S. C., Parritz, R., & Buss, K. (1996). Behavioral inhibition and stress reactivity: The moderating role of attachment security. *Child Development, 67,* 508–522.

Park, K. A., & Waters, E. (1989). Security of attachment and preschool friendships. *Child Development, 60,* 1076–1081.

Pastor, D. (1981). The quality of mother-infant attachment and its relationship to toddlers' initial sociability with peers. *Developmental Psychology, 17,* 326–335.

Pederson, D. R., & Moran, G. (1995). A categorical description of infant-mother relationships in the home and its relation to Q-Sort measures of infant-mother interaction. *Monographs of the Society for Research in Child Development, 60*(2–3, Serial No. 244).

Pederson, D. R., Moran, G., Sitko, C., Campbell, K., Ghesquire, K., & Acton, H. (1990). Maternal sensitivity and the security of infant-mother attachment: A Q-Sort study. *Child Development, 61,* 1974–1983.

Radke-Yarrow, M., Cummings, E. M., Kuczynski, L., & Chapman, M. (1985). Patterns of attachment in two- and three-year-olds in normal families and families with parental depression. *Child Development, 56,* 884–892.

Rende, R. D. (1993). Longitudinal relations between temperament traits and behavioral syndromes in middle childhood. *Journal of the American Academy of Child and Adolescent Psychiatry, 32,* 287–290.

Renken, B., Egeland, B., Marvinney, D., Mangelsdorf, S., & Sroufe, L. A. (1989). Early childhood antecedents of aggression and passive-withdrawal in early elementary school. *Journal of Personality, 57,* 257 281.

Rothbart, M. (1989). Temperament in childhood: A framework. In G. A. Kohnstamm, J. E. Bates, & Rothbart, M. K. (Eds.), *Temperament in childhood* (pp. 59–73). Chichester: Wiley.

Rothbart, M., Ahadi, S., & Hershey, K. L. (1994). Temperament and social behavior in childhood. *Merrill-Palmer Quarterly, 40,* 21–39.

Rothbart, M., & Bates, J. E. (1998). Temperament. In W. Damon (Series Ed.), & N. Eisenberg (Vol. Ed.), *Handbook of child psychology: Vol. 3. Social, emotional, and personality development* (5th ed., pp. 105–176). New York: Wiley.

Rothbart, M., & Derryberry, D. (1981). Development of individual differences in temperament. In M. E. Lamb & A. L. Brown (Eds.), *Advance in developmental psychology* (Vol. 1, pp. 37–86). Hillsdale, NJ: Erlbaum.

Rowe, D. C., & Plomin, R. (1977). Temperament in early childhood. *Journal of Personality Assessment, 41,* 150–156.

Rutter, M. (1982). Temperament: Concepts, issues, and problems. Temperamental differences in infants and young children. *London Foundations Symposium, 89,* 1–15.

Rutter, M. (1989). Temperament: Conceptual issues and clinical implications. In G. A. Kohnstamm, J. E. Bates, & M. K. Rothbart (Eds.), *Temperament in childhood* (pp. 463–479). Chichester: Wiley.

Rutter, M., Birch, H. G., Thomas, A., & Chess, S. (1964). Temperamental characteristics in infancy and the later development of behavioural disorders. *British Journal of Psychiatry, 110,* 651–661.

Sagi, A., Lamb, M. E., Lewkowicz, K. S., Shoham, R., Dvir, R., & Estes, D. (1985). Security of infant-mother, -father, and -metaplet attachments among Kibbutz-reared Israeli children. *Monographs of the Society for Research in Child Development, 50*(1–2, Serial No. 209).

Sameroff, A., & Chandler, M. J. (1975). Reproductive risk and the continuum of caretaking casualty. In F. D. Horowitz, M. Hetherington, S. Scarr-Salapatek, & G. Siegel (Eds.), *Review of child development research* (Vol. 4, pp. 187–244). Chicago: University of Chicago Press.

Sameroff, A., & Fiese, B. H. (1990). Transactional regulation and early intervention. In S. J. Meisels & J. P. Shonkoff (Eds.), *Handbook of early childhood intervention* (pp. 119–149). New York: Cambridge University Press.

Sanson, A., Smart, D., Prior, M., & Oberklaid, F. (1993). Precursors of hyperactivity and aggression. *Journal of the American Academy of Child and Adolescent Psychiatry, 32,* 1207–1216.

Seifer, R., Sameroff, A. J., Barrett, L. C., & Krafchuk, E. (1994). Infant temperament measured by multiple observations and mother report. *Child Development, 65,* 1478–1490.

Seifer, R., & Schiller, M. (1995). The role of parenting sensitivity, infant temperament, and dyadic interaction in attachment theory and assessment. *Monographs of the Society for Research in Child Development, 60,*(2–3, Serial No. 244).

Seifer, R., Schiller, M., Sameroff, A. J., Resnick, S., & Riordan, K. (1996). Attachment, maternal sensitivity, and infant temperament during the first year of life. *Developmental Psychology, 32,* 12–25.

Shaw, D. S., & Vondra, J. I. (1995). Infant attachment security and maternal predictors of early behavior problems. A longitudinal study of low-income families. *Journal of Abnormal Child Psychology, 23,* 335–357.

Slabach, E. H., Morrow, J., & Wachs, T. D. (1991). Questionnaire measurement of infant and child temperament: Current status and directions. In J. Strelau & A. Angleitner (Eds.), *Explorations in temperament: International perspective on theory and measurement* (pp. 205–234). New York: Plenum.

Spieker, S., & Booth, C. (1988). Maternal antecedents of attachment quality. In J. Belsky & T. Nezworski (Eds.), *Clinical implications of attachment* (pp. 95–135). Hillsdale, NJ: Erlbaum.

Sroufe, L. A. (1985). Attachment classification from the perspective of infant-caregiver relationships and infant temperament. *Child Development, 6,* 1–14.

Sroufe, L. A. (1996). *Emotional development: The organization of emotional life in the early years.* New York: Cambridge University Press.

Sroufe, L. A., Schork, E., Motti, E., Lawroski, N., & LaFreniere, P. (1984). The role of affect in emerging social competence. In C. Izard, J. Kagan, & R. Zajonc (Eds.), *Emotion, cognition, and behavior* (pp. 289–319). New York: Cambridge University Press.

Susman-Stillman, A., Kalkoske, M., Egeland, B., & Waldman, I. (1996). Infant temperament and maternal sensitivity as predictors of attachment security. *Infant Behavior and Development, 19,* 33–47.

Tellegen, A. (1982). *Brief manual for the Multidimensional Personality Questionnaire.* Minneapolis: University of Minnesota Press.

Teti, D. M., & Ablard, K. (1989). Security of attachment and infant-sibling relationships: A laboratory study. *Child Development, 60,* 1519–1528.

Teti, D. M., Nakagawa, M., Das, R., & Wirth, O. (1991). Security of attachment between preschoolers and their mothers: Relations among social interaction, parenting stress, and mothers' sorts of the attachment Q-set. *Developmental Psychology, 27,* 440–447.

Thomas, A., & Chess, S. (1977). *Temperament and development.* New York: Brunner/Mazel.

Thomas, A., Chess, S., & Birch, H. G. (1968). *Temperament and behavior disorders in children.* New York: New York University Press.

Thomas, A., Chess, S., Birch, H. G., Hertzig, M. E., & Korn, S. (1963). *Behavioral individuality in early childhood.* New York: New York University Press.

Thomas, A., Chess, S., & Korn, S. J. (1982). The reality of difficult temperament. *Merrill-Palmer Quarterly, 28,* 1–20.

Thompson, R. A., & Lamb, M. E. (1983). Security of attachment and stranger sociability in infancy. *Developmental Psychology, 19,* 184–191.

van Dam, M., & van IJzendoorn, M. H. (1988). Measuring attachment security: Concurrent and predictive validity of the parental attachment Q-Set. *Journal of Genetic Psychology, 149,* 447–457.

van den Boom, D. C. (1989). Neonatal irritability and the development of attachment. In G. Kohnstamm, J. E. Bates, & M. K. Rothbart (Eds.), *Temperament in childhood* (pp. 299–318). New York: Wiley.

van den Boom, D. C. (1994). The influence of temperament and mothering on attachment and exploration: An experimental manipulation of sensitive responsiveness among lower-class mothers with irritable infants. *Child Development, 65,* 1457–1477.

van IJzendoorn, M. H., & Kroonenberg, P. M. (1988). Cross-cultural patterns of attachment: A meta-analysis of the strange situation. *Child Development, 59,* 147–156.

Vaughn, B. E., Lefever, G. B., Seifer, R., & Barglow, P. (1989). Attachment behavior, attachment security, and temperament during infancy. *Child Development, 60,* 728–737.

Vaughn, B. E., Stevenson-Hinde, J., Waters, E., Kotsaftis, A., Lefever, G. B., Shouldice, A., Trudel, M., & Belsky, J. (1992). Attachment security and temperament in infancy and early childhood: Some conceptual clarifications. *Developmental Psychology, 28,* 463–473.

Vaughn, B. E., & Waters, E. (1990). Attachment behavior at home and in the laboratory: Q-sort observations and strange situation classifications of one-year-olds. *Child Development, 61,* 1965–1973.

Wachs, T. D., & Desai, S. (1993). Parent-report measures of toddler temperament and attachment: Their relation to each other and to the social microenvironment. *Infant Behavior and Development, 16,* 391–396.

Waters, E. (1987). *Attachment Behavior Q-Set (Revision 3.0).* Unpublished instrument, State University of New York at Stony Brook, Department of Psychology.

Waters, E. (1995). The Attachment Q-Set (Version 3.0). *Monographs of the Society for Research in Child Development, 60*(2–3, Serial No. 244).

Waters, E., & Deane, K. (1982). Infant-mother attachment: Theories, models, recent data, and some tasks for comparative developmental analysis. In L. W. Hoffman, R. A. Gandelman, & H. R. Schiffman (Eds.), *Parenting: Its causes and consequences* (pp. 19–54). Hillsdale, NJ: Erlbaum.

Waters, E., & Deane, K. (1985). Defining and assessing individual differences in attachment behavior: Q methodology and the organization of behavior in infancy and early childhood. *Monographs of the Society for Research in Child Development, 50*(1–2, Serial No. 209).

Waters, E., Vaughn, B., & Egeland, B. (1980). Individual differences in infant-mother attachment relationships at age one: Antecedents in neonatal behavior in an urban, economically disadvantaged sample. *Child Development, 51,* 208–216.

Waters, E., Wippman, J., & Sroufe, L. A. (1979). Attachment, positive affect, and competence in the peer group: Two studies in construct validation. *Child Development, 50,* 821–829.

Weber, R. A., Levitt, M. J., & Clark, M. C. (1986). Individual variation in attachment security and Strange Situation behavior: The role of maternal and infant temperament. *Child Development, 57,* 56–65.

THE FOUNDATION OF PIAGET'S THEORIES: MENTAL AND PHYSICAL ACTION

Harry Beilin

DEVELOPMENTAL PSYCHOLOGY PROGRAM
CITY UNIVERSITY OF NEW YORK GRADUATE SCHOOL
NEW YORK, NEW YORK 10016

Gary Fireman

DEPARTMENT OF PSYCHOLOGY
TEXAS TECH UNIVERSITY
LUBBOCK, TEXAS 79409

I. Active and Passive Acquisition of Knowledge

A distinctive feature of Piaget's psychological and epistemological theories is the central position given to action in the child's acquisition of knowledge. The idea was not new. It was posited in early pragmatism and in Marxist theory (as praxis). In the era of the dominance of stimulus–response behaviorism, however,

ADVANCES IN CHILD DEVELOPMENT
AND BEHAVIOR, VOL. 27

the idea was contrary to conventional wisdom. The behaviorist view was that the learner is essentially passive in the face of experience and that the environment determines the acquisition of skills and thought. With the advent of the cognitive revolution in psychology, from the late 1950s on, the acquisition of learning and knowledge came to be conceptualized as an active process, but without necessarily denying that passive learning could also occur. Piaget, for one, was unwilling to accept the latter possibility. He insisted that when children are exposed to didactic instruction and conventional knowledge, for example, they reconstruct these forms of knowledge to make them their own.

The conception of children as active in their own learning is not as direct and simple as may first appear. Piaget makes a number of contestable assertions about action. These assertions require analysis and evaluation before one can assume that they are reasonable candidates for a cognitive developmental theory.

Before embarking on that task, some definitions are in order. Piaget's concept of action goes beyond dictionary definitions of action, as "the process of producing an effect, or performing a function, or doing something." In some psychological (i.e., organismic) contexts, a human or animal is active if it causes changes in behavior. The foregoing senses of action are essentially physical. Consequently, persons may be called active or passive (if acted upon by outside force or agency). One may also refer to active or passive processes when internal states are by inference defined as such. Physiological processes are an example.

There is an additional sense of action identified with internal states. This is mental action, in which thought and comparable endogenous processes of mind act to effect behavior or other mental states. Piaget does not ordinarily refer to mental action as such but his concept of logical operations and operative thought fall within the rubric of mental action. He says, for example, mathematics uses operations and transformations "which are still actions although they are carried out mentally" (Piaget, 1967/1971, p. 6).

The basic argument of Piaget's theory throughout its various developments is that action is the source of knowledge in distinction to perception and language. Although perception and language are never independent of action, nonetheless for Piaget, they are subordinate to action as a source of knowledge. This position stands in opposition to the view, principally but not exclusively, held by empiricists that perception is the primary source of knowledge. To some others, language has that role.

A corollary to Piaget's assertion about the priority of action is that action as the primary source of knowledge is at first physical (material) and is then "interiorized" and becomes "operational" in thought. Physical action is thus transformed into mental action. Mental action has a number of forms in Piaget's theory, and a number of conceptual issues about its nature have arisen.

As already indicated, action itself requires definition. Piaget defined action and its function in mind in ways that appear more metaphorical than psychologically real.

In addition, Piaget claimed that action is both a domain of knowledge and a source of knowledge. This is either a contradiction or a paradox in that process is also product. In Piaget's theory, however, they may be in a complementary relation to one another.

Further, Piaget proposed that in the relation between action and thought, the nature of objects plays a subordinate role in the creation of knowledge. In Piaget's theory, the relation of logic to action and the reverse is crucial to the origin of knowledge. Piaget's later theory, in particular, emphasized the role of logical form and function in action.

Last, Piaget held that developmental change is so intimately related to the nature of knowledge that an understanding of development is incomplete without an understanding of the sources of change. Not all philosophers or psychologists are persuaded by this assertion, which played a large role in underpinning Piaget's constructivism.

II. The Priority of Action

In asserting that knowledge originated in action and not in perception, Piaget challenged directly the foundations of empiricist (including behaviorist) psychological theories. The objection to perception was part of Piaget's objection to "pure empiricism and its reduction of everything to experience." While acknowledging the necessity of experience for the early growth of knowledge (Piaget & Inhelder, 1969a, p. 125) he said that

> There is no "pure" experience in the sense of a simple recording of external factors without endogenous activity on the part of the subject. All physical experience results from actions on objects, for without actions modifying objects the latter would be inaccessible even to perception, since perception itself presupposes a series of activities such as establishing relationships. (p. 125)

Further,

> It is impossible simply to divide cognitive functions in perception ("the senses") and reason, because action as a whole is both the point of departure for reason and a continuous source of organization and reorganization for perception. (Piaget, 1961/1969, p. 361)

In other words, perception itself is dependent upon action, although it is hard to see how action would be possible in any meaningful sense without perception.

Another reason for rejecting perception as the origin of knowledge was, for Piaget, that action transforms objects (in mind) rather than simply discovering their existence (through perception). In each new action, discovery and transformation are thus inseparable. It would be misleading, Piaget held, to consider perception as giving us "reality," and action as merely transforming that reality. Rather, perception is a basic part of each action scheme, not separate from it. "The subject is not constrained by the characteristics of the object but directs his perceptual activities as if he were solving a problem: he explores, relates objects to their contexts, anticipates and samples" (Piaget, 1961/1969, p. 363).

As Piaget put it,

> While operations . . . tend to reduce the real to structures of deducible transformations, perception is of the *here and now* and serves the function of fitting each object or particular event into its available assimilative framework. Perception is not therefore the source of knowledge, because knowledge derives from the operative schemes of action as a whole. Perceptions function as connectors which establish constant and local contacts between actions or operations on the one hand, and objects or events on the other. (Piaget, 1961/1969, p. 359)

He asserted further that perceptual messages are transmitted in a figurative form, the only form available to it. These messages are decoded by being integrated into the system of transformations (p. 359).

In addition, objectivity is constructed from and in proportion to the activities of the subject. The first contact with the object produces "field effects," which also produce deformations of the object. These deformations are corrected by perceptual activities.

Another feature of perception that limits its role in knowledge acquisition is that it is an unreliable source of knowledge. It is probabilistic and may lead to illusions, whereas reliable knowledge is derived entirely from thought or operations.

After considering the 14 differences between perception and operational intelligence, as well as their similarities, and the 14 intermediate states between the two, Piaget concluded (1961/1969, p. 309) that continuous development from perception to cognition is possible for only two properties, proximity and mobility (i.e., distinguishing between parts of objects from centration to decentration; and from the rigidity of perceptual structures to increasing mobility of intellectual structures). Otherwise, Piaget declared action is the source of operations to a large extent, even if it is not wholly independent of perception.

Finally, the relative adequacy (objectivity) of any perception depends on a constructive process not direct contact. With a method that is cumulative and corrective, the subject builds a perception into a "system" that as nearly as possible conforms to the properties of the object. Thus, for Piaget, "perception enjoys no special privileges in the conquest of the object" (p. 366).

III. Action Proper

Inasmuch as action is the focus of concern in the explanation of the origin of knowledge, what is known of the nature of action itself? It is necessary to be clear about the sense in which action is understood. A problem arises from the fact that action implies motion and motion implies activity. Yet motion and activity are involved in all physical and psychological phenomena. Activity and motion at this level of description can be of little value in the explanation of particular psychological phenomena. Such an explanation merely reiterates the idea that life itself entails activity and activity is thus entailed in the explanation of all phenomena involving living things. Clearly, this is not what Piaget had in mind in making action the centerpiece of his constructivist psychology. If he had, the proposal would be essentially meaningless as an explanation of the acquisition and construction of knowledge.

What appears to be the case is that Piaget considered action in the sense of agency, that volition is basic to action and that the individual is an actor carrying out an action as a matter of intention, as Brentano would have it. If that were the case though, there would be no knowledge until the emergence of intentions in the child's mental repertoire, about the 7th or 8th month of life, at least by Piaget's accounting.

Another problem is in accounting for some kinds of knowledge whose origin is not individual, as in what Piaget referred to as "biological" knowledge, the knowledge, for example, that a particular species employs to avoid predators by becoming totally motionless, thus avoiding detection, or the knowledge that comes with knowing how to signal the location of food to others in the species. This knowledge is not constructed or created by any individual of the species but comes with birth into that species. No volition or intention is entailed in these actions, as far as is known. It is evident from other instances as well, that Piaget's notion of action was multifaceted and encompassed more than one conception of action. Further, the notion of action itself is embedded in a complex web of relations at various levels of abstraction.

What are the significant features of the development of action? First is the idea that action is, for the most part, organized. The next idea is that organization in action has a logical character. Is intention crucial to this developmental course? Only, it seems, for the functioning of active intelligence. Before the emergence of intentions and intentional action there is, however, a logic in action, and as Piaget made clear in his later works (in particular, Piaget & Garcia, 1991), these logical forms are a protologic that bears an anticipatory relationship to the more fully developed logical forms of operational intelligence.

There are thus two levels of action: first, physical action, as evident in the sensorimotor schemes, and then, with the start of representation, mental action in the so-called one-way operations, followed by reversible operations.

Physical action leads to a form of knowledge achieved by physical abstraction, similar to the behaviorists' notions of abstraction, except that Piaget's conception of physical abstraction always resulted in sensorimotor schemes, that is, it entailed assimilation to a structure. Mental action, however, entails a different constituting process, namely, reflective abstraction.

At what point can it be said that mental action becomes part of the child's cognitive repertoire? It appears that there is no all-or-nothing transition from physical action to mental action.

Although Piaget did not discuss them as such, one-way functions require mental actions, albeit of less intellectual complexity than fully operational thought. Piaget did not spell out what happens to make or transform a one-way set of functions into two-way functions. What accounts for the increased logical and operating functions is not clear, except that the transitions may occur as a product of equilibration processes (assimilation/accommodation/self-regulation-organization/reflective abstraction).

The theory of equilibration is an indispensable part of Piaget's account of the development of knowledge. In his later, revised, theory of equilibration (Piaget, 1975/1985, p. XVII) he wrote, "Knowledge does not proceed either from objects alone or from an innate program performed in the subject, but results, instead, from a succession of constructions producing new structures."

On an analogy to biological functions, assimilation is defined as "the incorporation of an external element, for example, an object or event into a sensorimotor or conceptual scheme of the subject" (p. 5).

A second complementary process that is likewise a "component of every cognitive equilibrium" is accommodation. Accommodation entails the differentiation of schemes that take into account the "peculiarities of the elements assimilated" (p. 6). In development accommodations are always secondary to assimilations.

A third subprocess in equilibration is regulation. Regulation occurs when "the results of an action modify the repetition of that action" either through correcting negative feedback or reinforcing positive feedback. Such regulations may be either automatic (and make self-organization, or autoregulation, possible), or active.

Reflective abstraction is for Piaget "an essential aspect of the constructive process tied . . . to the interplay of regulations" (p. 29). Reflective abstraction includes two processes: (a) "reflecting," the projection onto a higher level something from a lower level; and (b) "more or less conscious" "reflexion," "the cognitive reconstruction or reorganization of what is transferred from one level to another" (p. 29).

The driving force in cognitive development is perturbation or conflict (i.e., disequilibrium) that is either external or internal (p. 34).

How the equilibration mechanisms transform one level of logical processing into another more complex was not delineated. Piaget is often criticized on this point, and he often acknowledged the deficiency. But it should be said that Piaget at least proposed a partial answer in the proposal of an equilibration mechanism. Other investigators have offered other proposals, such as those of the neo-Piagetians who posit increases in working memory at these transition points, and information-processing theorists offer other possibilities. These alternatives, however, appear no more adequate than the biologically derived statements of Piaget.

The semilogical or preoperational period that follows the sensorimotor period is characterized not only by one-way functions but also by the appearance of correspondences and morphisms. That is, the child becomes capable of making comparisons between the states of objects and events and generates structures (called morphisms) that embody these comparisons. This form of logical thought differs from operational thought in that it does not entail transformations in objects that are characteristic of operational thought.

The later discovery of correspondences, in fact, led to a significant change in one of the core assumptions of Piaget's theory. Earlier, Piaget had made the general statement, "to think is to transform." All cognition and mature intelligence was said to be based on operations that involve the transformation of objects and events. The new assertion is modified by the addition of comparison and matching processes in thought, so that the new slogan should be "to think is to compare and transform."

The period defined by one-way operations and correspondences is thus possible with mental action only, in correspondences with the actions of comparing and matching, in one-way operations in relating, classifying, ordering, and generally transforming, albeit without operational (logical) reversibility.

In Piaget's early books, this period was referred to as the period of representational or representative intelligence. He recognized the marked transition that occurs between the sensorimotor (and practical intelligence) period and the period of representational intelligence that follows by virtue of the emergence of the semiotic (earlier referred to by Piaget as the "symbolic") function. The sensorimotor period, up to the 6th substage at least, is characterized primarily by practical intelligence driven by sensorimotor schemes and devoid of what Piaget would have clearly implied was mental action. One can only assume that for Piaget mental action did not define the competence of the child before the sixth substage and the period of representational intelligence that follows.

What is there in the sixth substage that permits mental action and may even initiate it? The primary change, and it was a momentous one for Piaget, was the emergence and initial functioning of the symbolic function. The symbolic function was evident in a variety of forms, in deferred imitation, in symbolic (or pretense) play, in mental "search," in drawing and dreaming.

Piaget later shifted his reference from symbolic to semiotic function because of his desire to place symbols and symbolic development within the larger framework of a theory of signs (or signification or meaning). For Piaget, symbols were defined as objects, material or abstract, that stand for or substitute for other objects or events or thoughts different in kind from themselves, or that stand for or suggest something else by reason of relationship, association, or connection. They are distinguished in turn from arbitrary or conventional signs (as in those of language).

The development of the semiotic function puts into mental space a system of representation that enables action to take place on a mental level. Thus, such physical actions as pushing, pulling, turning, rotating can now take place mentally through representation without the necessity of physical action. Not only is there "something" in mind to manipulate through such actions, but there is also "something" to store in memory, for later action, as in the instances of deferred imitation (of actions observed in others that are carried out at a later time).

IV. Mental Representation

A. GENERAL CONSIDERATIONS

What is the nature of the relation of mental action to mental representation? First, in modern theorizing as to the causes and origins of behavior, a singularly important role has been assigned to representation. In the era of early behaviorism in psychology and its counterparts in philosophy, representation and other mental activities and events were relegated to banished, metaphysical categories of explanation. At best, these were conceived as epiphenomena in need of being accounted for, not in themselves candidates for causal explanation.

The cognitive revolution has changed all that. Particularly with computational theories (information-processing theory and the like), representation has become a matter of intense interest and debate. In information-processing models, and computational models generally, it is assumed that information is represented in symbols and signs, and processing occurs with these symbols. Strings of symbols represent propositions in a computational syntax. The impetus for emphasizing representational aspects of mind in Piaget's theory has a different origin, but funtionally there is a parallel with that of computational theory. Representation is what makes cognition possible, it is the basis for constructing meanings in the subject's action on the world of physical and social objects. In a highly contested view, representation was said by Piaget not to appear until the sixth stage of sensorimotor development with the emergence of images and symbols (in the semiotic function).

On this basis Piaget identified the period following the sensorimotor as the period of representative intelligence. By implication, the earlier period of practical intelligence is devoid of symbolic forms. But if Piaget's discussion is unclear on this issue, it is apparent that representational forms do appear before the appearance of symbolic forms. Piaget declared that the earliest assimilations of the sensorimotor period are marked by the development of "schemes." A scheme was defined as something that can be repeated and generalized in an action. Something that can be repeated and generalized is presumed to have some structure. Inasmuch as these schemes derive from internal states to which new actions on subjects have been assimilated.

If these structures do have an enduring presence, then, presumably there is some form of representation in mind. How these are represented is left unclear except as they are labeled "sensorimotor schemes," to indicate the coordination of sensory information with motor responses. With development, these "schemes" became elaborated and integrated into quite complex systems. Again, the emphasis Piaget placed on these "schemes" was as schemes of action on objects. The presumption appears to be that a scheme represented in mind (such as the sucking scheme or the pushing scheme) exists ready for the time and occasion when they are required for and manifest in action.

The enduring nature of sensorimotor schemes is supplemented by a set of properties elucidated in his last work (Piaget & Garcia, 1991). He saw in these actions early forms of logic (protologic); that is, there is logical form inherent in these early action schemes. These protological forms were thus the earliest forms of representations in Piaget's later system, aside from the sensorimotor schemes themselves.

A problem arises in that representations are ordinarily thought of as static forms, in the way that external representations such as pictures are ordinarily static. Yet action schemes are dynamic. In what way, then, can a representation that is static embody coordinated actions that are dynamic?

The solution is simple enough. When not evoked, the representation in mind (and/or in the brain) is in a static form, as a picture would be, although for many reasons it is not in the form of a picture. In computational terms it is represented, as in a computer program, in the form of a symbolically coded statement or set of instructions, comparable to a Simon-Newell type of "production." When the scheme is called up, invoked, or activated, the representations are set in "motion" in the way a video or motion picture camera is started up. The stream of pictures that define the scheme is played through, or the static "production" begins to be processed as the program is run through. Instead of seeing the action-scheme as a motion picture we see output as the behavior of the child as it, pushes, pulls, reaches for, and so on.

Piaget did not discuss sensorimotor schemes in these terms, but I suggest it is implicit in the manner in which he discussed them and their properties. Margaret Boden (1979, 1989) also suggests that Piaget's sensorimotor schemes are not incompatible with computational theory assumptions concerning representational processes. Computationalists, such as Pylyshyn (1986) and Fodor (1975, 1981), assert that central to a theory of mind is the need to assume a form of mental representation that is capable of representing knowledge in all its variety. Their prime candidate is the propositional form with its mental representation in the form of "propositional attitudes" (e.g., "Johnny believes that . . . *proposition*"). These participate in what Fodor refers to as a "language of thought" (1975). Propositional attitudes suggest an underlying propositional logic of the kind that Piaget assumed in formal operational thought only, but this is not Fodor's position. Fodor's "propositions" have more of a sentential form in a language-like context. Fodor and Pylyshyn also assume that propositional attitudes and propositional forms of representation do not undergo developmental change but are constant in development (i.e., they are genetically determined).

Another form of representation assumed to characterize mental processing, the existence of which Fodor and Pylyshyn dispute, is the imagined (image) form that was studied by Shepard (1978) in his mental rotation experiments and discussed extensively in the debate with propositionalists over whether this form of representation is epiphenomenal (as Pylyshyn and Fodor maintain) or is an autonomous mental representational form, perceptual in origin. Kosslyn (1980), who asserts that both propositional and imaginal (analog) forms function in mental representation, takes a developmental view of their emergence and offers a model of a spatial display as can be generated by a cathode ray tube.

To oversimplify, two views are inherent in the foregoing discussion. There is opposition between a conception of mental functioning that stresses the representational features of mind, as in imaginal and computationally inspired theories, and a view of the Piagetian kind that, in addition to positing representational forms, requires a conception of action and action coordination. Intersecting with this distinction is the distinction between developmental and nondevelopmental views.

B. BRUNER'S PROPOSAL

Two attempts at explaining cognitive development in primarily representational terms are Bruner's (Bruner, Olver, & Greenfield, 1966) and more recent child's theory-of-mind theories (e.g., Perner, 1991). Bruner's early theory proposed to shift away from Piaget's (structuralist) schemes and logico-mathematical forms as critical sources in the development of knowledge to (functionally inspired) representational changes that occur in the progression from enactive, to iconic to symbolic representational forms in development. This progression appears to parallel the representations detailed by Piaget, with a change of emphasis. The enactive form may well be considered the representational aspect of sensorimotor schemes, collapsing signals and indices as signifiers into this representational form. Bruner's iconic representations are equivalent to Piaget's images (Piaget & Inhelder, 1966/1971), except that for Piaget images embodied some of the properties of symbols and some of perceptions. (Images, although representing object features are not direct copies but more like maps than photographs in their reduction of such features.) Bruner's symbols parallel Piaget's symbolic representation, although Bruner appears to collapse the Piagetian distinction between motivated (subject-generated) symbols and conventional signs.

Although Bruner's early theoretical position is consistently functionalist, he adapted the representational aspects of Piaget's theory without its equilibration component and particularly without its logical structuring. Instead it is concept-based, and at the time it was proposed, emphasized classification and concept matching. Although the subject in Bruner's theory is not the passive copy theorist of behaviorism, he did not, like Piaget, base acquisition of knowledge on the subject's action on objects. If anything, his emphasis is on concepts and language in the origins and workings of mind, and his more recent theories are based on the narrative aspects of knowing.

C. CHILD'S THEORY OF MIND

Child's theory of mind theory, referred to by some as theory theory (Russell, 1992) is an offshoot and development of some early Piagetian assertions, which these theorists for the most part reject. The core of the challenge is to Piaget's characterization of the young child, 2 to 6 years of age, as a realist, in the sense that the child believes that mental entities, dreams, images, language, and conceptions of various kinds have a substantive reality in the world external to themselves. For example, at first they do not understand dreams to take place in their own minds but are things they perceive in the world external to themselves. The theory theorists demonstrate fairly convincingly that in a variety of formats and contexts young children have a quite reasonable understanding of the differences between the contents of their own minds and the contents of other minds, the external world of objects and events. The counter-arguments of the theory theorists, however, go well beyond rejection of childhood realism. Although in Piaget's early work, the child was seen, in large measure, as developing a "conception" of the world (his early and some later books contain the term "conception" in their titles), he argued that the progression in these conceptions was from early egocentric thought to later social- and object-oriented conceptions. In addition, the picture of the world held in mind was fragmented, like a succession of discrete pictures, as in a slide show presentation, which only later became integrated and continuous, as in the projections of a motion picture.

The theory theorists assert, however—and this may be the heart of their position—that the young child has an integrated, nonegocentric, and reasonably coherent view of the world. It is more than a mere series of discrete conceptions. Rather it constitutes a theory of mind and by extension a theory of reality (at least of other minds) similar to that of adults. It is a "theory" by analogy to the properties of theories held by scientists and philosophers. Needless to say, there is some discomfort, even among members of this group, over the strong assertion about the likelihood that the young child has theories. But there is no denying that the child is conceived to have a less "distorted" conception of both mind and reality than was suggested by Piaget.

Piaget, in his own account of childhood "theories," said he did not mean that children's "philosophies" were articulated by them. Rather, the attribution of a philosophy to children was metaphorical and a regulative concept in the theorist and not a constitutive element in the child.

A further set of assumptions is shared by theory theorists, despite considerable differences about the details of these assumptions. These bear on representation. What is asserted is that children have an understanding of mental representation. Some say this happens at 4 years of age and older, others say the figure is 3.

The discussion is phrased in terms of mental representation, either implicitly or explicitly, adopting philosophers' representational theory of mind (Fodor, 1981). The principal components rely on representations as "propositional attitudes," together with intentions, and a belief/desire (i.e., folk) psychology. Belief is the core concept in these theories of mind (Russell, 1992). Much research up to now into child's theory of mind has been about the child's grasp of the idea of false belief, that is, in understanding the distinction between holding true beliefs and holding false beliefs.

The latter has been studied extensively, in the so-called false-belief task. The task is said to demonstrate when a child is capable of understanding that another child entertains a false belief about an object that lies hidden or not hidden in a box. The strongest claims concerning false belief are made by Perner (1991), who holds that the development of mental representation is the ability to represent the representational relation itself. According to Perner, children do not have a theory of mind until they have this metarepresentational capacity, which is not evident until the age of 4. The conclusions of others about the appearance of a theory of mind at 3 years or earlier, he holds, are based on evidence of having beliefs, but not on understanding the representational process itself. (Perner calls the child before 4 years a "situation theorist.")

The theory-theorist emphasis on representation (and metarepresentation) differs from Piaget's in a number of important respects. First, whereas Piaget's theory of representation was developmental, the theory-theorists adopt the representational theory-of-mind position that there is only one form of representation (the "propositional attitude"—or propositional forms of representation—from Pylyshyn and Fodor). A second assumption appears to be that this form of representation is innately given. Leslie is most explicit about this; arguing that a theory-of-mind module (following Fodor) is activated in the second year of life and makes representation and metarepresentation possible (Russell, 1992, pp. 500–501). Piaget characterized the second year as well as the time when the symbolic function emerges, but took no stand as to whether this could take a "propositional" form. Piaget's late work, which suggest that protological forms underly sensorimotor actions, would seem to imply a propositional or similar form of representation. Piaget, however, did not embrace that possibility.

Russell (1992, p. 512) in his critique of theory-of-mind theory holds that "theory of mind research inherits Piaget's problems but neglects his insights." It does so by neglecting to see "that thinking is as much mental action as it is mental representation" (p. 512). What this implies is that understanding about the nature of mind requires both the concept of mental action and mental representation. Whatever the representational theory of mind buys for the child's theory of mind, it does not buy into a description and explanation of the mechanism of change that accounts for the transitions, at 3 or 4 years, taking place in the child's conceptions of mind (or theory, if you will). By neglecting to do so one merely has a description of states in children's knowledge at different stages in their development, without accounting for the changes.

Russell's own suggestion is to look to cognitive neuropsychology for possible models of how to account for the possibility of reconciling novelty and the need to make decisions in a theory of mind. A likely candidate, he proposes, is a theory that posits a level of representations as well as an executive function to be able to distinguish actions that are willed from those that are not. Connectivist models of frontal lobe function appear to Russell to suggest mechanisms of change and offer a way of spelling out what Piaget intended by his use of the notion of autoregulation. And, as Russell points out, "if there is no autoregulation, there is no mind to theorize about" (p. 516).

D. SCHOPENHAUER AND THE WILL

Russell holds that although Piaget is often said to be a Kantian, and Piaget acknowledged that this is true in part, Piaget was in actuality more in harmony with Schopenhauer than with Kant. Schopenhauer (1859/1964) is clear about his own debt to Kant and built his philosophy on selected Kantian ideas.

The parallel between Piaget and Schopenhauer is seen in Schopenhauer's distinction between, and the need for, both representation and will in accounting for how the subject locates himself in and knows the world.

According to Schopenhauer, the knowing subject's view of the world, if it were merely to involve a representation of that world, would yield insufficient meaning of that world inasmuch as the subject is himself an individual rooted in the world. Thus, although his knowledge of the world rests on representation, it is given entirely through the medium of his own body, which is an object among objects. This is the starting point for the perception of the world (1859/1964, p. 99). Piaget and others such as Baldwin (1899) and Vygotsky (1935/1979), had a comparable idea in noting that children maintain an egocentric view of the world until they are able to see themselves as objects relative to other objects.

Further, according to Schopenhauer, individuals are defined only through their identity with their bodies, and experience those bodies in two different ways: first, in intelligent perception as representation, the individual is seen as an object among other objects subject to the laws of those objects (such as that of causality); second, in what is known by the word *will,* in which every act of the individual's will is inevitably a movement of the body. An act cannot be willed without awareness that it appears as a movement of the body.

The act of will and the action of the body, however, are not two different objective states connected in a cause–effect relation. Rather, they are one and the same, even though they are given in two different ways: first directly, and then in perception that provides the basis of understanding. The action of the body is nothing but the objectification of the act of will. For Schopenhauer, this applies not only to motivated movement, but also to involuntary movement in response to stimuli. He says, "indeed . . . the whole body is nothing but the objectified will, i.e., will that has become representation" (p. 100).

He adds that the resolution to act in the future exists only in reason, in the abstract. Only action itself objectifies the resolve; until then it is "mere" intention that can be altered: "Only in reflection are willing and acting different; in reality, they are the same" (pp. 100–101).

To the difficult question as to whether the truth of these assertions can be demonstrated, Schopenhauer noted that by their inherent nature they did not fall into the four criteria of truth determination he himself had outlined: the logical, empirical, transcendental, and metalogical. He proposed instead another criterion, which he called philosophical, and which was to be known by direct knowledge only, not indirectly, by inference (p. 102).

The parallels between Piaget and Schopenhauer are apparent in the shared view that representation is not enough to account for the individual's knowledge of the world. The other necessary component, which Schopenhauer called "will," is paralleled by Piaget's notion of "action." How close is Schopenhauer's will to Piaget's action? Schopenhauer's identity of will with body and (physical) movement would at first seem to be what Piaget meant by action. Schopenhauer, although he distinguished the act of will from the actions of the body, insists they are one and the same, with the movement of the body the objectification of the will. The evidence for this was that the act cannot be willed without awareness (consciousness) of the bodily movement it causes. Although this appears to imply that will occurs only with conscious acts only, Schopenhauer extended its reference to involuntary stimuli and ostensibly to "voluntary" acts that occur without consciousness.

Piaget's proposal, with its developmental focus, suggested a two-step process in which actions are integrated at first into sensorimotor schemes that lack intentionality. They could be seen as having the status of involuntary responses to stimuli, which might be true of the youngest infants were it not that somewhat older ones tend to be selective in their movements toward and away from objects. Only later in the sensorimotor period, according to Piaget, does "true" intentionality enter the child's behavioral repertoire. Although Piaget attempted to account for the ways in which the processes of knowledge acquisition are cumulatively acquired, thus differing from both Schopenhauer and Kant, who imply they are a feature of human capacities from the start. Piaget, as did Schopenhauer, stressed the origin of knowledge in action and its genesis in (bodily) movements.

Piaget departed from Schopenhauer's view that these assertions, as philosophical truths, are nontestable or beyond establishment as scientific truths, that they are only subjectively knowable. Piaget's position as a constructive realist, as I view him, appeared to hold that (physical) reality is the ultimate arbiter of our theories about the mind, even though the closer one comes to that reality the farther it seems to recede. Nevertheless, in his pursuit of epistemological truths through scientific (i.e., psychological) means, Piaget was more a scientist than a traditional philosopher.

Although Piaget's conception of mental action was not fully developed until his elaborations of the late theory, the essential features of his ideas about mental action appeared in his quite early descriptions of infant development. A few of these features have already been mentioned. The earliest evidence of the infant's actions on the world are first assimilated into existing (innate) structures. These assimilated actions become organized into more and more elaborate action schemes or sensorimotor schemes. These schemes are at first unmotivated in the sense that they do not reflect true intentionality. Piaget's criteria for recognizing true intentionality were fairly strict: Children display intentionality only when they truly search for objects that disappear, not merely when they track objects with their eyes through possible trajectories, although the latter is certainly an advance over losing interest in an object as soon as it disappears.

The transition of physical action to mental action takes place as the former is internalized by virtue of symbolic and imaginal representational forms that become available to the child in the second year. From this point on, the child may be said to have the full apparatus for rational thought, except that the mental action available to the child is limited in the logical forms it can take. The most important limitation of mental action prior to 6 or 7 years is its semilogical nature in that the logical actions that are possible are "one-way" functions only; that is, they lack logical reversibility. This immediately suggests that mental action is intimately related to its logical forms and properties. But mental action is still not fully realized until the development of formal operations, because the concrete operations that are available in the period from about 6–7 years to about 11–12 years are tied to the manipulation of concrete (actual) materials or events. Full liberation of thought is achieved only when mental action occurs in respect to the hypothetical.

E. INTENTIONALITY

Two issues require fuller explanation. The intentional or purposive character of action and mental action, and the logical status of mental action. In the latter case, we need to know what in fact is meant by mental action. In what sense is mental logic "action," and in what sense is it not? That is, our usual model of action is physical movement, activity in a physical sense. Is mental action analogous to physical action? If not, what is mental action?

Further, is all mental action purposive? If we can differentiate purposive or motivated physical action from nonpurposive, or unmotivated, even involuntary action, is this also true of mental action?

The question of purposiveness is tied to the matter of intention in mental life. The nature of intentions and general questions in regard to intentionality have become matters of serious concern to both contemporary psychology and philosophy of mind. To Piaget, the examination of intentions was critical to establishing the dividing line between mere action and habit from true intelligence.

In laying out the development course in the achievement of intellectual functions in childhood, Piaget grappled with determining what criteria were decisive in identifying true intellectual functioning. He first considered identifying an act as intentional in representational terms. He rejected this possibility on two grounds. If one defines representation broadly, so as to encompass all consciousness of meanings, then intention would exist with the simplest associations, beginning as early as first reflex use. On the other hand, if representation is taken in a stricter, more limited sense, with the onset of language and individual symbols, it would come too late (in the second year). Instead, according to Piaget, intention can first be recognized when the child begins to set aside obstacles in seeking a goal. When 2-month-old children suck their thumbs, the action can be called intentional, because the coordination of the hand and sucking is simple and direct. When an 8-month-old sets aside an obstacle to reach a goal, this is intentional because the need activated by the stimulus of the act (i.e., by the object to be grasped) is realized only after a series of intermediary acts that involve the obstacles set aside. Intention thus arises from consciousness of either desire or of the direction of the act, or both.

This awareness is itself a function of the number of intermediary acts. The awareness or consciousness in intention, however, is the reverse of the consciousness of nonintentional acts. In nonintentional acts, as in the performance of a habit, consciousness arises from carrying out the action or resulting from the action. In intentional acts the consciousness is of the very action that is to be performed. In this, Piaget's views are very much in accord with Bergson (1937/1911). In intentional acts, then, there is a goal to reach and the means to achieve that goal.

Achieving a level of action that is intentional is a gradual achievement for Piaget. In the third stage of the sensorimotor period one finds behavior patterns that are "almost" intentional in that, for example, "almost intentional" searching is necessary to reproduce movements that had been performed fortuitously. These acts are not truly intentional or constitute acts of true intelligence because there is no differentiation of means and ends, at least not until after the event and the act is repeated with no novel adaptations. The fourth stage of sensorimotor development, with an adaptation of means to new circumstances, includes the first manifestation of truly intelligent acts and the manifestation of intentions by use of intermediate means to achieve a goal.

Thus, one sees in infancy the manner in which intentions are intimately tied to actions by way of the conscious awareness of goals and the means of achieving such goals. Two conditions are necessary for this development, the progressive differentiation of means and ends, and consciousness of the direction of acts from their inception to their results. Piaget implied that an object of desire (goal), in response to some need, is the motive force in intention. This is associated as well with "consciousness of values" (1923/1955, p. 149), in which the intermediary acts (means) take on values or interests as means.

In contemporary philosophy of mind, intentionality (as distinguished from intentions) refers to the quality or state of being conscious of intending an object, and takes three forms: idea, judgment, and desire. Put more simply, in intentionalist theories of mind (and in folk psychology), intentions are defined in terms of beliefs and desires, and in folk psychology the assumption is made that such beliefs and desires are the causal agents in the production of action and behavior. Piaget's theory is clearly more complex in that intentions are intimately tied to actions and have both functional and structural aspects. They are functional in their roles in adaptive intelligence and have a structural side in that they are tied to the combination and organization of schemes in which some schemes act as means and are subordinated to others that are goals.

The discussion of the infant achievement of intentional action normally implies a desire aspect to intentions, with subsidiary interests and values attached to objects, particularly as goals. However, beliefs play an increasingly important role after the sensorimotor period. In a child about 3 years old, Piaget saw "the beginnings of formulated reasoning that begins to be incorporated into the language of the subject" (1923/1955, p. 234). This newly developed form of reasoning produces the basis of the construction of a conception of "reality supposedly deeper than the merely given world" (p. 234). It is the work of an act of conscious realization "in which the child is able to distinguish the reality immediate to his senses" and which "precedes events and underlies all phenomena" (p. 234). Piaget referred to the latter as "intention." It is also the time when the child first ascribes intentions to other people and then to things. Further, these intentions, ascribed to people and to things, become the principal categories of child thought. From the conscious realization of psychological operations relative to intentions, and not from perception of world objects and events, arise the fundamental categories or primitive functions of thought (p. 236): the implicatory function and the explicatory function. They are two aspects of every mental activity.

In the explicatory function the mind turns to the external world, and through it the child develops (in the years from 3 to 7–8) the concepts of causality, reality, time, and place. In the implicatory function, the mind turns inward to the analysis of intentions and their relations, which yield classificatory concepts, names, numbers, and logical relations (p. 238). Each function has two poles. A psychological pole in common with each is the starting point and point of divergence for the two functions (explicatory and implicatory). Piaget called this function "mixed" and regarded it as the basis of psychological justification and explanation and drew from both the nature of explanation and implication.

It is at this point that the belief aspect of intentions may be said to take ascendancy in the intellectual functions of mind, although the desire aspect continues as a motivational force. At 3 years the child's understanding begins to play an increasingly important role in understanding of the child's own mind (and its relation to reality of the world), as well as to the beliefs and desires (intentions) of others. It is to these very issues in the development of mind that so-called theory-theories and child's theory-of-mind research is focused.

V. The Logic of Meaning and Action

As we have seen, a central thesis of Piaget's was that logic resides in action, a tenet that defined his position from the start. From this focal point the entire architecture of his theory was developed over his long years of active research. Until his final years he maintained that schemes led progressively to the period of formal operations (at 10–12 years), when the 16 binary operations of propositional logic were attained. This became the canonical view of Piaget's theory. It still is for those unfamiliar with Piaget's last works. As Garcia points out, this became the classic view because hypothetical deductive thinking starts at this level of development and because the 16 binary operations are related in the well-known INRC group [through the logical relations of inversion (N), reciprocity (R), the correlative (C), and identity (I)], which Piaget asserted is used by the subject in physical problem solving and reasoning.

The last work on meaning (Piaget & Garcia, 1991), which entailed an intensive examination of the logics upon which Piaget had relied to that point, the so-called extensional or truth table logics, led to one of the most radical changes in Piaget's theory.

This late redirection of the theory had two main features. The first was the "discovery" of the 16 binary combinations at the level of the coordinations among actions in the sensorimotor period. However, the coordinations are not the structured wholes of the integrated INRC combinations but combinations of *pairs of actions* in which "each combination is performed differently according to varying contexts" (Piaget & Garcia, 1991, p. 163).

Further, when considered in their own right and in the context of their meanings, these early combinations and operations are isomorphic with the 16 binary operations of propositional logic. This in itself constitutes a striking departure from the earlier statements of the theory. Although isomorphic with later logical operations, they are still sensorimotor coordinations and thus are said to be protological forms.

This change in the theory lends credence and support to allegations by various critics of the appearance of logical anticipations of formal operations at ages earlier than those observed by Piaget in his earlier work. The change also lends support to the pioneering, and largely neglected, work of Jonas Langer (1980, 1986), who studied protological forms in the first years of the child's activity. For a long time Langer's work appeared as though he was outlogicizing Piaget by extending logical forms into the earliest action, although it was always clear from the Piagetian view that the origins of logic resided in the earliest actions. The new work of Piaget's not only placed the origins of logic in the organization of schemes but argued specifically that the protological coordinations of pairs of actions are isomorphic with the later, truly logical ones and apply as well to statements as to actions.

The second feature of the theory's redirection is the new thesis, that even at the most elementary levels, knowledge involves some "inferential dimension" (Piaget & Garcia, 1991, p. 159). At the most elementary levels this inferential dimension consists of implications between meanings, which are attributed to properties, to objects, and to actions themselves. The late reemphasis on meanings in Piaget's theory is significant in a number of ways. Meanings have always been associated in the theory with the process of assimilation and with assimilation schemes; that is, they were said to acquire meaning by virtue of the assimilation of objects to existing structures. In the older theory these meanings/assimilation schemes were subordinated to the schemes, operations, and logical structures that progressively constituted the logico-mathematical structure of an extensional logic, the Boolean logic, and truth table logic that defined the group structures of formal operations. With the emphasis on these earlier extensional (quantified) logics what was deemphasized and even neglected was the intensional (qualitative) meaning side of a complementary relation that Piaget always insisted defined the construction of knowledge.

Developments in new logics in recent years led some to be incorporated into Piaget's theory, altering some important features and even assumptions of the theory. Such was the case with category theory, which led to a new characterization of the developments of the preoperational periods with Piaget's theory of correspondences and morphisms. This addition to the theory required a fundamental change in the classical view of the theory that all cognition entails transformation. The new logical forms, based on actions of comparison, and comparison of states that could lead to new forms (morphisms), acquired a status that essentially denied the ubiquity of transformations, although the new logical forms had a relationship to the operations (and transformations) that followed their development.

However, a more profound development in logical theory led to the late examination and ultimate proposal to restructure the entire logical architecture of the theory. Unfortunately, the proposal was only programmatic, and with Piaget's death the project of restructuring was never completed. In this proposal the logical theory of Anderson and Belnap (1975), the relevance or implicational logic, led to a shift in balance between intensional and extensional logics in favor of the former.

In one sense, the shift was only from extensional logical operations, defined by conjunction, union, disjunction, and so on, with their linguistic correlates in the linguistic operations ("and," "or," etc.) to the intentional relations of implication.

In Piaget's parallel to the Anderson and Belnap proposals, the logical theory was assimilated to a psychological adaptation in which the basic psychological process was one of drawing inferences. The Piaget proposal was that inferences themselves "are just implications between meanings (which are attributed to properties, to objects, and to the actions themselves)" (Piaget & Garcia, 1991, p. 159).

The new assertion was that the very earliest action coordinations require inferences to be made by the subjects themselves in regard to actions and objects. Inasmuch as inferences are mental actions that, as indicated, have logical properties, that is implications, inferences introduced powerful mental devices into the child's repertoire that were inconceivable in Piaget's standard theory. The latter assertion requires some clarification and justification and to have its implications drawn out, since the proposal makes claims for profound competencies in the very youngest children.

For Piaget and Garcia, to begin with, an object, a property of an object, and an action are not simply "observed." The young child's attribution of an assimilation scheme to each of these entities that gives them meaning always includes an interpretation of what is observed. Such interpretations require a process of inference. Within the framework of schemes, Piaget and Garcia defined the meaning of an object as "what can be done with the object," which applies to both sensorimotor schemes and preoperational schemes following the emergence of the semiotic function (1991, p. 159). In addition to the "use" definition of meaning, there is an ascriptive aspect in what can be said of objects (that is, descriptions) as well as what can be thought of them, when the child classifies or relates them.

The meaning of actions themselves resides in "what they lead to." These extend then to any actions of the subject that engage an external reality or to a reality the subject has generated, as in logico-mathematical forms. Neither elementary actions nor "higher-order" actions are ever autonomous or isolated; they are always linked together in schemes and among schemes, with increasingly elaborated meanings derived from their applications. For Piaget, the most general link among actions was the relation of implication.

The relations among actions were said by Piaget to be of two kinds, causal and implicative. The former apply to objects and arise once actions have taken place with respect to them. Implicative relations are between meanings and may be anticipated. In the transition that takes place from material (physical) actions in coordinated action schema to the anticipated, and thus, inferential coordinates or compositions is said to lie the beginnings of logic. The justification for identifying these inferential compositions as logical is based on the assertion that although actions in themselves are neither true nor false, and are useful or efficient only with respect to attaining a goal, action implications, which are entailed in anticipations, may, like statements or propositions, be either true or false. Thus they would meet a necessary condition for being considered "logical." It is in this sense that Piaget's late theory placed logic (or protologic) in the earliest and most "primitive" levels of development.

This early or protologic is of course not the formal logic that holds between statements or propositions. Rather it is a "logic of meanings" that is founded on implications between meanings or what Piaget and Garcia hold to be the same thing, implications between actions (1991, p. 160).

From the observer's point of view, meaning implications drawn by children in their actions are reducible to combinations of implications and their possible negations. They are thus inferential. Empirically, three kinds of inferences appear ontogenetically. First, subjects (in their anticipations) reason and infer only about physical or material objects. Next, inferences in anticipations go beyond the observable. These action implications are not the logical consequences of empirical observations but derive from "reflective abstraction." Last, are inferences based on "reasons."

Piaget linked up the logic of meanings with the process of abstraction elaborated earlier in the theory of equilibration, in which empirical abstraction is differentiated from reflective (and reflected) abstractions that lead to logic-mathematical knowledge. The former, by contrast, results in physical knowledge. In the new formulation, the early protologic is based on references that accompany the earliest anticipations of action coordinations.

Meaning implications can be viewed in other ways as well. Among these, Piaget and Garcia differentiate the various forms or degrees (of logical power) of such implications. The first of these levels are "local" implications, where the meanings of actions are defined by their observed outcomes. These implications are thus data-driven and context-bound. "Systematic" implications follow. Here implications progressively improved step-by-step become part of a system of relations. Although the first judgments of possibility and impossibility appear at this point, these inferences do not attain necessary "reasons." Last are "structural" implications. These refer to the internal organization of earlier composed structures. Accompanying or reflecting this level of organization is understanding by the subject of the "reason" for observed general (empirical) facts. What at the second (systemic) level were general relationships now become necessary.

The elaboration of the logic of meanings has significant implications for Piaget's general theory and research program relating to the extensional logics on which Piaget based his theory in its structuralist (or classical phase). Piaget argued that with the emergence of the semiotic functions (and the possibility of language acquisition in the second year) action implications accompany statements and thus meaning implications between statements. Inasmuch as implications are determined by meanings, they cannot be reduced to extensions. From this, Piaget concluded that a logic of meanings has to be constructed with its main building block the "meaning implication."

In this logic, meaning implications can entail other embodiments (which he called "inherences"). These correspond to "extensive nestings" and hence to truth values. But, he maintained, consistent with the logical implications of Anderson and Belnap's implicational logic, the latter extensive nestings and their truth values are "partial" and are determined by meanings. Thus, meaning takes priority over truth determination. In this, Piaget reversed the earlier priority given to extensional and truth table logic over intensional logic and meaning. But for Piaget, meaning and truth were still two sides of the same coin, not to be dissociated from one another as appeared to be Frege's intent in differentiating between *sinn* (meaning) and *bedeutung* (extension, reference, or truth).

We see then in Piaget's assumption and assertions that knowledge derives from action a complex architecture, which, by its nature, serves mind with a variety of functions that enable the epistemic as well as actual subject to adapt to a world of objects that are at least equally complex.

VI. On Piaget's Logical Models

Piaget made extensive use of theoretical models from other disciplines for almost the entire history of his own theories. The sources of these models varied from sociology, psychoanalysis, mathematics, and logic. The most contentious was the use he made of logical models in defining the nature of cognitive development.

At issue has been whether his adaptation of these models and various concepts, such as "structure," were merely metaphorical or had psychological reality. In the case of structure, for example, he held that although structures were not observable as such, they are located at levels "which can be reached by abstracting forms . . . the detection [of which] calls for a special effort of reflective abstraction" (Piaget, 1968/1970, p. 136). In other words, they have psychological reality.

It is likewise the case that for Piaget logical and mathematical systems are "the mirror of thought," as evidence from the origins of intelligence suggests (p. 53). Axiomatized logical theories are, thus, parallels of underlying structures of thought. This, then, justifies the mapping of logical and mathematical models onto systems of developing cognitive structures. As he contends,

> It is much more likely that logic is in fact an axiomatization of the forms of equilibrium that characterize thought, an autonomous axiomatization . . . one, which like all axiomatizations, serves to formalize preliminary data. (Piaget & Inhelder, 1963/1969b, p. 153)

Some critics, rightly or wrongly, have assumed that Piaget's empirical research was driven by his psychological and logical theories. In one instance at least, he recounts how he arrived at his truth-table logical model independently of Inhelder's research on logical thought in adolescence. Only later did they realize that the logical model could be mapped onto the psychological data (Inhelder & Piaget, 1958, p. xxiii).

Some logicians have also criticized Piaget and Inhelder's use of logic and their assertions about children's logical abilities. Papert, in defense of Piaget's program, wrote that Piaget in starting a new field (i.e., genetic epistemology) had no choice but to use existing instruments (i.e., logic) that were developed for other purposes (Piaget & Garcia, 1991, p. x).

With Piaget's late theory, questions about the psychological reality of Piaget's claims arises anew. In addition, what of the empirical data reported? Were the data predetermined by the "guiding hypothesis" that "general and local meanings consist of attributions of actions to objects" (Piaget & Garcia, 1991, p. 13)? With equally compelling interpretations of the data possible, what makes entailment logic the privileged model for interpretation? In an implicit reply to this question, Garcia argued there is "convergence" between Anderson and Belnap's entailment logic and the updated operatory (empirical) logic of the later theory that was "not purely coincidental" (p. 157). This convergence was said to buttress the claims for the new approach in the logic of meaning. "Meanings result," Garcia asserts "from an attribution of assimilation schemes to objects, the properties of which are not 'pure' observables but always involve an interpretation of the 'data' " (p. 157).

Seen historically, it cannot be pure chance that Piaget's earlier revolutionary turn to truth-table (extensional) logic should have occurred during the era when structuralist theories (Piaget, 1969/1970) were sweeping through the biological and social sciences (generally in the 1960s to early 1980s). Equally so, it cannot be pure chance that Piaget and Garcia's (1991) later logic of meanings should have appeared coinciding with the poststructuralist, and even postmodernist, turn to hermeneutics, semiotics, and other interpretive theories and the emphasis on meaning rather than on truth. Nevertheless, Piaget's later theory maintains a certain consistency. It is not just meaning that he was concerned with, but a logic of meanings. Although he moved to intensional (qualitative) logic, he did not wholly reject his earlier extensional (truth-table) logic. Rather, he saw the need to revise it, in light of the new developments in his theory.

In addition, the later theory offers a new conception of action, and provides a strikingly different context for viewing Piaget's theory of cognitive development.

VII. Summary and Conclusions

Piaget's late theory of action and action implication was the realization of a long history of development. A review of that history shows the central place of action in all of his theoretical assertions, despite the waxing and waning of other important features of his theories. Action was said to be the primary source of knowledge with perception and language in secondary roles. Action is for the most part not only organized but there is logic in action. Action, which is at first physical, becomes internalized and transformed into mental action and mental representation, largely in the development of the symbolic or semiotic function in the sensorimotor period.

A number of alternative theories of cognitive development place primary emphasis on mental representation. Piaget provided it with an important place as well, but subordinated it to mental action in the form of operations. In this, as Russell claims, he paralleled Schopenhauer's distinction between representation and will.

Piaget's theory of action was intimately related to the gradual development of intentionality in childhood. Intentions were tied to actions by way of the conscious awareness of goals and the means to achieve them.

Mental action, following the sensorimotor period, was limited in its logical form to semilogical or one-way functions. These forms were said by Piaget to lack logical reversibility, which was achieved only in the sixth or seventh year, in concrete operations. Mental action was not to be fully realized until the development of formal operations, with hypothetical reasoning, in adolescence, according to the classical Piagetian formulation.

This view of the child's logical development, which relied heavily on truth-table (extensional) logic, underwent a number of changes. First from the addition of other logics: category theory and the theory of functions among them. In his last theory, however, an even more radical change occurred. With the collaboration of R. Garcia, he proposed a logic of meanings that would require a recasting of his earlier truth-table-based operatory logic that he claimed explained the development of logical thought and problem solving. The new logic of meanings, influenced by Anderson and Belnap's (1975) logic of entailment, placed new emphasis on inferential processes in the sensorimotor period, introduced protological forms in the actions of the very young child, and proposed that knowledge has an inferential dimension. The consequence was that the late theory shifted emphasis to intensional (qualitative) logic and meaning from the earlier extensional (quantitative) logic and truth testing.

The profound changes in Piaget's late theory requires a serious reevaluation of Piaget's entire corpus of research and theory; a task which is yet to be done. Seen in a new light, the late theory is much closer to intellectual currents associated with hermeneutic and semiotic traditions in their concern with meaning and interpretation and less, if at all, with truth. This, despite Piaget's couching of the new theory in a logical mode.

The late theory added significant new elements to the theory of action and action-implication, and suggest that Piaget's, and his collaborator's, new research data, which were interpreted within the new theoretical framework, require corroboration and review.

The question as to whether Piaget's assertions are at root metaphorical and lack psychological reality, which has followed his theories from its earliest days, arises as well with the assertions of the late theory. Possibly, even more so, since even a limited historical review of his theories points to a considerable concurrence between changes in the fundamental assumptions of his theories and intellectual currents of the times.

In hindsight, Piaget's theories appear as "works in progress," down to his last theory. Yet, even in the end, he charted the direction of possible further progress.

ACKNOWLEDGMENTS

A portion of the present chapter was delivered at the conference celebrating the 100th anniversary of Jean Piaget's birth, "La Epistemologia Genetica y la Ciencia Contemporanea," in Mexico City, Mexico, April 25, 1996. I thank Terrance Brown for reading that paper when illness kept me from attending the conference. I also thank Hayne Reese for insightful comments on an earlier draft of this chapter. I am grateful as well to Walter Golman for editorial assistance in the preparation of the manuscript.

REFERENCES

Anderson, A. R., & Belnap, N. D. (1975). *The logic of relevance and necessity.* Princeton, NJ: Princeton University Press.

Baldwin, J. M. (1899). *Social and ethical interpretations in mental development: A study in social psychology* (2nd ed.). New York: Macmillan.

Bergson, H. (1911). *Creative evolution.* New York: Henry Holt. (Original work published 1937)

Boden, M. (1979). *Piaget.* Brighton, England: Harvester Press.

Boden, M. (1989). *Artificial Intelligence in psychology: Interdisciplinary essays.* Cambridge, MA: MIT Press.

Bruner, J., Olver, R. R., & Greenfield, P. M. (Eds.). (1966). *Studies in cognitive growth.* New York: Wiley.

Fodor, J. A. (1975). *The language of thought.* Cambridge, MA: Harvard University Press.

Fodor, J. A. (1981). *RePresentations: Philosophical essays on the foundations of cognitive science.* Cambridge, MA: MIT Press.

Inhelder, B., & Piaget, J. (1958). *The growth of logical thinking from childhood to adolescence: An essay on the construction of formal operational structures.* New York: Basic Books.

Kosslyn, S. M. (1980). *Image and mind.* Cambridge, MA: Harvard University Press.

Langer, J. (1980). *The origins of logic: Six to twelve months.* New York: Academic Press.

Langer, J. (1986). *The origins of logic: One to two years.* New York: Academic Press.

Perner, J. (1991). *Understanding the representational mind.* Cambridge, MA: MIT Press.

Piaget, J. (1955). *The language and thought of the child.* New York: Meridian Books. (Original work published 1923)

Piaget, J. (1969). *The mechanisms of perception.* London: Routledge & Kegan Paul. (Original work published 1961)

Piaget, J. (1970). *Structuralism.* New York: Basic Books. (Original work published 1968)

Piaget, J. (1971). *Biology and knowledge.* Chicago: University of Chicago Press. (Original work published 1967)

Piaget, J. (1985). *The equilibration of cognitive structures: A central problem of intellectual development.* Chicago: University of Chicago Press. (Original work published 1975)

Piaget, J., & Garcia, R. (1991). *Toward a logic of meanings.* Hillsdale, NJ: Erlbaum.

Piaget, J., & Inhelder, B. (1969a). The gaps in empiricism. In A. Koestler & J. R. Smythies (Eds.), *Beyond reductionism: The Alpach symposium, 1968. New perspectives in the life sciences* (pp. 118–160). London: Hutchinson.

Piaget, J., & Inhelder, B. (1969b). Intellectual operations and their development. In P. Fraisse & J. Piaget (Eds.), *Experimental psychology: Its scope and method: Vol. 7. Intelligence* (pp. 144–205). London: Routledge & Kegan Paul. (Original work published 1963)

Piaget, J., & Inhelder, B. (1971). *Mental imagery in the child.* London: Routledge & Kegan Paul. (Original work published 1966)245

Pylyshyn, Z. (1986). *Computation and cognition.* Cambridge, MA: MIT Press.

Russell, J. (1992). Book review. The theory theory: So good they need it twice? *Cognitive Development, 7,* 485–519.

Schopenhauer, A. (1969). *The world as will and representation* (Vol. 1). New York: Dover. (Original work published 1859)

Shepard, R. N. (1978). The mental image. *American Psychologist, 33,* 125–137.

Vygotsky, L. S. (1979). Consciousness as a problem in the psychology of behavior. *Soviet Psychology, 17*(4), 3–35. (Original work published 1935)

Author Index

A

Abdi, H., 90, 92
Ablard, K., 197, 219
Achenbach, T. M., 189, 214
Acredolo, L. P., 173, 174, 175, 177, 179
Action, H., 196, 218
Adams, A., 173, 175, 177
Adams, A. K., 74, 92
Aguiar, A., 139, 145, 146, 149, 150, 151, 152, 155, 157, 160, 161, 163, 166, 168, 170, 177, 178, 179
Ahadi, S., 187, 218
Ahmed, A., 138, 140, 177
Ahn, W.-K., 60, 90, 92
Ainsworth, M. D. S., 183, 191, 192, 193, 196, 198, 199, 201, 202, 205, 214
Akhtar, N., 3, 53
Alansky, J. A., 203, 212, 216
Alderton, D., 165, 179
Alderton, D. L., 165, 178
Allen, S. E. M., 40, 46
Anderson, A., 3, 32, 46
Anderson, A. R., 239, 240, 244, 245
Anderson, J. R., 145, 177
Anderson, S. R., 27, 46
Andersson, K., 207, 214
Andreas, D., 198, 204, 206, 217
Arend, R., 183, 189, 195, 196, 198, 214, 217, 218
Aslin, R. N., 101, 129, 131
Atran, S., 74, 90, 91, 92
Au, T. K., 87, 92

B

Baer, D. M., 105, 130
Bai, D. L, 173, 175, 177
Baillargeon, R., 17, 46, 87, 93, 101, 103, 104, 111, 113, 117, 118, 124, 128, 130, 132, 133, 135, 139, 146, 150, 152, 155, 157, 160, 161, 163, 166, 168, 170, 177, 178
Baldwin, D. A., 46

Baldwin, J. M., 233, 245
Banks, M. S., 125, 131
Bard, E., 3, 32, 46
Barglow, P., 202, 220
Barnett, R. K., 33, 36, 39, 53
Baron, A., 105, 130
Barrett, K. C., 173, 174, 175, 178
Barrett, L. C., 189, 219
Barrett, S. E., 90, 92
Barsalou, L. W., 86, 88, 92, 93
Bartsch, K., 79, 93, 137, 180
Bates, E., 14, 38, 46, 48
Bates, J., 189, 202, 214
Bates, J. E., 186, 187, 188, 189, 195, 214, 216, 218
Bayles, K., 188, 189, 214
Begun, J. S., 23, 47
Behrend, D., 6, 46
Bell, R. Q., 183, 214
Bell, S. M., 183, 214
Belnap, N. D., 239, 240, 244, 245
Belsky, J., 193, 200, 201, 206–209, 210, 212, 214, 217, 220
Bem, S., 58, 93
Benson, J. B., 178
Benveniste, E., 87, 93
Bergson, H., 236, 245
Berlin, M., 195, 217, 218
Berlin, S., 211, 212, 217
Berlyne, D. E., 105, 130
Bern, D. J., 215
Bernstein Ratner, N., 34, 46
Bertenthal, B. I., 108, 130, 173, 175, 177, 178
Best, C. T., 39, 53
Bettiger, J. G., 165, 179
Bever, T. G., 39, 40, 47
Bhatt, R. S., 104, 117, 118, 130
Biederman, L., 105, 115, 130
Bierwisch, M., 11, 46
Bigelow, E., 139, 140, 179
Bijou, S. W., 105, 130
Binns, H., 189, 217
Birch, H. G., 184, 185, 189, 219, 220
Bjork, R. A., 165, 180

Subject Index

A

Action, Piaget theory
  characteristics, 224–228
  features of development, 225
  intentionality, 235–238
  knowledge acquisition, 221–223
  late theory prospects, 244–245
  logic of meaning, 238–242
  logical models, 242–243
  mental representation relationship, 228–230, 244
  perception relationship, 223–224
  physical versus mental action, 222, 225
  representative intelligence period, 227–228
  Schopenhauer's will concept homology, 233–235
  semiotic function, 227–228
  sensorimotor schemes, 229
  thought relationship, 223
Attachment
  classification of infants
    continuum, 209
    disorganized, 194, 209
    insecure-avoidant, 194, 205–206
    insecure-resistant, 194, 205–206
    secure, 194, 205–206
  definition, 191
  evaluation
    Attachment Q-set, 195–197, 209–212
    Strange Situation procedure, 192–196, 201–207, 209
  manifestations, 191–192
  predictive validity, 195–197
  quality of care effects, 192
  temperament comparison
    empirical evidence on relations
      Attachment Q-set evaluation, 209–212
      extreme temperament group examination, 204–205
      goodness-of-fit model evidence, 207–209
      observational tests of temperament, 203–204

      parents' reports of temperament, 202–203
    reactivity distinctions from Strange Situation test, 205–207
    individual differences in Strange Situation test, 201–202
    overview, 182–184, 197–198, 213
    parenting sensitivity versus temperament, 198
    temperament contributions to attachment, 198–200
    transactional models, 200–201, 207–209

B

Ball tasks, *see* Containment tasks
Brain transplant, essentialist perceptions of children, 63–64

C

Categorization, *see* Object categorization, infancy
Child's theory of mind, mental representation, 231–233
Containment tasks, ball tasks in infant perseveration testing
  block and box task results comparison, 165–166
  container and no-container conditions
    familiarization phase, 157
    overview, 156–157
    perseveration results and interpretation, 158–160
    test phase, 157–158
  occluder and basket conditions
    overview, 160–161
    perseveration results and interpretation, 162
  procedure, 156
  related findings, 162–163
  performance by age, 166–168, 171–172

Contents of Previous Volumes

ISBN 0-12-009727-3